Winchester

ARCHAEOLOGICAL HISTORIES

Series editors: Thomas Harrison, Duncan Garrow and Michele George

An important series charting the history of sites, buildings and towns from their construction to the present day. Each title examines not only the physical history and uses of the site but also its broader context: its role in political history, in the history of scholarship, and in the popular imagination.

Avebury, Mark Gillings and Joshua Pollard
Butrint: At the Crossroads of the Mediterranean, Richard Hodges
Carthage, Sandra Bingham and Eve MacDonald
Dura-Europos, J. A. Baird
Hadrian's Wall: Creating Division, Matthew Symonds
Knossos: Myth, History and Archaeology, James Whitley
Pompeii, Alison E. Cooley
Stonehenge: A Brief History, Mike Parker Pearson
Tarquinia, Robert Leighton
Troy: Myth, City, Icon, Naoíse Mac Sweeney
Ur: The City of the Moon God, Harriet Crawford

Winchester
City of Kings

Susanne Haselgrove with Katherine Barclay

BLOOMSBURY ACADEMIC
LONDON • NEW YORK • OXFORD • NEW DELHI • SYDNEY

BLOOMSBURY ACADEMIC
Bloomsbury Publishing Plc, 50 Bedford Square, London, WC1B 3DP, UK
Bloomsbury Publishing Inc, 1385 Broadway, New York, NY 10018, USA
Bloomsbury Publishing Ireland, 29 Earlsfort Terrace, Dublin 2, D02 AY28, Ireland

BLOOMSBURY, BLOOMSBURY ACADEMIC and the Diana logo are trademarks of
Bloomsbury Publishing Plc

First published in Great Britain 2025

Copyright © Susanne Haselgrove and Katherine Barclay, 2025

Susanne Haselgrove and Katherine Barclay have asserted their right under the Copyright,
Designs and Patents Act, 1988, to be identified as Author of this work.

For legal purposes the Acknowledgements on p. xi constitute an extension of
this copyright page.

Cover design: Terry Woodley
Cover image © Medieval West Gate, Winchester, Hampshire, UK
Nadia Isakova/Alamy Stock Photo

All rights reserved. No part of this publication may be: i) reproduced or transmitted in
any form, electronic or mechanical, including photocopying, recording or by means
of any information storage or retrieval system without prior permission in writing from
the publishers; or ii) used or reproduced in any way for the training, development or
operation of artificial intelligence (AI) technologies, including generative AI technologies.
The rights holders expressly reserve this publication from the text and data mining
exception as per Article 4(3) of the Digital Single Market Directive (EU) 2019/790.

Bloomsbury Publishing Plc does not have any control over, or responsibility for, any
third-party websites referred to or in this book. All internet addresses given in this book
were correct at the time of going to press. The author and publisher regret
any inconvenience caused if addresses have changed or sites have ceased
to exist, but can accept no responsibility for any such changes.

A catalogue record for this book is available from the British Library.

A catalog record for this book is available from the Library of Congress.

ISBN: HB: 978-1-3503-9978-5
PB: 978-1-3503-9977-8
ePDF: 978-1-3503-9979-2
eBook: 978-1-3503-9980-8

Series: Archaeological Histories

Typeset by RefineCatch Ltd, Bungay, Suffolk
Printed and bound in Great Britain

For product safety related questions contact productsafety@bloomsbury.com.

To find out more about our authors and books, visit www.bloomsbury.com
and sign up for our newsletters.

Martin Biddle at the site of the Anglo-Saxon Minsters.

To Martin Biddle, for his inestimable contributions

CONTENTS

List of Illustrations ix
Preface and Acknowledgements xi

Introduction 1

1   The Uniqueness of Winchester 7
    Background 7
    Archaeological evidence 7
    Historical and documentary sources 11
    Standing buildings 13
    Destruction, absence and sampling bias 14

2   The Archaeological Story 18
    Early explorations 18
    John Leland 18
    Winchester Cathedral 19
    Early investigations 20
    Early twentieth-century archaeological investigations 21
    The Biddle achievement 22
    Later work 27
    Lankhills 27
    St Mary Magdalen 28
    Winchester Cathedral mortuary chests 28
    Barton Farm Hessian camp 29

3   The Early Settlements 30
    The situation of Winchester 30
    The prehistoric landscape 30
    Prehistoric human activity 31

4   The Rise and Fall of *Venta Belgarum* 43
    Foundation and early history 43
    Mid-second to third centuries 50

Later Roman Winchester 50
Fourth-century Winchester and the Germanic transition 52
Germanic presence 55
Epilogue 57

5 **The Golden Age of Early Medieval Winchester** 58
The early medieval context 58
Documentary evidence 58
Archaeological evidence 60
Surviving Britons 61
Bede's *Uintancaestir* ('Walled place of *Venta*') 62
Late eighth and ninth centuries 64
Tenth century 68
Aethelred and the eleventh century 82

6 **Medieval Winchester** 87
Introduction 87
The citizens of Winchester 87
Royal Winchester 95
Ecclesiastical Winchester 99
Late Medieval Winchester 111

7 **Reduced Horizons** 114
Tudor times 114
Stuart highs and lows, Georgian gentility 120
The Victorian city 123

8 **The Legacy of Past Glories and New Beginnings** 128
Twentieth-century developments 128
Twenty-first century 135

Afterword 142

Chronology 144
Dramatis Personae 148
Notes 151
Further Reading 151
Bibliography 152
Index 172

ILLUSTRATIONS

	Frontispiece: Martin Biddle at the site of the Anglo-Saxon Minsters	v
0.1	The location of Winchester	2
1.1	The West Window at Winchster Cathedral	6
1.2	The development of Winchester from the mid- to late second century BCE to 1870	8
1.3	Part of an archaeological section drawn for publication from 'field' drawings made to scale on site during the excavation	16
2.1	Sites excavated by the Winchester Excavations Committee, 1961–71	23
2.2	Looking N-W over excavation of the remains of the West Hall, Wolvesey Palace, 1970	24
2.3	Martin Biddle examining the construction of the Round Table during its removal for restoration	26
3.1	Neolithic sites and finds in the Winchester area	32
3.2	Beaker and Early Bronze Age sites and finds in the Winchester area	34
3.3	Early Iron Age sites and finds in the Winchester area	36
4.1	Roman Winchester by *c*. 90 CE	42
4.2	Wooden statuette of a matron of *Venta* found at Lower Brook Street	46
4.3	Roman Winchester by *c*. 350, including all known observations of significant Roman buildings	51
5.1	Winchester *c*. 410–650	59
5.2	Three-dimensional views of the development of Old Minster from *c*. 648 to 992–4	63
5.3	Winchester's Roman street plan overlain by the Anglo-Saxon street-plan of the mid- to late ninth century	66
5.4	Excavation in 1968 at Old Minster: the north apse and northern half of the central space of the double-apsed link-building or *martyrium* built *c*. 971–5 around the grave of Swithun	74
5.5	Old Minster at 992–4 from the S-W with New Minster in the background	77

6.1	View N-W across Lower Brook Street excavation in 1966, over the remains of St Mary's church	90
6.2	The royal quarter of Winchester in 1093 on the eve of the demolition of Old Minster	95
6.3	Winchester Castle: outline plans of the principal elements in the late twelfth and thirteenth centuries	96
6.4	Excavation at Winchester Castle in 1967, with the foundation of the twelfth-century Great Tower	97
6.5	Winchester Castle: looking S-W at Great Hall and the visitors' centre	98
6.6	The size of Old Minster as completed in 992–4 compared with the outline of the Norman cathedral as built 1079–*c.* 1120	99
6.7	New Minster, the site of the demolished Old Minster, and the nave of the new cathedral under construction *c.* 1120	100
6.8	Winchester Cathedral, Norman tower and north transept, and Perpendicular nave	101
6.9	Hyde Abbey's fifteenth-century southern gatehouse, seen from inside the abbey precinct	103
6.10	Wolvesey Palace today (2024)	105
6.11	The alms-houses and church at St Cross, seen from the water meadows, site of the abbey's fishponds	107
7.1	King Arthur's Round Table today	115
7.2	Winchester Castle in the late seventeenth century, showing the plan of the palace, or King's House, as built in 1683–5	121
8.1	Alfred in bronze as the heroic warrior king, by Hamo Thornycroft, erected in 1901, dominates the east end of The Broadway	129
8.2	*A Promise Honoured*, by Simon Smith	131
8.3	Winchester College Cloister designed by Herbert Baker	133
8.4	Twyford Down protests (1991–3)	134
8.5	Licoricia and her son, by Ian Rank-Broadley	138
8.6	Winchester from St Giles Hill	139
8.7	Looking through Westgate down High St, *c.* 1900	141

PREFACE AND ACKNOWLEDGEMENTS

This book has had a long gestation, beginning with Bloomsbury's initial approach to Katherine in 2021, when she invited Susanne to be part of the author team. Because of her many other responsibilities to the Winchester Studies publication process, Katherine was less involved in the initial writing of the book than planned, but has contributed hugely to its final form. Both of us were part of the team of 3,000 who participated in Winchester Excavations' Committee's (WEC) famous excavations' campaign of the 1960s and 1970s directed by Martin Biddle. Katherine continued in the post-excavation team at the Winchester Research Unit and became Assistant Director in 1985. After a variety of archaeological roles, Susanne had a career change in 1982 but returned to WEC in 2012 as its Secretary, as well as co-organizing its successful 2014 international conference – *Winchester: Archaeology and Memory*.

In summarizing Winchester's rich past, we have indeed been standing on the shoulders of giants, especially those of Professor Martin Biddle, who had the vision of the sort of interdisciplinary study of Winchester's past we have sought to emulate. That vision has produced to date eleven volumes of both archaeological and documentary research in the Winchester Studies series, with six volumes still to come https://www.winchesterstudies.org.uk/publications/. Our partner, Archaeopress, is now making current and forthcoming publications available in both print and e-book form, as well as making past publications available as digital open access. In addition to his many academic contributions, Martin also brought Winchester's past to a wider audience through lectures, popular books, TV programmes and podcasts; we hope that this book will fulfil a similar purpose. We have been fortunate to be able to use the wealth of other research and publications, which chart Winchester's historical, archaeological, social and cultural life, from the far past to the present day.

We are most grateful to Winchester Excavations Committee's Chairman, Barbara Bryant, for all her support for Winchester's heritage over many years, and for the production of this book. Pru Kemball's work is invaluable to WEC's publication processes and to this book's later stages, especially in sourcing its illustrations. We thank Lily Mac Mahon and her predecessors as Commissioning Editors at Bloomsbury, as well as other colleagues from the team who have brought this book to publication, especially Lisa Carden and Merv Honeywood.

Susanne Haselgrove and Katherine Barclay
March 2025

Introduction

The Great West Window is a patchwork of fragments of medieval glass, but element of the original scheme may be made out.
CROOK 2006: 38

The City of Winchester is the county town of Hampshire, located about 100 kilometres south-east of London and 18 kilometres north of the port of Southampton. A rich range of evidence helps us understand the development of the town (Chapter 1) and how its archaeological past has been uniquely excavated, analysed and disseminated (Chapter 2). Chapter 3 discusses the traces of prehistoric activity that have been found in and around Winchester – the present city is essentially a Roman creation. Unlike other Roman towns, *Venta* had no immediate antecedents on the site, although there were significant earlier Iron Age settlements on the nearby hillfort of St Catherine's Hill and within Oram's Arbour, immediately to the east of what became the Roman settlement. Chapter 4 draws attention to aspects of the foundation of *Venta*, including its very early defences, and to the discovery of the largest letter (and therefore probably the largest inscription) so far found in Roman Britain (see below 50).

The early history of *Venta* is the first indication of a theme that regularly recurs in the city's history – there is something about Winchester which makes it special and draws in successive rulers and creatives. In the nineteenth century, John Keats lyrically described Winchester as 'the pleasantest Town I ever was in and has the most recommendations of any' (Keats 2011: 233–4). While Roman *Venta* effectively disappeared, there is evidence of a high-status Germanic presence within the Roman walled area, although much of the town appears to have been turned over to agriculture. Chapter 5 explores evidence of continuity in Winchester's hinterland as well as within the town itself which probably contributed to a decision by Cenwulf, the ruler of Wessex (642–5 and 648–72), to commission a church there in the seventh century that would later be known as the Old Minster. Although the rulers of the new kingdom of England were always peripatetic, Winchester saw a continuing royal investment in the creation of a unique collection of magnificent churches which housed their bones and those of

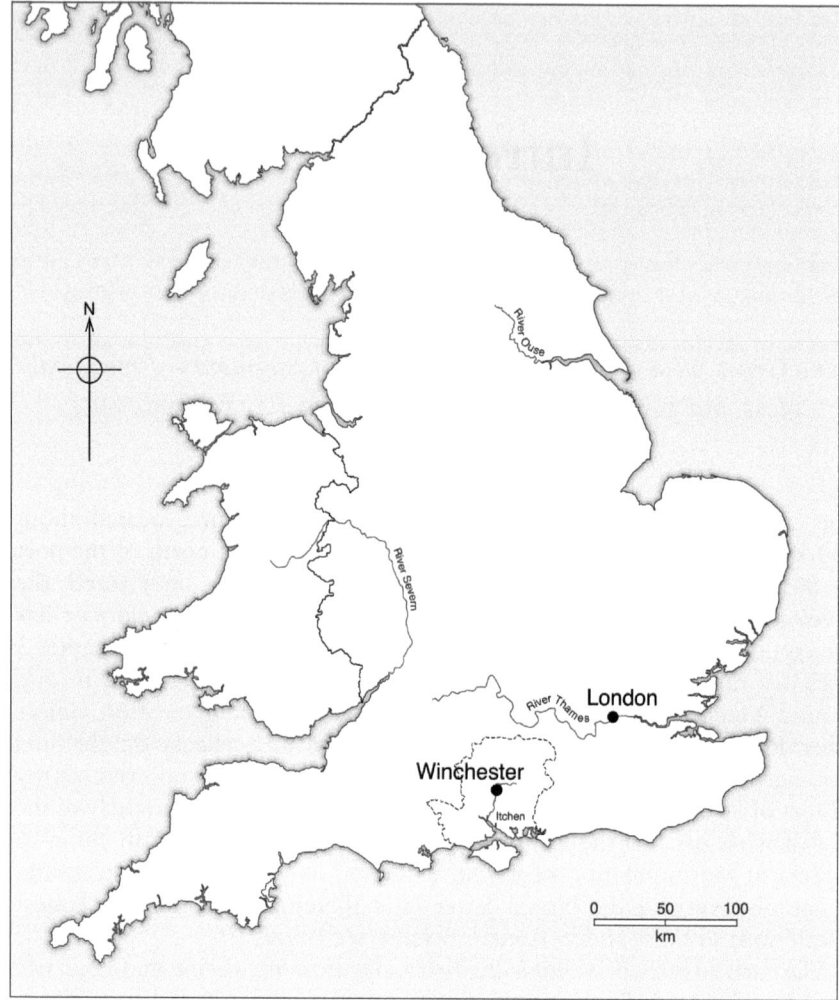

FIGURE 0.1 *The location of Winchester* © WEC.

the increasingly important saint, Swithun. Under King Alfred, the kingdom of Wessex established both supremacy amongst the English kingdoms and the promotion of learning, which was continued by key religious figures such as Bishop Aethelwold. Winchester became an artistic powerhouse, producing exceptional manuscripts such as the *Benedictional of St Aethelwold* and the *New Minster Charter*, as well as the European-inspired artefacts of the 'Winchester School', whose influence also spread into the Scandinavian-controlled areas of the Danelaw. Unlike his predecessor Aethelred, when the Danish ruler Cnut came to power, he took pains to associate himself with Winchester, including donating a great golden cross to New Minster and possibly commissioning an Anglo-Scandinavian freeze for its decoration – a symbol of a shared history.

As we consider in Chapter 6, whilst after 1066 the centre of royal power shifted to London, Winchester continued to have a 'pull' for Norman kings, whose large castle dominated the town. The bishopric of Winchester was the richest in England and so was held by a number of the most notable clerics of the medieval period. Among them was Henri de Blois, who commissioned at Wolvesey Palace 'a house like a palace with a very strong tower', as well the Winchester Bible. During the medieval period Winchester became associated with the Arthurian Court in the increasingly popular Romances, culminating in Thomas Malory eventually identifying it explicitly with Camelot. It was probably this Arthurian connection that prompted Edward I to commission the 'replica' Round Table which still hangs in the surviving medieval Great Hall of the Castle with decoration updated by Henry VIII. Winchester's distinctiveness is shown too by the fact that Benedict, the son of the entrepreneur Licoricia, was the only Jew in medieval England to be elected as a guildsman. However, despite the choice of Winchester by William of Wykeham as the site of his College in 1392, and the continuing importance of the shrine of St Swithun as a pilgrimage centre, the later medieval period saw Winchester decline considerably. One major factor was the loss of royal attention, but most devastating was the Black Death and its resultant severe population loss, from which Winchester did not recover until the mid-nineteenth century.

Nevertheless, for the newly crowned Henry Tudor, Winchester's heritage – and especially the supposed connection with King Arthur – led to his arranging for his heir to be born in the town and christened after the king in the Cathedral. Chapter 7 explores this and the continuing interest by Tudor and Stuart monarchs in the town, which saw Henry VIII having the Round Table repainted and shown off to the Emperor Charles V, Mary I marrying Phillip of Spain in the Cathedral, and Charles II commissioning Christopher Wren to build for him an 'English Versailles'. Charles' death put an end to this project, and Winchester increasingly became a provincial town, albeit enlivened periodically by the presence of 'the regiments' described by Jane Austen. With the increase in antiquarianism and interest in the antecedents of the British Empire, Winchester, its key figures and buildings, became the focus of both research and tourism facilitated by the coming of the railways in the nineteenth century.

Chapter 8 opens with what was the apogee of this imperial project – the commemoration of the millennium of King Alfred's death, including the erection of his statue in the city and the related celebrations which extended beyond Winchester to the United States. During the First World War, Winchester's geographical location prompted the building of transit camps for more than two million Allied soldiers, although this important episode in the city's history was not commemorated until 2014. However,

Winchester's chivalric heritage explicitly inspired the neo-medieval War Cloister that commemorates the 500 Winchester College alumni who died in this conflict; Herbert Baker's creation remains the largest private war memorial in Europe. Heritage (and its preservation) was a significant factor in the late twentieth-century campaigns to alter the proposed route of the M3 motorway which, although ultimately unsuccessful, is recognized as a key part of the formation of the modern environmental movement. In the twenty-first century, King Alfred and Winchester have again gained a place in popular culture through Bernard Cornwell's *Last Kingdom* novels and the television series based on them, and most prominently through featuring in Ubisoft's *Assassin's Creed Valhalla* computer game. In recent years Winchester has featured regularly in newspaper surveys as both the 'best' and 'happiest' place to live in England; the criteria for these judgments vary but capture some shared expression of there being something special about Winchester. Local author, Roger Lloyd drew inspiration from it for his own fictional city:

> From the tower . . . it looked unutterably beautiful, with its haphazard mingling of trees and houses, of streets studded with unexpected gardens and fishponds, and the shadows thrown by tower, turrets and crenelated parapets of the Cathedral. Here surely was the slowly beating heart of England . . . A backwater? Perhaps, but there was grace and content in it . . . infecting the whole life of the nation, and of other nations far beyond the seas of the world.
>
> LLOYD 1962: 2–3

FIGURE 1.1 *The West Window at Winchester Cathedral* © Roger Utting.

1

The Uniqueness of Winchester

Background

In exploring Winchester's exceptional history, it may be that the best metaphor is the magnificent west window of Winchester Cathedral, which was broken apart by the Parliamentarian forces in 1642; at the Restoration, its fragments were reassembled:

> The Great West Window is a patchwork of fragments of medieval glass, but elements of the original scheme may be made out.
>
> CROOK 2006: 38

The past can never be fully reconstructed but, as the following sections will illustrate, the historical, archaeological and cultural evidence for Winchester is both extensive and wide-ranging, portraying a credible picture of the lives of Winchester's citizens through the centuries. What makes understanding Winchester's history unique is the range of evidence available to show how its fortunes waxed and waned from its prehistoric roots to its recent status – a micro-city, and one of the most desirable places to live in England (see below, 138–40).

Archaeological evidence

After nineteenth-century antiquarian investigations, from 1926 Sydney Ward Evans was the first to document systematically the archaeological finds coming from 'watching briefs' on hundreds of building sites in Winchester. In the mid-twentieth century (Ottaway 2017: 11), under the direction of Frank Cottrill (from 1947) Winchester's first paid Museum curator), systematic recording of watching briefs continued and a programme of rescue excavations was instigated in advance of redevelopment (Cunliffe 1964; Collis 1978). From 1961 to 1971 the then newly formed charity, Winchester Excavations Committee (WEC), carried out the largest programme of archaeological excavations ever undertaken in a British city

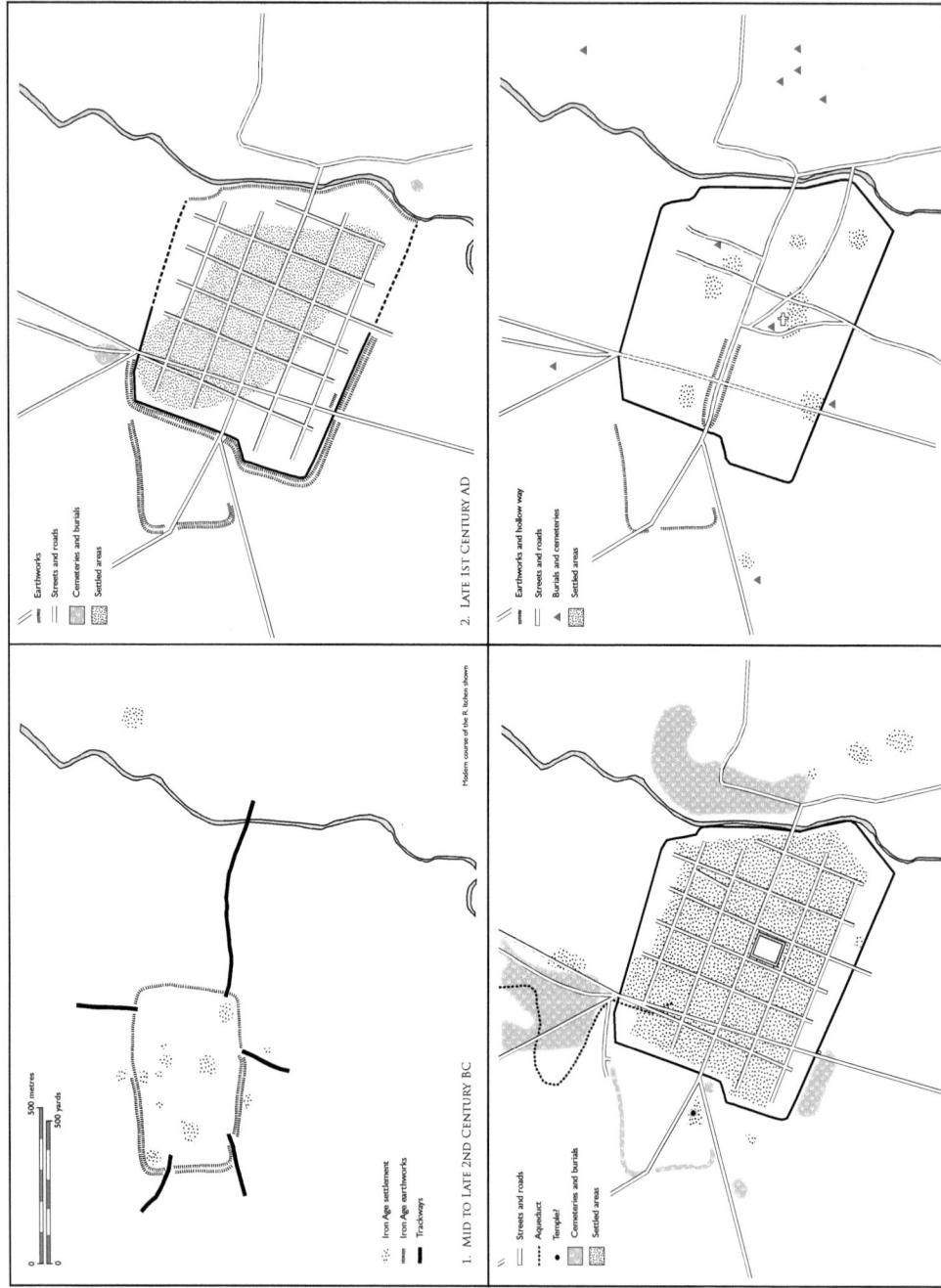

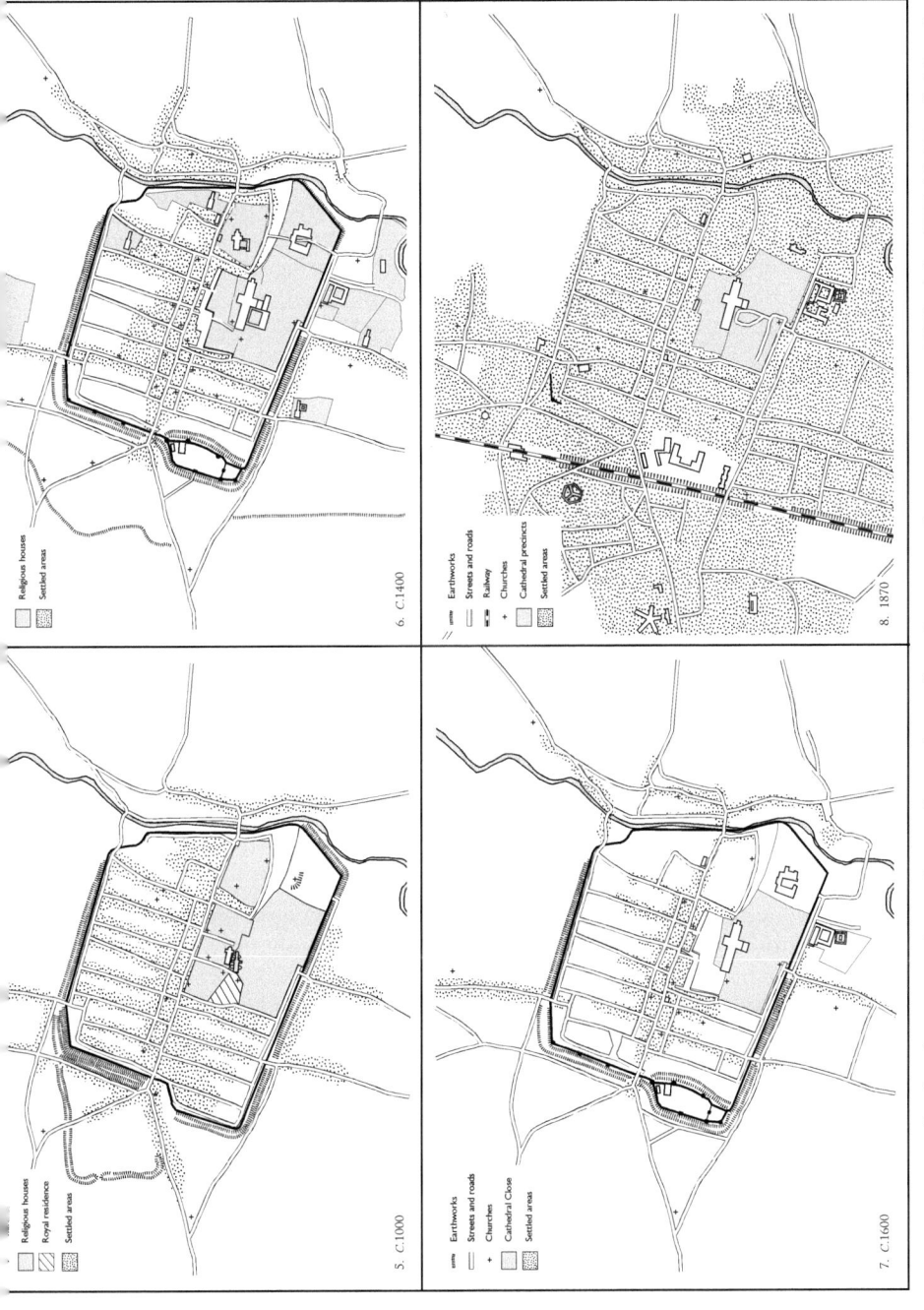

FIGURE 1.2 The development of Winchester from the mid- to late second century BCE to 1870. After WS 11, Fig. 1. Map by Giles Darkes © WEC and HTT 2017.

with 3,000 people (in total) digging on its sites (Biddle 2021b). The excavation programme used ground-breaking techniques to reveal for the first-time complete urban neighbourhoods, as well as the development of the city's major landmarks (Collis 2011). Winchester is extremely fortunate that the WEC excavations beside its Cathedral and at Wolvesey were carried out as research excavations unconstrained by the pressures of rescue projects. Innovatively the centre of interest was the city itself, the urban phenomenon (Biddle 1964: 188) and how it developed (Biddle 1974; Wood 2022b). Post-excavation analysis, research and scientific investigations add to the story of how Winchester's people lived and died, the crops they ate, the diseases they suffered from, their work and where they worshipped. (Biddle 1990; Biddle 2012; Biddle, Renfrew and Ottaway 2022). Since the WEC excavation programme was completed, further archaeological investigations have added to the evidence base both within the walled core of the city and beyond (Ottaway 2017), notably:

1. investigations of the town's northern later Roman cemeteries revealed both general information about the funerary practices and demography of its inhabitants as well as intriguing clues about some of the earliest Germanic settlers in late Roman *Britannia* (Clarke 2023)
2. research at the leper hospital at St Mary Magdalen enabled an archaeological and historical reassessment of the social context of leprosy and the status of its hospitals in medieval society (Roffey 2020)
3. at Hyde Abbey, archaeological, historical and osteological analysis provided evidence of both the translation of royal burials from the New Minster and the development of the medieval abbey (Qualmann, Scobie and Zant 2021)
4. recent historical and scientific research has shed light on the identities of the individuals whose remains are contained in the Cathedral's mortuary chests (Crook 2022; Jarman 2023)
5. excavations at Abbot's Barton found significant traces of the briefly occupied camp of the 8,000 Hessian militia that had been mapped in pictorial detail in the eighteenth century (McCulloch and Osgood 2018)
6. at Morn Hill, excavations have revealed details of the major World War One transit camp (Napier 2021)

How archaeological research in the city has evolved and illuminated its past will be explored further in Chapter 2 below (19). In line with Martin Biddle's emphasis on using all sources to understand Winchester's development (Biddle 1965: 261), in addition to the outcomes of the excavations, volumes in the Winchester Studies (WS) series use documentary and art-historical sources to illuminate the town's past (25–6).

Historical and documentary sources

From the early medieval period onwards, major texts such as the *Anglo-Saxon Chronicle* (Irvine 2002) and Asser's *Life of King Alfred* (Keynes and Lapidge 1983) highlight key Winchester events. The wide range of charters, court judgements, manorial rolls and property records show the formal side of town life (e.g. Keene 1985; Ramble 2003; James 2009: 13) as well as details of the everyday lives of its inhabitants (Keene 1985: 2022). In addition to its royal and noble inhabitants, other records describe some of the remarkable people who lived in the town, including the medieval Jewish entrepreneur Licoricia (Keene 1985: 385, 1835; Brown and McCartney 2004; Bartlett 2009) and the thirteenth-century laundress, Juliana de la Floude (Keene 1985: 715) (90). Keene (1985) showed that, using documentary sources, it is possible to reconstruct histories of medieval places and people; his survey includes Winchester's urban parishes, public buildings, commercial sites and, remarkably, 1,128 private properties. There is a biographical register of over 8,000 medieval property holders. Together, these have enabled his analysis and discussion of the administrative setting, topographical development, economic fortunes and social structure of the town.

The Bishopric of Winchester's Pipe Rolls (dating from 1208 to 1456–7) document the annual records of each of the Bishop's estates across southern England (Page 2002: 12–13) and include evidence of the building works undertaken at his Palace at Wolvesey, enhancing the archaeological evidence from the site (ibid.: 14). There are also extensive records of the agriculture practices on the Bishop's estates, which help to explain how these major architectural projects were resourced (Titov 2022: 104–13; also see below, 92–3).

From the early medieval and medieval periods, the wealth of Winchester's ecclesiastical houses enabled the creation of exceptional manuscripts (Chedzey 2003). They show the design influences of their creators and the interconnectedness of elites, including tapping into trade routes to bring lapis lazuli from Afghanistan to illuminate the Winchester Bible (Donovan 2021: 153). One notable Anglo-Saxon example is *The Benedictional of Aethelwold* (Deshman 1995), made for the eponymous bishop during the revival of Benedictine monasticism in the second half of the tenth century (Chedzey 2003: 2). Art historians have identified how the style of the early medieval Winchester School spread widely not only within England, but also to Continental Europe (Brownrigg 1978) (77–8). Henri de Blois, a Norman bishop, was the likely patron for the Winchester Bible produced between 1150 and 1175, which is the largest surviving twelfth-century English Bible (Donavan 2021). Detailed analysis of it provides insights into how such books were created (ibid.: 156–71); the excavations at Lower Brook Street also produced tools thought to have been associated with manuscript production (Biddle 1990: II 274).

The post-plague decline of the town during the fifteenth century is recorded in an appeal made to Henry VI asking for a reduction in taxes (Carpenter-Turner 1980: 78), although later that same century Henry VII arranged for his wife, Elizabeth, to give birth to their first child in Winchester: their son, Arthur, was born there in 1486 (Breverton 2019: 76); and in 1554 the wedding of Mary I and Philip of Spain took place in the Cathedral (Samson 2005). As will be shown in Chapter 6, the town, although by then in physical decline, still had an historical resonance prompting this and the earlier visit of the Emperor Charles V to see Henry VIII's newly refurbished Round Table (Biddle 2000a: 455) (116).

In the twentieth and twenty-first centuries, we are familiar with the association of Winchester with King Alfred (Keynes 1999; Yorke, 1999). However, in Winchester's earlier past, it had much stronger links with other icons. John Leland's sixteenth-century account of his visit to the town mentions its Anglo-Saxon roots but gives much more attention to King Arthur, following Thomas Malory's identification of Winchester as Camelot (Anderson 1991) and the presence of the Round Table (Biddle 2000a). Even less well known to modern audiences are exploits of the medieval fictional knight, Guy of Warwick, one of whose notable combats supposedly took place in Winchester where, after many other adventures, Guy assisted King Athelstan by killing the Danish giant Colebrand (Rouse 2005).

Nineteenth-century Census data demonstrates the rapid growth of Winchester's population to a new post-Plague high of 19,670 in 1891 (James 2009: 142); these data provide, for the first time, a comprehensive picture of Winchester's citizens, including their occupations, origins and overall demographics. Increasingly, civic records also provide greater details of the lives of 'ordinary' people, including how the city's dampness and poor drainage contributed to frequent cholera outbreaks, especially in the Brooks area which had been redeveloped for working-class housing (Carpenter Turner 1980; 168). A growing interest in Winchester's past prompted an increasing number of visitors including, in 1819, the poet John Keats, who composed his ode *To Autumn* after a walk in the water meadows (Margraff, Turley, Archer and Thomas 2012: 801).

The start of the twentieth century in Winchester was marked by a major celebration of the millennium of King Alfred with a significant amount of the funding for the iconic statue of the King raised in the United States (Yorke 1999: 7). However, the Alfred of this commemoration was as much, if not more, a Victorian imperial icon as a ninth-century one; Arthur Conan Doyle commented 'What we are really commemorating is . . . the greatness of those institutions which he founded . . . He was an educationalist on a scale we have hardly yet attained . . . He inaugurated a navy and obtained that command of the Channel which during 1000 years has hardly ever been relaxed' (Bowker 1902: 20–1).

During the First World War, two transit camps were established at Winnall Down and Morn Hill respectively. Some two million British, American and

Allied troops passed through its gates on the way to the Western Front via Southampton, to which it was connected by a specially constructed railway line with a dedicated station. It is estimated that the camp housed 50,000 people at any one time – double the then resident population of Winchester (Eddelstone 2015: 30). In the late twentieth century, Winchester re-emerged in the national and international headlines, as plans were developed to complete the M3 motorway past the city. An eight-year campaign was launched in 1985 to save the chalk downland of Twyford Down in the face of plans to route the M3 through it (Bryant 1996). Part of the justification for the objection was the city's heritage, summarized by Martin Biddle: 'Here, perhaps alone in modern urban England, it was possible to walk from the twentieth century to the prehistoric past' (ibid.: vii). Although the campaign failed, it formed a crucial part in the evolution of environmental campaigning (ibid.: 297).

In the twenty-first century, Winchester's early heritage again reached a wide audience through Bernard Cornwell's books and the linked *Last Kingdom* television series about the hero Uhtred (e.g. Cornwell 2004) and his support of Alfred and his family. With images derived from the Ubisoft computer game *Assassin's Creed Valhalla,* which has scenes set in Winchester, *878 AD* opened in 2022 as 'an Anglo-Saxon experience' to give visitors an imaginary interactive view of Winchester in the mid-ninth century. In 2016 Winchester was voted 'The Best Place to Live' by the *Sunday Times.* In 2017, however, the City lost its crown because it was 'too popular', although it saw a revival in 2023 and 2024. Winchester's most recent Local Plan has 'Conserving and Enhancing the Historic Environment' as one of its key points, noting that 'Heritage assets contribute towards the character, diversity and distinctiveness of the district' (see below Chapter 8).

Standing buildings

Winchester has major surviving buildings that tell their own stories, but which also influence the twenty-first-century layout and life of the city (Morris and Hoverd 1994). Although partly modified, the line of the Roman walls essentially defines the historic core of the city, and many of the main routes into Winchester follow the line of their Roman predecessors (Ottaway 2017: 17–18). Even more strikingly, perhaps, the street system of the modern city centre is still essentially Anglo-Saxon (ibid.: 18). The Norman and medieval Cathedral demonstrates the evolution of church architecture from the Romanesque (Crook 1993) to Burne-Jones' stained glass (Boyd and Dear 1998: 18). It is the burial place of kings and bishops (Crook 2022; Jarman 2023), of major authors including Jane Austen and Isaak Walton, and was a 1960s pop icon in the eponymous song by the New Vaudeville Band. The fourteenth-century buildings of Winchester College, erected at the order of Bishop William of Wykeham, survive as the core of the modern school (Harvey 1982); as noted above, its War Cloister, opened in 1924 (Kernot 1927: 80–4), is the largest private war memorial in Europe (Mowl 2024).

The Hospital of St Cross and Alms-house of Noble Poverty was founded by Bishop Henri de Blois in the twelfth century (Crook 2011: 2–3), from when much of its church survives (ibid.: 9–23); most of the other standing buildings date from the fourteenth (ibid.: 39–46) to sixteenth centuries (ibid.: 47–61). It seems likely that a nineteenth-century enquiry into its finances was also partly the inspiration for Anthony Trollope's *The Warden*; the author was a pupil at Winchester College so would have been familiar with the institution (Sabben-Clare 1992: 47–8). Wolvesey Palace is a testament to the power and wealth of the Bishops of Winchester, with the medieval remains of a fortified 'keep' and what were once lavishly decorated private apartments (Biddle 2021). Winchester Castle's medieval Great Hall is second only in size to Westminster Hall (Biddle and Keene 2017: 40); as noted above, it houses the iconic Round Table (Biddle 2000a) and was the scene of the trial of Sir Walter Raleigh in 1603, the so-called Bloody Assizes held after the seventeenth-century rebellion by the Duke of Monmouth, and the twentieth-century trial of eight IRA bombers.

At the site of Winchester's Castle, the shell of the King's House and other buildings from the unfinished Royal Palace were used to house prisoners of war and refugee clergy until 1796 when they were leased to the Barrack Department for military use (Thomas and Clayre 2017: 60). During the eighteenth and nineteenth centuries, these Peninsula Barracks housed a significant military presence – the 'regiments' with which Jane Austen was familiar when she moved to nearby Chawton (Worsley 2017: 231). These barracks again connect Winchester to wider political and colonial aspirations: they housed 3,000 troops during the Napoleonic Wars and numerous regiments temporarily between 1815 and 1856. The military museums that now occupy the site include not only two devoted to the Rifles, but also the Gurkha Museum, which relates their worldwide history and presence in twentieth-century Winchester (Lewis 1965) (124).

Destruction, absence and sampling bias

Despite the richness of this record, much has been lost. Documentary sources record the burning of Winchester's Anglo-Saxon settlement in 860 (James 2009: 51), and the destruction of the town during the civil war between Stephen and Matilda (Hanley 2021: 163). The Reformation saw considerable destruction at the Cathedral (Streeter 2012: 345–6a), its monastic buildings, treasures and many of its written records (Crook 2003: 227), as well as the Shrine of St Swithun. Nunnaminster and the monastic buildings of Hyde Abbey were also destroyed; both were quarried for stone for many centuries (Hare 1999: 15–16); the Cathedral, the Castle, and the town suffered further damage during the Civil War (Richardson 1992). Although the documentary sources for Winchester do record some notable women, such as Licoricia (Keene 1985: 353, Bartlet 2009) and Juliana de la Floude (both mentioned above (11)), the lives of women are largely absent (Ramirez 2023: xiv). Generally, people of colour, people with disabilities and other minorities, as well as ordinary individuals, are under-represented in the historical record (Bengry 2021; Nubin 2021; Virdi 2021) until the twentieth century (Bussey 2002). To date, little research in Winchester has been devoted to the impact of transatlantic slavery, although the Diocese[1] of Winchester has commissioned work on the Church's role and involvement including a walk around sites of significance in the Hampshire countryside

Notably, Alfred is recorded as visiting Winchester only once during his lifetime, in 896, although he was buried in the town (Yorke 1999: 5); Lavelle has argued that the absence of mentions of the town may be the result of his biographer Asser's own attitude to Winchester (2020: 323), emphasizing again that all written records are the author's creation (Carr 2018). Alfred's popular association with Winchester is predominately the result of a nineteenth- and twentieth-century civic publicity campaign (Yorke 1999: 5), although his popularity had been rising in general since the eighteenth century (Keynes 1999: 271). Many charters were forged in the medieval period to support claims of disputed lands (Brooks 1982; Thomas and Hessayon 2009: 186–7; Hooke 2011: 165). Church documents have their own stories to tell, especially of the 'backsliders', 'pagans' and 'heretics' of their own time (Morris 2021: 26–7; Wood 2022a: 40) and the changing doctrinal context (Hare 1999: 5).

Titow highlights that because of the keeping of systematic records, there is a much richer understanding of medieval agriculture practised on the great estates of the Church and major landlords than of peasants or even smaller landlords who did not have literate reeves and bailiffs to record them (2022: 89). Very few documents survive relating to Winchester Cathedral in the high medieval period (Crook 2003: 227): its first 'historical' source dates from the fifteenth century (ibid.: 229). The Arthurian strand in the town's history is a complex interweaving of several factors: royal patronage, leading to the creation of the Round Table at the behest of Edward I; literary creativity by Thomas Malory in his identification of Camelot as Winchester; and Henry VII's insecurities about his claim to the throne, resulting in his eagerness to root his dynasty in Winchester's established royal timeline (James 2009: 113; Kendrick 1950: 33–44).

In 2009, James noted that only 5 per cent of the city's archaeology had been investigated (2009: 25) and while excavations continue, it is important to appreciate that our interpretations are based on 'glimpses' rather than 'wide shots' of the past citizens of Winchester. In his ground-breaking

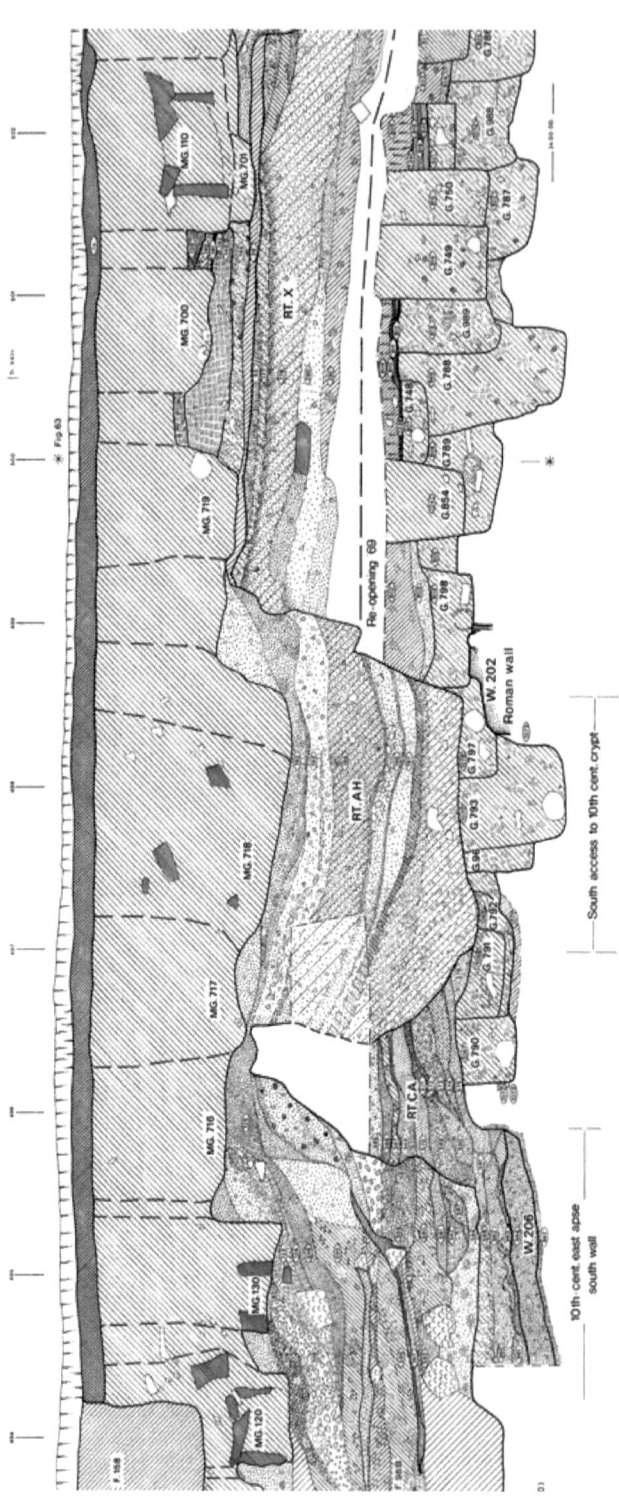

FIGURE 1.3 Part of an archaeological section drawn for publication from 'field' drawings made to scale on site during the excavation. It runs from south (left) to north and represents c. 9 metres across the east end of Old Minster in 980–992/4. The deeper narrow 'pits' across the bottom of the drawing represent graves dug before 980 when the extension of the east end was first laid out. Larger 'sweeps' of layers above the graves represent layers of rubble and other features, lines of the debris surviving after demolition. Deeper pits above represent graves of the cemetery which covered the site of the demolished Old Minster from about 1200 to the end of burial here c. 1540. © WEC.

introduction to the 'New Archaeology' of the 1970s, David Clarke argued that:

> all archaeological distributions artificially portrayed on flat map projections were once distributed over complex surfaces – topographic, demographic, ecological surfaces etc.
>
> CLARKE 1972: 15

In a continuously occupied urban settlement, many earlier levels will be destroyed by later activity (Carver 1987: 11; Barker 1993: 73) and often, pre-development investigations are of observations in service trenches, and other 'random' insights into the city's past determined by modern priorities (Ottaway 2017: 11), rather than following a research design seeking to understand past communities better (Barker 1993: 73). In Winchester, archaeological investigations have seen little coherent settlement evidence before the Iron Age, and evidence of the period between late Roman-dated contexts and the seventh century remains sparse (Morris and Biddle 2023: 80–1). The Old and New Minsters were demolished around the time of the erection of the Norman cathedral; the importance and continuing use of the site of Old Minster for burials resulted in the destruction of earlier levels (Kjølbye-Biddle 1975; Barker 1993: 126).

Local geology influences the picture of the past we have in the present; at Winchester, the lack of good local building stone meant that many domestic buildings were built predominately of wood, and when a stone building fell out of use, its constituent parts were 'recovered' and reused (Carver 1987 14; Ottaway: 2017: 252). Traces of timber building are ephemeral, and 'robber' trenches dug to retrieve stone cause considerable damage to archaeological evidence, as is documented for Winchester (Biddle and Kjølbye-Biddle 1969) and more generally (Carver 1987: 14; Barker 1993: 33–4). Obviously, the choices made by past societies also have an impact on what we can discern about them in the present. Carver argues 'When the opportunity allows, displaced householders will take their valuables with them' (ibid.: 14), so in many cases archaeological evidence consists of broken, discarded or waste items (ibid.: 69). Outside the walled circuit – where Roman law prescribed that burials should be made – later settlement was generally less intense, so more archaeological traces survive. Both archaeological and scientific analyses from Winchester's cemeteries have yielded considerable evidence of its past populations (Clarke 1979 and 2023; Stuckert 2017).

2

The Archaeological Story

Early explorations

Before reviewing Winchester's modern archaeological investigations, this section will summarise how its historical, literary and mythological associations – along with its surviving monuments – made the town the subject of antiquarian interest from at least the sixteenth century.

John Leland

Later chapters will explore in more detail Winchester's associations with Arthurian legend and how this became important to the Tudor dynasty (Biddle 2000a, James 2009: 113; also see below 114) but it is important to identify that this strand of history underpins the first account of Winchester's standing monuments and history, written by John Leland, 'King's Antiquary' (Johnson 2011: 299). Leland has been described as the 'first archaeological traveller in the English-speaking world' (ibid.) and was commissioned by Henry VIII (1509–47) to undertake a journey of inspection of England between 1536 and 1544 (Leland 1544; Rouse 2005). As Lawton has argued Leland, was not a 'simple' observer:

> Leland's task is then to correct history, to reinvent the past. He consults older chronicles, not newer ones, tracing from Bede as historan and Joseph of Arimathea as proto evangelist a line of independent authority for the English church ... and generally sharing the highly medieval Tudor passion for King Arthur.
>
> LAWTON 2001: 35

Leland's description of Winchester appears in two accounts. First, in *The Itinerary*, after describing the general decay of the town, the extent of its walls and the state of its churches, he describes Hyde Abbey:

> The bones of Alfredus, king of the West-Saxons, and of Edward his sunne and king, were translated from Newanminstre and layid in a tumbe

before the high altare at Hyde. On the south side of Hyde Abbay is a medow caullid Denmark, wher the fame is that Guido Erle of Warwik killid great Colebrande the Dane *singulari certamine*.

LELAND 1907: 272

His other reference comes in *Assertio inclytissimi Arturi Regis Britanniae*:

In ye castle ... standeth fixed ye table at the walle side of ye kinges Hal, which (for ye maiesty of Arthure) they cal ye round table. And wherefore? Because neyther the memorie nor felowship of the round Trowpe of Knightes as yet falles out of Noble mens mindes, in the latter age of the world.

WAINWRIGHT 2000: 484

In this account, Leland combines three key elements in the perception of early modern Winchester: the historical burial place of King Alfred and the kings of Wessex; the location of Guy of Warwick's battle site at a place called Denmark; and the identification of the Round Table and its association with the court of King Arthur (Rouse 2005: 139).

Winchester Cathedral

The Duke of Clarendon undertook a survey of the Cathedral's funerary monuments, subsequently published in 1715 and supplemented by an introduction by Samuel Gale, which provides useful evidence of their original positions before the nineteenth-century 'reorganizations' (Crook 2003: 232). In 1759 the Bishop of London, Robert Lowth, produced a life of William of Wykeham which also included an analysis of the Cathedral fabric; he was the first person to suggest that the Cathedral was not of Saxon origin and to identify that the work that Wykeham commissioned on the nave was not new, but rather a remodelling of the structure commissioned by Bishop Walkelin (ibid.: 233). Very soon after, Thomas Wharton expanded this account with descriptions of the traces of the medieval buildings then visible in the Cathedral Close (ibid.: 233–4). John Milner's two-volume *History, Civil and Ecclesiastical, and Survey of the Antiquities of Winchester* accepted much of the previous 'mythical' history of the Cathedral but he was the first architectural historian to use comparative data to support his theory that the retrochoir was thirteenth century, by analogy with Salisbury Cathedral (ibid.: 236).

With the dawn of the nineteenth century, antiquarian scholarship accelerated generally (Rogers 1993; Cowell 2008: 55–9) and for the Cathedral in particular. In 1817, the Winchester volume of John Britton's *Cathedral Antiquities* was published. It was the first to challenge the 'British' mythological origins of the Cathedral and also to assert that 'no architectural part of the present church is strictly Saxon' (Crook 2003: 237). The next major analysis of the standing Cathedral fabric was made by Professor Willis in a lecture he gave to a meeting of the Archaeological Institute in 1845 (ibid.: 238). Willis realized that the recently cleared crypt provided the plan of the Norman east end of the Cathedral and rightly identified the sequence of the remodelling of the Romanesque nave. In 1886, Dean Kitchen (unwittingly) revealed part of the New Minster on Cathedral Green during his search for Saint Swithun's grave (Biddle 1964: 206). Further archaeological discoveries were made during the underpinning work carried out between 1905 and 1912; these included both a Roman mosaic and part of a medieval funerary monument (Ottaway 2017: 10).

Early investigations

The earliest record of an archaeological discovery was that of a Roman tessellated pavement observed in 1693 during the construction of Christopher Wren's palace for Charles II (Ottaway 2017: 10). Milner's account of Winchester's antiquities also records discoveries at Hyde Abbey when the abandoned site was used in 1785 for building the new Bridewell Prison:

> At almost every stoke of the mattock or spade some ancient sepulchre was violated, the venerable contents of which were treated with marked indignity. A great number of stone coffins were dug up with a variety of other curious artefacts . . . (including) a beautiful crosier.
>
> MILNER 1789: 227

Although this thirteenth-century crozier found its way to the Victoria & Albert Museum (Campbell 1987), it appears that most of the excavated artefacts, as well as the remains of the abbey buildings, did not survive (Qualmann, Scobie and Zant 2021: 46). The lure of King Alfred's reburial site at the Abbey continued to prompt a number of investigations in the nineteenth and early twentieth centuries that were largely 'unscientific', although John Mellor did recover bones which two centuries later were to form the basis of illuminating scientific research (ibid.: 275–95; Albert and Tucker 2015: 209–28).

During the nineteenth century, there were a number of discoveries of (predominately) Roman remains recorded in and around the town, including several 'tessellated pavements' as well as high-quality bronzes, an inscribed altar and burials. These early finds have been re-evaluated and published recently (Morris and Biddle 2023: 5–6) and will be discussed below (43). Winchester's past and surviving historical landmarks made it a 'suitable' location for meetings of learned societies hosting in 1845 both the British Archaeological Association and the Archaeological Institute (James 2009: 17–18). The following year, this national interest in Winchester's past prompted its citizens to decide to create a museum (ibid.: 19). Designated the City Museum in 1851, it was housed in a number of locations before being established in one of the first purpose-built museums in the UK in 1903; another museum had also been created in the surviving Westgate of the city in 1898 (ibid.). The founding in 1885 of the Hampshire Field Club and Archaeology Society prompted – and continues to promote – the study of the county's heritage (Taylor 1985: 5). In 1923, the Ordnance Survey published a map of 'Celtic' and Roman Winchester documenting where finds had been made and proposing what the street plan might have been. In 1924, the Royal Archaeological Institute (1924: 313–76) returned to the city and heard papers on Roman and medieval Winchester as well as visiting a number of sites in Winchester and other parts of Hampshire.

Early twentieth-century archaeological investigations

The first systematic archaeological excavation was carried out from 1925–8, not in the city itself but nearby at St Catherine's Hill, on land owned by Winchester College and led by three of its former students (Hawkes, Myres and Stevens 1930). Although today this excavation is remembered primarily for the Iron Age hillfort evidence (37), the authors had a more complex and interesting rationale for their researches:

> It has been our aim to focus all the available evidence on the continuous story of a single very limited area, and to shew the effects upon it of those many changes and chances whose interplay in the course of centuries has produced the History of England.
>
> ibid.: preface

Because of these research aims, in addition to excavation reports, the publication contains detailed analyses of documentary sources relating to the chapel which once stood on the hill's summit, discussions of the remains of the maze sited there and an account of the part St Catherine's Hill played in the life of Winchester College (ibid.), an approach that arguably foreshadows that of Martin Biddle in using all sources to illuminate Winchester's past (Biddle 1964: 188).

For more than thirty years this research excavation remained a 'one off', with the majority of archaeological knowledge of Winchester's past being derived from 'rescue' contexts. Sydney Ward Evans came to the city in 1926 and soon identified himself as 'Honorary Archaeologist' carrying out watching briefs on hundreds of building sites and funding information boards documenting what had been found. He correctly identified the Iron Age date of the earthworks at Oram's Arbour and recorded six Roman cemeteries

(Ottaway 2017: 11). In 1947 Winchester City Council employed its first paid Winchester Museum Curator, Frank Cottrill, who both updated the museum exhibitions and oversaw the first systematic excavations programme within the city (Collis 2011: 75). Between 1953 and 1961 Cottrill organized programmes of excavations on key sites in advance of road widening and development (Ottaway 2017: 11). Whilst he and the museum staff oversaw the watching briefs and ad hoc excavations, systematic digs were led by young archaeologists, two of whom, in particular, went on to be among the most significant archaeologists of their generation – Barry Cunliffe and John Collis. The publication of these excavations made major contributions to understanding Winchester's development (Cunliffe 1964, Collis 1978).

The Biddle achievement

Martin Biddle's contributions to the development of open-area archaeology techniques, meticulous recording, systematic post-excavation processes with a dedicated team, interdisciplinary research and the de facto invention of the discipline of urban archaeology, has been widely acknowledged (Carver 1987: 104–5; Collis 2011; Hilts 2015; Ottaway 2017: 13–15; Wood 2022b) and his excavation and post-excavation methodologies were set out in full detail in WS 7ii ((Biddle 1990: 9–23). From Biddle's various publications, it is evident that his innovations were underpinned by a continuing willingness to learn from what he encountered and to adapt what he was doing either at the time or subsequently (Barker 1993: 46). Whilst an undergraduate at Cambridge, Biddle was influenced by the archaeozoological approaches being pioneered by Eric Higgs and published a joint article with him on the animal bones from the excavations at Arreton Down (Higgs and Biddle 1960). Unusually for the time, animal bones were collected at all of Biddle's excavations in Winchester; environmental evidence was also sampled, especially where there were waterlogged deposits, providing evidence of agriculture, food processing and diet (Biddle, Renfrew and Ottaway 2022). Biddle's early experience of urban excavations in the Middle East were steeped in the tradition of cutting and recording of deep sections established by Sir Mortimer Wheeler (1954; Collis 2011: 75), but at the sites of the Assize Courts and Brook Street he realized that the site would be understood best if dug as a whole, retaining the use of standing sections for answering specific questions (Barker 1993: 113 and 117; Morris and Biddle 2023: 15–16). To ensure that nothing was lost, however, he also instigated new methods of recording and post-excavation analysis (ibid.: 16–23). When Birthe Kjølbye (later Biddle) suggested that metric rather than imperial measurements would better fit the complexities of the excavations at Cathedral Green, he not only adopted them – and her methodological approach – there, but across most of the Winchester excavations (Collis 2011: 76–9; Biddle 2021b: 24; Morris and Biddle 2023: 17).

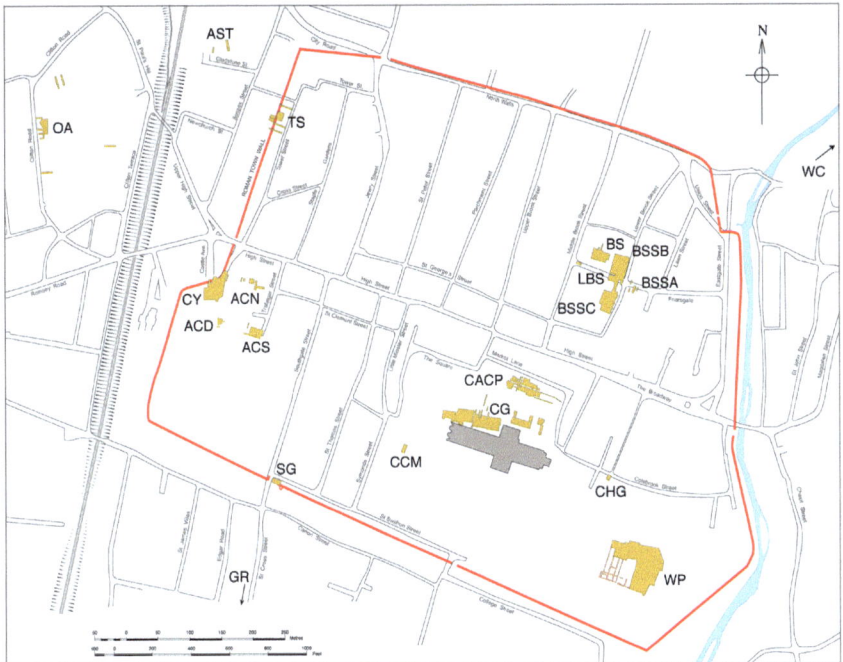

FIGURE 2.1 *Sites excavated by the Winchester Excavations Committee, 1961–71*
© WEC.

ACD, *Assize Courts Ditch*; ACN, *Assize Courts North*; ACS, *Assize Courts South*; AST *Ashley Terrace*; BS/LBS, *Lower Brook St*; CACP, *Cathedral Car Park*; CCM, *Cathedral Close Mound:* CHG, *Colebrook House Garden*; CG, *Cathedral Green*; SG, *Southgate St*; TS, *Tower St*; WC, *Winnall Cemetery*; WP, *Wolvesey Palace*.

After visiting Poland, Biddle recognized that the post-excavation programme of the scale the Winchester excavations demanded would require the establishment of the Polish model of long-term post-excavations team for the first time in the UK (ibid.: 23; Ottaway 1992: 10–11), rather than the temporary staffing that was the norm at the time (Cooper and Yarrow 2002). Therefore, in 1968, with funding from local and central government as well as from charitable trusts, the Winchester Research Unit was established to undertake the analysis and publication of his excavations (Biddle 2021b: 230). As Collis has identified, this organization model was adopted widely in British archaeology, notably in York, Oxford and London, to support an integrated and multidisciplinary approach to understanding a city's past (2011: 77–8).

What is also evident is that Biddle had the charisma and ability to engage, which captured the attention both of his archaeological colleagues and more widely. His presentation of the outcomes of the 1961 excavations had led to

FIGURE 2.2 *Looking N-W over excavation of the remains of the West Hall, Wolvesey Palace* © WEC.

a meeting of hundreds of Winchester's citizens that established the Winchester Excavations Committee (WEC) (Biddle 2021b: 20) and also secured funding from both Winchester City and Hampshire County Councils. After visiting the Lower Brook Street excavations, Professor Urban T. Holmes Jr invited Biddle to visit Chapel Hill, University of North Carolina, which led to the recruitment of student volunteers from there and the nearby Duke University, as well as substantial funding from both universities and from the US National Endowment for the Humanities (ibid.: 21).

With a team of volunteers (3,000 over the complete excavations' campaign), supervised by more experienced archaeologists schooled in the Winchester method (Collis 2011: 22; Morris and Biddle 2023: 17), four major sites and eighteen smaller sites were excavated between 1961 and 1971 (ibid.: 15). These major sites were Cathedral Green, Wolvesey Palace, Castle Yard and Lower Brook Street. However important the results from individual sites have been, what distinguishes the Winchester project is Martin Biddle's vision and aim for it, which he articulated first in the second interim report:

> to undertake excavations ... aimed at studying the development of Winchester as a town from its earliest origins to the establishment of the modern city. The centre of interest is the city itself, not any one period of its past, nor any one part of its remains.
>
> BIDDLE 1964: 188

These were restated and amplified in the following year:

> Important research programmes into various scientific problems, biological, botanical and physical have begun and throughout emphasis has been, and will continue to be, laid on the use of all available evidence, documentary, archaeological, scientific, to study the development of Winchester as an urban environment and of the inhabitants in inter-relation with that environment over a period of two thousand years.
>
> BIDDLE 1965: 261

This approach has led to the publication of four major volumes of Winchester Studies whose focus is documentary research: WS 1 *Winchester in the Early Middle Ages,* WS 2 *Survey of Medieval Winchester,* WS 4.ii *The Cult of St Swithun,* and WS 4.iii *Property and Piety in Early Medieval Winchester,* as well as the following five thematic archaeological volumes:

WS7ii *Object and Economy in Medieval Winchester* (Biddle et al. 1990). Under Martin Biddle's leadership, a team of eighty-three contributors analysed the post-Roman small finds from all the excavations to provide insights into Winchester's industries and trade as well as its cultural, economic and social life.

WS8 *The Winchester Mint and Coins and Related Finds from the Excavations of 1961–71* (Biddle 2012). With a catalogue of the known coins produced by Yvonne Harvey, this volume documents and illustrates more than 3,000 silver pennies produced under royal authority at the Winchester Mint between the reigns of King Alfred and Henry III.

WS9.1 *The People of Early Winchester* (Stuckert 2017). This volume presents the demography, physical characteristics, dental health, disease and trauma evidenced in 2,000 burials from the Winchester area dating from mid-third to the mid-sixteenth century, illuminating the lives, health, and disorders as well as causes of death of Winchester's inhabitants.

WS10 *Environment and Agriculture of Early Winchester* (Biddle, Renfrew and Ottaway 2022). This study draws on the contributions of a wide range of scholars using archaeological, documentary and paleoenvironmental evidence to illustrate the natural environment of Winchester and its immediate surroundings, and to explore the human interactions with that environment through agriculture, gardening and horticulture from the late Iron Age to the early post-medieval period.

WS3.1 *Venta Belgarum: Prehistoric, Roman, and Post-Roman Winchester* (Morris and Biddle 2023). With a team of sixty-four contributors, this is a detailed study of the archaeology of Roman Winchester based on the excavation of fourteen sites and the analysis of 4,000 artefacts. The archaeology of the Winchester area in prehistory is also included, as well as a description of what happened in the town between the end of organized Roman life and the seventh century.

Two further thematic Winchester Studies volumes (on ceramics and on animal bones, respectively) are in preparation, along with the site-based publications of the Anglo-Saxon Minsters, Lower Brook Street, Winchester Castle and Wolvesey Palace. In addition, WS11 *Winchester: British Historic Towns Atlas – Volume VI: 6* (Biddle and Keene 2017) was published jointly with the Historic Towns' Trust: it is centred on a detailed map of the town showing Winchester's historic buildings and structures as they were in 1800. A series of further maps show Winchester at key points in its history, charting its development and changing shape. Although not in the Winchester Studies series, *King Arthur's Round Table: An Archaeological Investigation* was published for the Winchester Excavations Committee (Biddle 2000a), with the Research Unit's same commitment to interdisciplinary approaches. The multi-author volume contains (in addition to Biddle's own analyses) contributions on iconography, dating, the Round Table in literature and legend as well as its links to the foundation of the Order of the Garter.

After the WEC excavations finished, in 1972 Biddle instigated the formation of the Winchester Rescue Archaeology Group (WARG) as volunteer support to Winchester City Council's newly appointed Rescue

FIGURE 2.3 *Martin Biddle examining the construction of the Round Table during its removal for restoration. Photo: Bob Pendreigh.*

Archaeologist (Ottaway 2017: 15). This support included finding and fitting out premises in which he could work (Old, Backhouse and WARG 2022: 16) as well as undertaking excavations and post-excavation work, producing regular newsletters and outreach activities (ibid.: 24–5). Over the next fifteen years, WARG published the results of 200 excavation projects (ibid.: 40–82), including major excavations at St Cross and St Elizabeth's Church (ibid.: 25–32) (108 and 94). WARG also plays a key role in the various community-based projects that form part of Hyde 900's continuing programme of activities in and around the site of Hyde Abbey (ibid.: 82–5). In 2005 WARG added Local History to its title, continuing to arrange lectures and visits as well as annual excavations; it assists with the curation of the city's archaeological archive, and with post-excavation work for the Winchester Research Unit.

In addition to the production of Winchester Studies and his contribution to archaeology nationally and internationally – which earned him an OBE in 1997 and a CBE in 2014 – Martin Biddle has made the results of his discoveries accessible to the people of Winchester through regular public lectures and provided advice to Winchester Cathedral and the City Council as well as overseeing the study of the Round Table. In recognition of these contributions, in 2010 he was made an Honorary Freeman of the City of Winchester. One key part of these achievements was the personal and professional partnership with his wife, Birthe Kjølbye-Biddle, who also co-directed many excavations outside Winchester. Following her direction of the site of Cathedral Green, Birthe was working on the publication of the Anglo-Saxon Minsters until shortly before her death in 2010.

Later work

Patrick Ottaway has summarized how archaeology in the city progressed from 1972 onwards, mainly through the work of archaeologists employed by Winchester City Council and latterly through excavations funded by developers (Ottaway 2017: 15–17). The final section of this chapter will outline four of these projects which have made key contributions to Winchester's archaeology.

Lankhills

Although he dug at Wolvesey Palace, where he was trained in WEC methods, Giles Clarke began the excavation of the Roman cemetery at Lankhills in 1967 while he was still a research student, and it was staffed primarily by pupils from Winchester's secondary schools. The Winchester Research Unit oversaw its publication; hence it became *Winchester Studies 4.1* (Clarke 1979: 1–3). Later excavations extended the sample of graves (Booth et al. 2010) and samples from over fifty skeletons have been subjected to isotope analysis, generally taken to indicate where an individual grew up (Clarke 2023: 1226). Taking the results together with the funerary rites, Clarke now argues that:

> the Lankhills cemetery contained more people of non-local childhood than was suspected in the 1970s. Some of the burials then thought to be of people of local origin appear not to be so, and it may be the intrusive group included additional or different elements.
>
> ibid.: 1244

Further isotope and DNA analysis is currently underway on a larger sample of the skeletons, as is a further exploration of comparable burials in mainland Europe, which together may help us to understand better the late to post-Roman period in Winchester (56). It seems likely that the application of the 'Twigstats' methodology will further assist in a better understanding of the population make-up of these individuals and late Roman populations of Britain more generally (Spiedal et al. 2025: 123).

St Mary Magdalen

The ten-year research programme carried out by the University of Winchester at the site of the medieval leper hospital of St Mary Magdalen revealed a series of carefully curated burials (Roffey and Tucker 2012) as well as a succession of buildings (Roffey 2020). The combination of osteological, archaeological and historical research led to a major re-evaluation of the treatment of people with leprosy, suggesting that the first phase of the site was effectively also a religious community (Roffey 2020: 545) and reflecting the concept of leprosy as a mark of divine favour and a 'passport to paradise' (Rawcliffe 2009: 58–9). (110).

Winchester Cathedral mortuary chests

In 2010, Winchester Cathedral instigated a research programme jointly with anthropologists from the University of Bristol to study the skeletal remains contained in a number of mortuary chests that were traditionally identified as housing the remains of a number of early medieval rulers and churchmen (Crook 2022: 136). Preliminary analysis was published in 2019 reporting on how the team identified which bones belong together (Yorke 2021b: 61). Coupled with the radiocarbon dating that was undertaken, it seems likely that the female burial is Queen Emma, who married both the Saxon king, Aethelred and later the Danish King, Cnut (Jarman 2023: 310–18). Jarman has used the burials and their related documentary sources to provide an overview of late Anglo-Saxon England, as well as exploring what the history of the burials reveals about the evolution of the Anglo-Saxon and Anglo-Scandinavian dynasties and how Winchester (and its Minsters and Cathedral) fit within the history of England more generally (Jarman 2023) (86).

Barton Farm Hessian Camp

Between July 1756 and April 1757, 3,000 mercenary troops from the German state of Hesse were stationed just outside Winchester as part of the defence against a possible French invasion at the start of the Seven Years' War (McCulloch and Osgood 2018: 20); William Godson produced a drawing of the camp (ibid.: 21). In 2015, in advance of the Barton Farm development, a geophysical survey revealed square features that matched what was depicted on the drawing as field kitchens; subsequent excavations revealed more details of these kitchens, as well as the soldiers' living accommodation also as depicted in the drawing (ibid.: 22–3). The team from Pre Construct Archaeology undertaking the excavation were supplemented by three members of *Operation Nightingale* – the Ministry of Defence scheme using archaeology to aid the recovery of wounded ex-service personnel. One of these former soldiers brought an interpretation of what was found inspired by his own experience:

> Transit accommodation, and any situation where soldiers are grouped together for extended periods of time in less than comfortable surroundings, is where the real bonds of brotherhood and friendship are made.
>
> ibid.: 25

3

The Early Settlements

The situation of Winchester

Winchester lies in the gap that the River Itchen has dissected through the west–east chalk ridge on the southern margin of the Hampshire Chalk Downs (Ottoway 2017: 22–3); the Itchen is a typical shallow Wessex chalk stream that rises to the north-east of the city at Hinton Marsh. To the east, west and north, the city is surrounded by upland downs; to the south is the Hampshire Basin leading to the sea at Southampton. The natural environment of Winchester therefore can be considered as two zones: the river valley; and the surrounding chalk down. From Teg Down in the west and Compton Down in the south-west, the downs descend gently to the river valley, while the promontories and slopes of Magdalen Hill Down and Twyford Down drop steeply to the river (Renfrew and Ottaway 2022: 26)

The prehistoric landscape

The evolution of the landscape in Winchester and its surrounding areas has been reconstructed from a number of paleoenvironmental studies based on pollen and mollusc analysis; from these, it appears that the first clearances of the deciduous woodlands began in the late fifth or early fourth millennium and can be associated plausibly with the beginning of arable agriculture (Bradley 2019: 39–40). Borehole samples taken from the site of the Pilgrim School (on the Itchen floodplain and within the later walled town) suggest that although that area would have been too wet for human habitation, the wetland environments could have served as seasonal pasture. These pollen cores include an increasing representation of cereal pollen and a decrease in that from trees, indicating that arable agriculture was taking place on nearby drier land in the later prehistoric periods (Champness, Teague and Ford 2012: 36). However, although pollen cores from Winnall Downs imply some woodland clearance from the Mesolithic period onwards (10,000 to 4,000 BCE) (Morris and Biddle 2023: 33), mollusc evidence from downland environments suggests that woodland persisted there until the Bronze Age (Ottaway 2017: 28). By the end of that era, the whole Winchester environs show evidence of woodlands, pasture and arable land. implying mixed agriculture supported by woodland management in line with the general pattern in Southern England (ibid.; Bradley 2019: 263–4).

Prehistoric human activity

Preservation

Generally, the downland areas give a clearer idea of prehistoric settlement than the walled area of the city, as Patrick Ottaway has identified:

> The changing pattern of human settlement has had an important effect on the survival and visibility of archaeological remains. Like many of Britain's historic towns and cities, the various periods of occupation in Winchester more or less overlie one another ... (and) as a consequence of this stratification the remains of earlier periods can be more or less compromised by the impact of activities in later ones.
>
> OTTAWAY 2017: 28

Palaeolithic remains

While it was still connected to mainland Europe, the earliest humans colonized Great Britain during interglacial periods; although there are a small number of stratified Palaeolithic sites, human activity is attested to predominately by stone tools that have a high potential for survival but often little or no context (Pryor 2004: 58). Ottaway has argued that the modern distribution of these tools in Hampshire as whole is the product of:

> the extent of collection by various parties, the incidence of quarrying and the emergence of rivers from constrained valleys through the chalk into broader valleys on Tertiary rocks.
>
> 2017: 41

Against this background, the finds of hand axes and other stone tools discovered in the Winchester area, and assigned a date by typological analysis, testify to human activity there in the period 800,000–10,000 BCE (Morris and Biddle 2023: 32). In the Mesolithic period, the main evidence is also of stone tool fragments, although (as noted above) pollen cores give evidence of human intervention in the natural environment, resulting by 4690–4330 BCE in a decline in tree pollen as well as a rise in grass pollen (including cereals) and herbs (ibid.: 33). Bradley identifies (2019: 36) that this change may be the result of systematic burning which would have increased the food supply and also enabled the concentration of game animals.

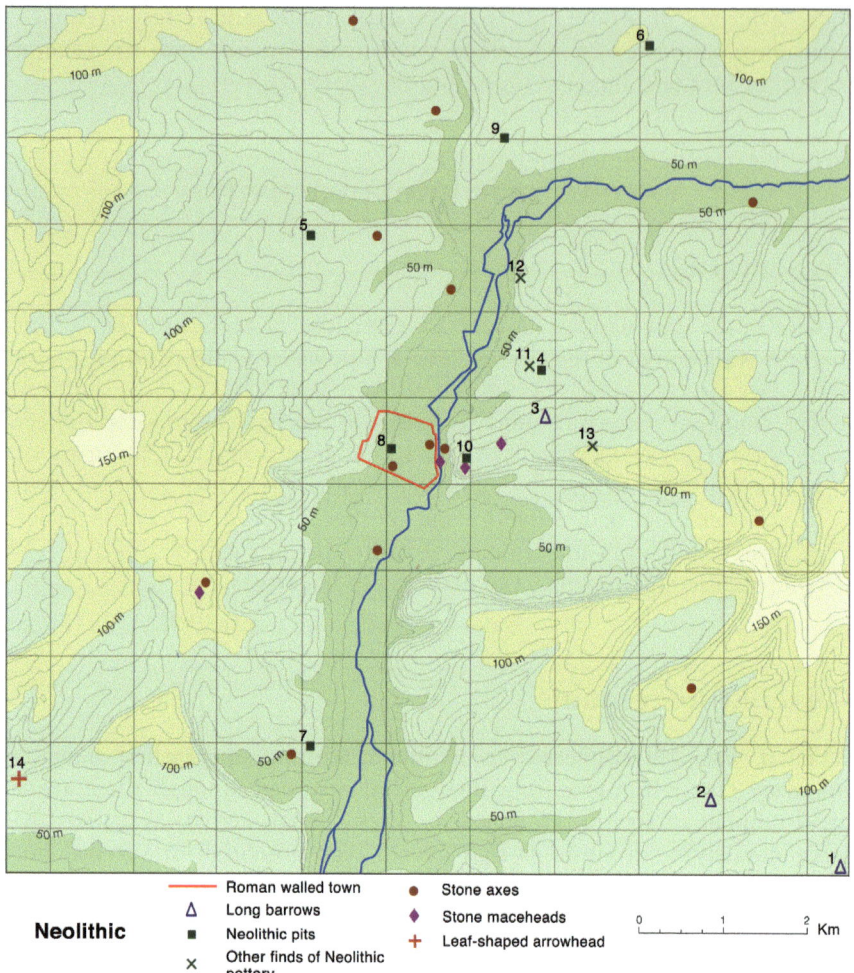

FIGURE 3.1 *Neolithic sites and finds in the Winchester area* © WEC.

1 Longwood House; 2 Morestead Warren; 3 St Swithun's School; 4 Winnall Down; 5 Barton Farm; 6 Burntwood Farm; 7 South Winchester Park and Ride; 8 Little Minster Street; 9 Lovedon Lane; 10 Northbrook Avenue; 11 Easton Lane; 12 Easton Down; 13 former Victoria Hospital; 14 east of Hursley.

The Neolithic period

Recent research indicates a complex transition between the Mesolithic and Neolithic periods, recognizing that rather than being a 'Neolithic Revolution' (Childe 1923: 48), human management of animals and the landscape was a process of evolution (Thomas 1999, Pryor 2004: 135–7, Bradley 2019: 34–8). At some point settled 'mixed farming' became the predominant form of subsistence with pottery types, animals and forms of monumental architecture that have clear links with Europe (Bradley 2019: 40). Petrological analysis has also produced evidence for long-distance transport of axes from the Western Alps to Britain in the early Neolithic, suggesting complex human interactions over considerable distances (Pétrequin et al. 2012).

The earliest identifiable Neolithic monument near Winchester is a ring ditch excavated at Winnall Down and dated to 4690 +/− 90 BP; no other internal or external features were associated with this earthwork (Fasham 1985: 19–24). Traces of other earthworks are a possible ploughed-out long barrow, just north of St Swithun's School on Magdalen Hill, and further away to the south-east of Winchester, the long barrows at Longwood House and Morstead Warren. Within and around the city, pits with Neolithic pottery have been found at ten sites, as well as flint axes at thirteen locations and mace heads from a further four (Morris and Biddle 2023: 33, 36). Overall, in the Neolithic there is evidence for a variety of agricultural settlements (managing both crops and animals), that were generating sufficient surpluses for communities to invest in the construction of a variety of communal monuments such as Durrington Walls, Stonehenge and Woodhenge, all less than a day's walk from the Winchester area (Bradley 2019: 124–30, 143–8).

The Bronze Age

In the Bronze Age, a new ceramic type – 'Beaker pottery' – appears, associated with single inhumation burials, continental-style archery equipment and objects of gold and copper dating to *c.* 2450 BCE (Bradley 2019: 249, Armit and Reich 2021: 1464). There has always been a consensus that the origins of this Bronze Age culture lies in mainland Europe, but there has been a debate about the nature of the process by which these changes were adopted (ibid.: 1465). In 2018 an analysis of the genome-wide data was published, from 400 individuals in Britain and Europe dating from the Neolithic period to the Middle Bronze Age, including 226 associated with distinctive Beaker Complex artefacts (Olalde et al. 2018). The authors argued that the European data show that whilst populations in Iberia and Central Europe shared Beaker culture, genetically they differed considerably: the former predominately shared the genetic profile of their Neolithic ancestors, whilst the latter evidenced lineages derived from the Yamnaya cultures of the Eurasian Steppe (ibid., Armit and Reich 2021: 1467). Developing the argument further, Armit and Reich identified that in the UK the analysis revealed none of the Steppe profile in the Neolithic profiles sampled but did show that 90 per cent of the sample of Beaker-associated burials had the Steppe profile; mitochondrial haplogroups not previously present in Britain led the authors to suggest that women had also moved in substantial numbers (ibid.: 1468). Furthermore, this genetic profile continues to predominate in samples from later periods. These results prompted the authors to argue that this evidence:

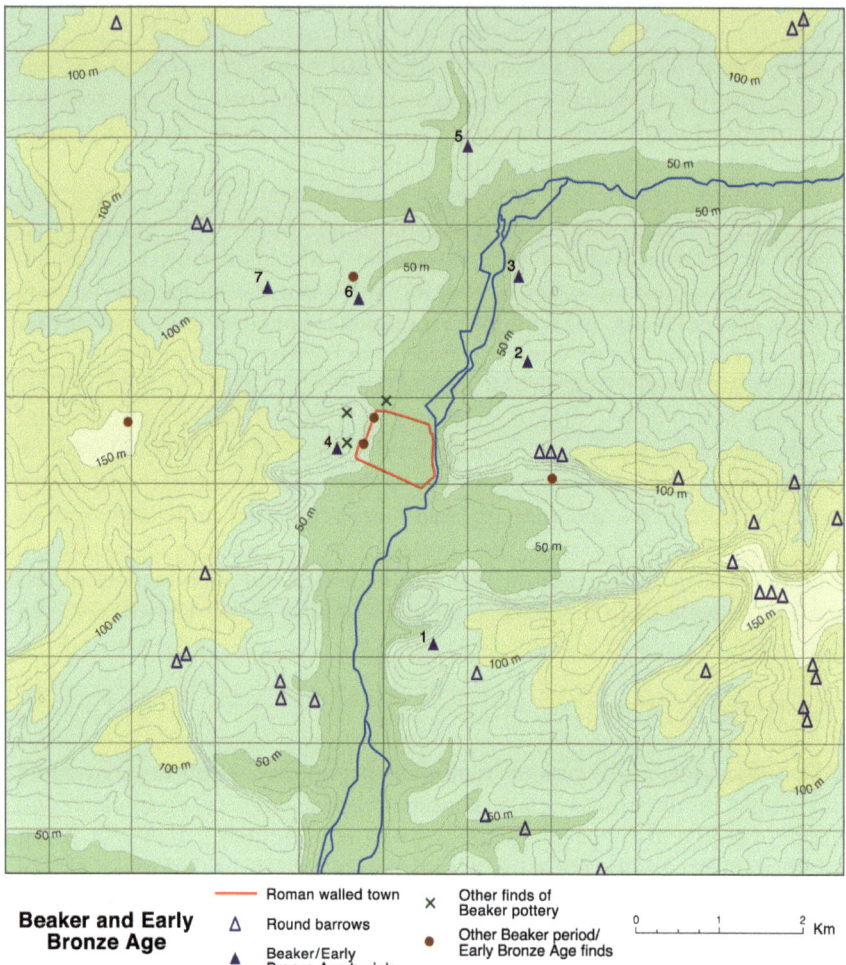

FIGURE 3.2 *Beaker and Early Bronze Age sites and finds in the Winchester area* © WEC.

1 Twyford Down; 2 Easton Lane; 3 Easton Down; 4 Mews Lane; 5 Kings Worthy; 6 Barton Farm; 7 Rowlings Road.

shows a replacement of 93 % of the gene pool in Britain, suggesting that the arrival of the Beaker Complex correlates with a massive turnover of population during the final centuries of the third millennium BC.

ibid.: 1473

Although there have been some challenges to these arguments, the methodology and conclusions appear to now be accepted generally (Armit and Reich 2021: 1470) and it seems possible that this population movement was enabled by the decline in the pre-existing Neolithic populations (ibid.:

1471). Certainly, radiocarbon dating of burnt cereals appears to show a sharp drop in agricultural activity at the start of the Middle Neolithic, *c.* 3350 BCE; there is a further decline at *c.* 2850 BCE as well as a remarkably low level of arable cultivation that persists until *c.* 2450 BCE (Stevens and Fuller 2012, 2015: fig. 1). Recent studies of ancient DNA from Scandinavian sites have demonstrated regular outbreaks of bubonic plague in the indigenous Neolithic communities, which the researchers suggest may have resulted in their decline and eventual replacement (Seersholm et al. 2024); whether this also happened in the UK must await comparable studies. As there is a considerable degree of continuity in the overall archaeological record, it seems likely that the arrival of people with the Steppe DNA/Beaker assemblage was a gradual process that also included a continuing veneration of existing sacred sites such as Stonehenge, where there are developments associated with Beaker assemblages (Armit and Reich 2021: 1472).

The Bronze Age discoveries from the Winchester area come predominately from cemetery sites (including round barrows), where both inhumations and cremations are associated with Beaker pottery and the later 'Deverel-Rimbury' wares; there are also several pits containing domestic waste, including pottery (Ottaway 2017: 58, Morris and Biddle 2023: 36). A small number of settlement sites have been discovered on the downland areas, however, where there is less disturbance from later activity (Morris and Biddle: 36–8). At Easton Lane, in addition to cremation and inhumation burials, evidence has been found both of domestic buildings and of what have been interpreted as field boundaries: the ditches cover an area of 15 hectares and environmental evidence indicates they were laid out over open downland (Ottaway 2017: 54). They suggested that the site, dating from the Middle Bronze Age, may have played a role in the regional trade networks as it is in a commanding position above the River Itchen and could have controlled the surrounding routeways (Fasham, Farwell and Whinney 1989: 54). Although none of the Winchester bones was included in the DNA study referred to above, the greater organization of the landscape and more evidence of domestic and funerary activity could plausibly be attributed to incoming people occupying land that had fallen out of use.

The Iron Age

In 2007, Haselgrove and Pope introduced their collection of research papers with this assessment:

> The Earlier Iron Age is a period which has consistently managed to elude study in British prehistoric studies ... Nevertheless, the Earlier Iron Age encompasses a period of major social change in later prehistory which we have consistently failed to characterise, let alone understand.
>
> HASELGROVE and POPE 2007: 1

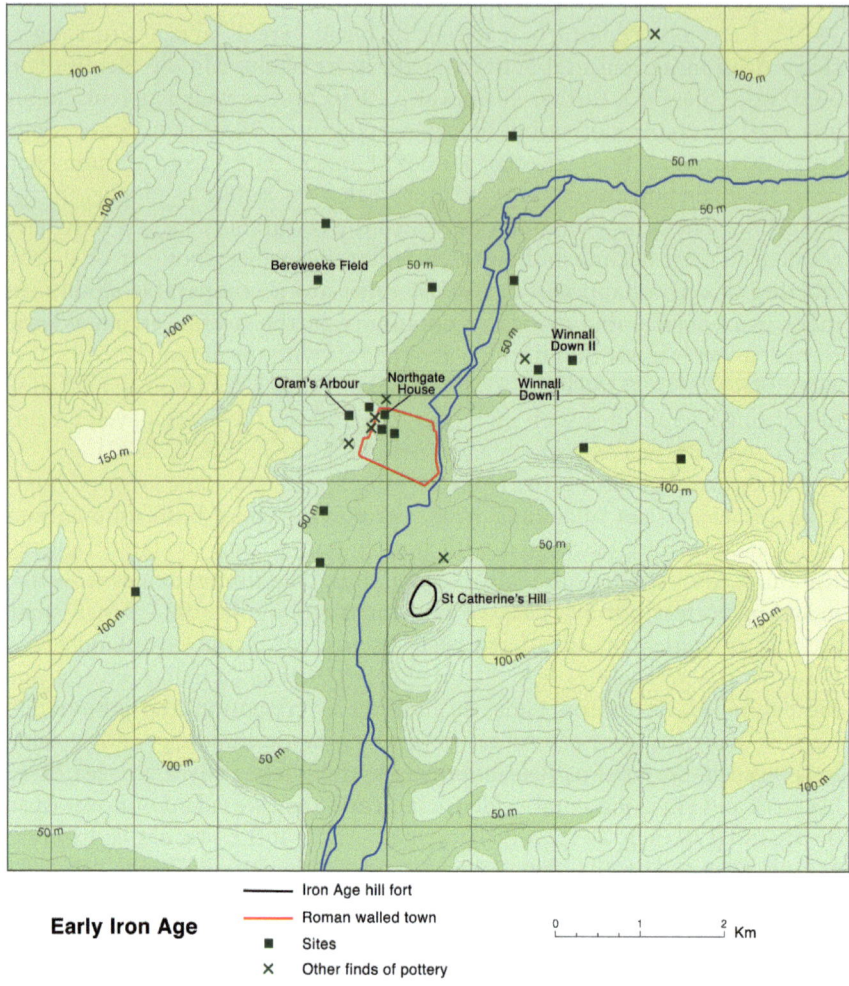

FIGURE 3.3 *Early Iron Age sites and finds in the Winchester area* © WEC.

The production of bronze requires copper, tin and sometimes lead, all of which had restricted availability, so networks of control and distribution were needed for the creation of bronze artefacts as well as for their subsequent circulation. Iron is much more common and relatively easy to work, however, which might have impacted the economic and social fabric of society (Bradley 2019: 271). Needham (2007: 40), proposes that 800 BCE should be identified as a point when a range of evidence marks a significant societal change lasting perhaps for a century. Recent radiocarbon dating from the midden at East Chisenbury, Wiltshire, indicates that in Wessex that transition may extend to the mid-fifth century BCE, as despite the decline of bronze objects in circulation, there is evidence of a continuing use of bronze and renewed exchange networks with Brittany and Normandy (Waddington et al. 2019: 2). Furthermore, Webley (2015: 124–5) has identified a considerable degree of commonality in the forms of everyday objects – iron artefacts, querns, loom-weights and weaving combs – in both Britain and Europe. The recent 'Twigstats' DNA analysis has suggested that 'In Britain, the ancestries of Iron Age and Roman individuals form a tight cluster ... shifted relative to available preceding Bronze Age individuals from Ireland and Orkney, and adjacent to, but distinct from, available individuals in Iron Age and Roman central Europe' (Spiedal et al. 2025: 123). It seems likely that further applications of this methodology will enable a better understanding of the extent to which change was the result of the transmission of ideas or the migration of peoples.

As was outlined above (21), a series of excavations was carried out at St Catherine's Hill where the still-surviving bank and ditch enclose an area of 9 hectares; the limited but well-recorded excavations revealed four periods of construction of the entrance works which came to an end with the intense burning of the ramparts' facings (Hawkes, Myres and Stevens 1930: 67). Excavation of the interior was very limited and revealed no postholes, but a number of pits were discovered (ibid.: 85–92) and although the pottery found has not been reviewed recently, it parallels that dated elsewhere as fourth to second century BCE. No late Iron Age pottery was found, suggesting that – like many other Wessex hillforts – it was abandoned by the middle of the second century BCE (Ottaway 2017: 61). Davis (2015: 48) has usefully summarized the consensus for the origins, use and abandonment of the Wessex hillforts:

1. There is considerable variation in the occupation evidence at Early Iron Age hillforts and it is likely that they were created for a number of different purposes (e.g. enclosure for pastoral activities, defined space for ritual, storage for agricultural surplus, defence, territorial marker), many of which were not mutually exclusive.

2. Middle Iron Age hillforts exhibit evidence of intensive internal activity and were strongly defended, with multiple lines of ramparts and complex entranceways. This suggests a major social change, perhaps even the result of long, drawn-out conflict between different communities.

Whilst there was an established consensus that the primary driver for hillfort construction was defence (e.g. Collis 1981), some authors argue that the motivation for construction was linked to ideas of community prestige rather than a reaction to a crisis (e.g. Sharples 2010).

Although the subject of more recent systematic excavations, the Oram's Arbour enclosure of 20 hectares, underlying the western edge of the Roman walled town, also remains enigmatic (Collis 2019; Morris and Biddle 2023:

42–7). Only 3 per cent of its enclosed area has been excavated under controlled conditions (Ottaway 2017: 64) and where evidence of occupation *has* been explored, the area excavated has been too small to provide complete plans of structures and/or they were disturbed by later activity (ibid.; Morris and Biddle 2023: 45). It appears that the site was first enclosed in the Middle Iron Age but the lack of evidence from both sites means that it is impossible to say whether Oram's Arbour and St Catherine's Hill were used concurrently or successively (ibid.: 43). Excavations of the ditch of the enclosure and its western entrance show signs of recutting and, although not closely datable, there is evidence of domestic activity which appears to have continued until the second century BCE (Biddle 1967: 254–5). Oram's Arbour is unusual in that it is sited on a slope and overlooked by rising ground, thereby limiting its defensiveness (Morris and Biddle 2023: 45). However, the investment of resources to enclose an area four times the size of the majority of 'developed' hillforts in Wessex (Morris and Biddle 2023: 45) leads these authors to argue that it:

> served as some form of regional political centre for which good communications were essential, with other factors (e.g., defence, concentration of population, religion, exchange, production) perhaps also being of importance, although our evidence for exchange, production, and storage at Oram's Arbour is at present limited.
>
> ibid.: 46

Based on the excavation evidence, Ottaway has drawn attention to evidence of a hollow way from the north approaching the enclosure's northern entrance and leading to a point that would later become the north gate of the Roman town (Qualmann et al. 2004: 48). He also suggests that another entrance was probably located at the south-west corner of the enclosure, where a hollow way (on the line of the modern Romsey Road) crossed the line of the enclosure defences (Ottaway 2017: 65). He further hypotheses that there would be an opening on the eastern side relating to a route descending to the river and goes on to argue that the enclosure was deliberately located at the junction of these two major trackways in order to compel long distance traffic to enter it, creating a focal point for trade and commerce (ibid.: 73, Biddle 1967: 254–5). As will be explored below (44), even though there is no evidence of intensive activity at Oram's Arbour in the immediate pre-Roman period, the site appears to have influenced the layout of the Roman town.

Much less ambiguous are the mixed arable agricultural settlements around Winchester that used the downland areas increasingly intensively; they are characterized by roundhouses, storage pits, granaries, loom weights, quern stones and enclosure systems delineating the landscape (Ottaway 2017: 60, 66–9). From Winnall Down, carbonized seed remains of spelt wheat and barley are associated with weed remains that suggest that both downland and the river valley were being cultivated (Fasham 1985: 112–17). Furthermore, eighteen pits at the site produced the partial skeletons of a range of animals including cattle, sheep, pigs and dogs, apparently deposited deliberately and interpreted as ritual activity (Ottaway 2017: 68), widely paralleled at Iron Age and Roman sites in lowland England (Bradley 2019: 289). Finds from an enclosed settlement at Bereweeke Down include sherds of non-local pottery, of ceramic vessels for salt probably from the coast, and an iron ingot, suggesting connections beyond the local area (Ottaway 2017: 68–9).

Protohistory and the coming of Rome

There is evidence that Britain had regular contact with Europe for millennia; as of the first century BCE, however, that contact was with the literate world of what became the Roman Empire (de la Bédoyère 2013: 11–12). For the first time there are written descriptions of British people, how their societies were organized and even records of named individuals; because he actually visited Britain, Caesar's account has been particularly influential (ibid.: 18–19). However, as Beard has identified:

> It is not exactly a neutral document. Caesar had a shrewd eye for his public image, and the Commentaries is a carefully contrived justification of his conduct and parade of his military skill. But it is an early example of what we might call imperial ethnology . . . His is a wonderfully Roman vision of people he clearly did not entirely understand.
>
> BEARD 2015: 284

Linguistic research has called into question some of the names of individuals and 'tribes' that Caesar's account identified (Laycock 2008: 26–7). Nevertheless, there can be no doubt that Britain had moved onto the Roman agenda as a target for conquest and that members of the British elite evolved strong links with the imperial court, where some of them spent time as hostages (Russell and Laycock 2011: 24). Graafstahl has argued recently that the evidence of systematic road building in the Gallic and Germanic provinces, as well as the construction of a fortified transport corridor along the Rhine, suggest a premeditated invasion plan begun in the reign of Caligula well before the Claudian invasion of Britain (2023: 42–4). What is certain, however, is that following that invasion, a century-long military conquest was undertaken that, for the first time, created a single political entity for most of Britain – the Roman province of *Britannia* (de la Bédoyère 2013: 23–58). The detail of what happened where and exactly when continues to be disputed (Laycock 2008) but formally, until the early fifth century, Britain was an integral economic and political part of the Roman Empire (de la Bédoyère 2013: 8).

At Winchester, in the eastern part of the Oram's Arbour enclosure, the later Middle Iron Age features are overlain by a 10- to 40-centimetre-thick layer of featureless soil or turf (possibly plough soil) that Morris and Biddle identify as a 'pause horizon' indicating a hiatus in occupation, and which was in turn overlain and/or cut by the earliest Roman layers (Morris and Biddle 2023: 47). Furthermore, no examples of late indigenous Iron Age pottery or imported wares have been found in Winchester itself, although these have been discovered nearby at the rural site of Owslebury (Collis 2019: 70). Not far from this site was found the exceptional collection of gold jewellery known as the 'Winchester Hoard' (Hill et al. 2005). Morris has also catalogued the 113 Iron Age coins that have been found in a 10-by-10 kilometre square centred on Winchester (Morris and Biddle 2023: 599–611). All these finds suggest that people in the area were part of the network of trade and complex social organization that developed in southern Britain in the late Iron Age, stimulated by a closer relationship with the Roman Empire (Webley 2015: 133). Particularly because of the coin evidence, Morris and Biddle argue that the area was part of the territory controlled by the Atrebatic dynasty of Commius, thought to have covered the modern counties of Hampshire, Surrey, Berkshire and Sussex with major population centres at Silchester and Chichester (Morris and Biddle 2023: 48).

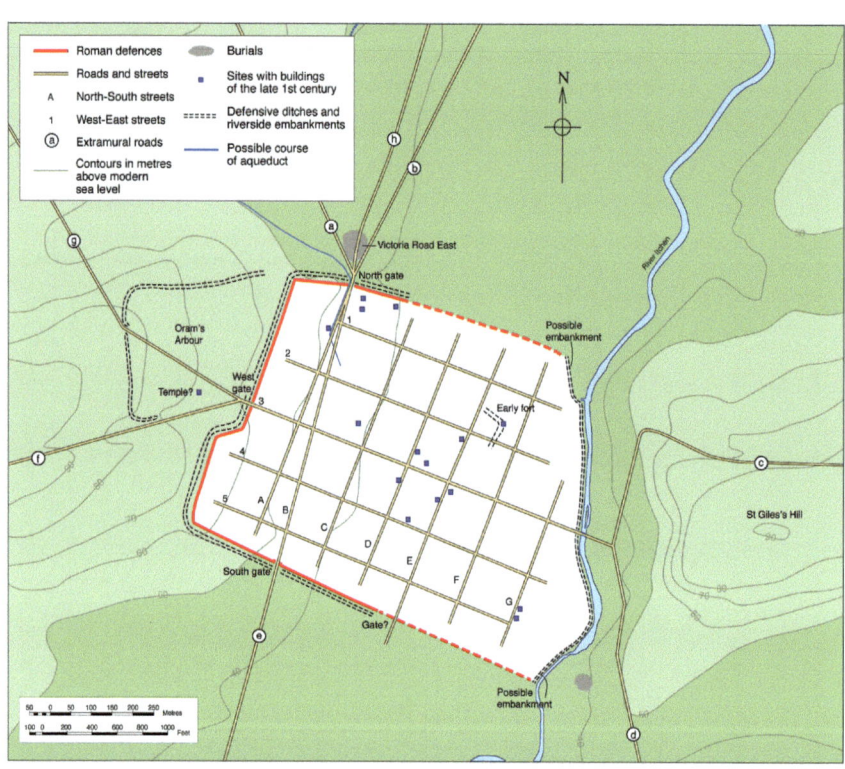

FIGURE 4.1 *Roman Winchester by* c. 90 CE © WEC.

4

The Rise and Fall of
Venta Belgarum

Foundation and early history

Before turning to the details of what we know about late Iron Age and early Roman Winchester, it is important to remember that what has been reported about Roman Britain is a product of the period in which it was discovered as well as of its original era (Carver 1987: 22). Because of their admiration for the classical world, nineteenth- and early twentieth-century scholars pictured a 'Romanized' Britain, the product of another Empire with which the elites of the British Empire deeply empathized:

> Successive generations from Haverfield (1912) onwards saw the Roman occupation of Britain in much the same light as they viewed the British occupation of India, as a benign and civilising force, rather than an agent for exploitation and repression, as any colonial occupation might now be regarded.
>
> HARDING 2020: 7

In the twenty-first century in particular, questions have been raised about the degree and depth of Romanization that the archaeological record can be deemed to demonstrate (e.g. Laycock 2008; Russell and Laycock 2011). The new town of *Venta Belgarum* was certainly an innovation, where people lived in houses very different from their Iron Age predecessors, and used pottery made with the Romans' superior technology; some people could afford prestige goods that travelled along the new metalled roads from the port at *Clausentum,* including imports from Europe (Cotton and Gathercole 1958). However, palaeobotanical and osteological evidence confirm the Roman town was firmly embedded in its agrarian hinterland, in all likelihood strongly linked to the elites that controlled it, probably the same dynasties from pre-Roman times (Laycock 2008: 17). In legal terms, everyone was a subject of the Roman Empire – from the third century a citizen if free – but it is likely that their personal sense of cultural identity was more complex and certainly not uniform (Gardner 2013: 3–6). These themes will be revisited below in relation to the late Roman/Germanic transition (55).

Although significant Roman remains have been discovered in Winchester, the later intensive occupation within the walled town has compromised the evidence, especially for the close dating of structures: artefacts were disturbed and redeposited. Morris and Biddle (2023: 581) identify that the majority of Roman finds from the 1961–71 excavations come from post-Roman contexts; many other Roman finds came from watching briefs and other rescue contexts where opportunities for systematic recording were severely limited (ibid.: 581). In excavations beyond the walls of the Roman town, the later disturbance was less severe, so the cemetery evidence is extensive and largely recently excavated, providing a significant sample of Winchester's Roman populations (Stuckert 2016: 7–123; Clarke 2023).

At Lower Brook Street, a mid-first-century ditch and associated features were discovered which Morris and Biddle (2023: 53) identify as the north-east angle of an enclosure that may have been a military fort associated with the Roman army campaigns of 43–7 CE and could have controlled the nearby putative ford across the River Itchen (ibid.: 91). Although Zant (1993: 50) argued that the high level of the water table made this unlikely, Ottaway (2017: 85) has countered that the water table may not have been so high, and this view is confirmed by Morris and Biddle (2023: 373). However, Ottaway also proposes that timber buildings set on a deliberately constructed terrace on higher ground in the north-west of the town at Oram's Arbour could be the remains of a fort (ibid.: 88), although Morris and Biddle (2023: 56) characterize it as 'non-military'. What is certain is that these timber buildings were burnt down and sealed by a thick layer of burnt daub dated by the presence of Neronian Samian pottery (54–68 CE) (ibid.: 57); by analogy with the much more extensive burnt levels at London and Colchester, some have argued that this may be evidence of destruction during the Boudiccan revolt (Cunliffe 1964: 21–3; Russell and Laycock 2011: 61, 234).

Parallels from the wider Roman Empire suggest that the military would have been involved in the layout of the town (Russell and Laycock 2011: 64) as well as the road system, which for Winchester appears to start in the early post-Conquest period and is substantial, with five or six metalled roads being constructed (Ottaway 2017: 85–8). The military probably at least oversaw the first stage of the defences which appear to have been laid out in the Flavian period *c.* 70 CE (Morris and Biddle 2023: 58). Winchester is very unusual in having defences erected in this period; the only other known examples are at Colchester, Gloucester and Lincoln – three *coloniae* based on former legionary fortresses (ibid.: 58; de la Bédoyère 2013: 133) – and the *municipium* of St Albans, whose residents had the intermediate status of 'Latin' (ibid.). Bounded by the River Itchen on its eastern side, the earth and timber rampart enclosed an area of 58 hectares, making Winchester the largest defended town in the province until the widespread erection of town defences in the second half of the second century (Morris and Biddle 2023: 58–9). Within the walls, a regular grid was laid out with seven streets running north–south and five east–west to form thirty-nine blocks (*insulae*) (ibid.: 61–2). King has detailed the occurrences of the name *Venta Belgarum*:

> *Venta (Ouenta in Greek* transliteration) by Ptolemy, *Venta Belgarum* or *Velgarum* in the Antonine Itinerary, *Venta Velgarom* in the Ravenna Cosmography, and also as *Venta* by Bede who also links *Venta* to *Wintancaestir.*
>
> KING 2020: 13

Two-part place names are common in Roman Britain and refer to what seem to be at the level below the *municipa* – *civitas* capitals serving as administrative centres for the surrounding area (de la Bédoyère 2013: 83–91, 134–5). Although *Venta* is most commonly translated as a 'marketplace', deriving from a Brittonic word, Jackson pointed out that it does not have a clear Celtic etymology, and it does not survive in 'successor' languages of Breton or Cornish (Jackson 1970: 80). More recently, Delamarre derives the word from Gallo-Brittonic **wenta*, and Indo-European **gwhen-ta*, with the meaning 'place of slaughtering of animals' or 'place of sacrifice of animals' (2010–12: 126–9). King suggests (2020: 17) that this interpretation could relate to sacrificial activity within the Oram's Arbour enclosure, which was respected by the Roman defensive line and so might have been a place of significance for the local population. He raises another linguistic connection for *'venta'* (ibid.: 18) through its appearance in the name of the nymph named as *Coventina* associated with a spring and a shrine near the Roman fort of Carrawburgh (Allason-Jones and McKay 1985). King also identifies Indo-European **auent-* 'to wet; a spring', from which river names can be derived (2020: 18). In later centuries, a Romano-Celtic temple was built in the low-lying Brooks area and a wooden statue of an ex-voto or possibly a goddess was found preserved by waterlogged conditions (Henig 2023: 857).

However, this does not resolve why decisions about siting the civitas at Winchester were made. King (2020: 24–5) has also suggested a European (Belgic) origin for the *Atrebates*, who he believes were the main Iron Age 'tribe' of the area, and that the attachment of the *Belgarum* element to the name of the new Winchester settlement in some way relates back to their origin story. What is clear is that something significant prompted these considerable investments of human and other resources making Winchester a special place, possibly building on the Oram's Arbour heritage. For whatever reason, as Morris and Biddle have argued (2023: 59), the developments at Winchester were undertaken either after the death of Togidumnus, when the territory was absorbed fully into the Roman *Britannia,* or more likely during the flourishing of Togidubnus' kingdom in

FIGURE 4.2 *Wooden statuette of a matron of* Venta *displaying the key and folded cloth, attributes of her status, found at Lower Brook Street* © WEC.

the years after the Boudiccan revolt, when he may have been rewarded for his loyalty to Rome.

Whatever the exact circumstances of *Venta*'s foundation, it seems likely that Romanized magnates of the area would have invested in the creation of the new town to demonstrate their close relations with the imperial authorities (Russell and Laycock 2011: 14). However, there is not enough evidence to say much more than this; perhaps they settled some of their tenants in the town especially if they had skills to benefit from an increased market, or these elites might have contributed to some part of the urban project either through paying for a specific feature like a statue, through taxation or providing free or enslaved workers to undertake some of the construction work (de la Bédoyère 2013: 226–7). Although these may lie in the unexcavated areas of *Venta*, the current lack of substantial, high-status buildings suggests that these local elites may not have moved into *Venta* but rather erected Romanized buildings in the countryside, for example, at the Sparsholt villa (Johnston and Dicks 2014). They are likely, however, to have visited to take part in dispensing justice and other aspects of local government (de la Bédoyère 2013: 143–9). Other people with skills and with some economic independence from the local area or further afield could also have been attracted to *Venta* by its greater opportunities; epigraphic evidence from other towns suggests that people settled in Britain from the wider Roman Empire (Russell and Laycock 2011: 16–17). Whoever paid for it, at the heart of *Venta Belgarum* was a *forum*, where Roman administrative and economic operations were directed, which de la Bédoyère has described generically as:

An open piazza surrounded on three sides by a covered portico behind which were commercial buildings. The fourth side was formed by the *basilica* ... [with] a central nave flanked by one or two aisles ... At one end, a raised dais provided an area for public pronouncements and hearing. The *curia*, one of the rooms flanking the outer aisle, hosted meetings of the town council, and other rooms stored census and taxation archives, and records of judicial decisions.

DE LA BÉDOYÈRE 2013: 140

The area of *Venta*'s probable f*orum* was greatly disturbed by later activity but has produced traces of buildings and a collection of decorative architectural fragments (from both British and European sources) presumably associated with the *forum*, but which cannot be dated or ascribed to any particular phase except by analogy with dated examples from elsewhere (Blagg and Biddle 2023). What they do provide, however, is further evidence of the investment in demonstrating the Romanized character of *Venta* (Russell and Laycock 2011: 64).

Evidence of military involvement in the early development of *Venta* comes from the town's only (almost) complete inscription that was found in 1854 reused in the wall of the Old County Jail in Jewry Street and which has been reviewed recently by Tomlin (2023). In translation it reads: 'To the Italian, German, Gallic, and British Mother (Goddesses), Antonius Lucretianus *beneficiarius consularis* restored (this)' (ibid.: 830). Epigraphic dating for this inscription gives a date range starting in the late first and extending to the late second century CE. These *beneficiarii consularis* were legionary officers, seconded to the governor's staff and are known from elsewhere in Britain, predominately on Hadrian's Wall and in places with strong military connections (Shallmayer 1990: 15–31). As these officers reported directly to the provincial Governor, they were people of significance but all that the other inscriptions suggest is that they had a role in communications with a dedication 'to the god who devised roads and paths' (Shallmayer 1990 No. 19), although a fragmentary petition from *Vindolanda* contains a complaint to a *beneficarius* from a foreigner that he had been beaten unjustly, which Tomlin (2023: 831) interprets as suggesting that they also had a police function. Whether or not this is correct, the *beneficarius* was clearly seen as person who had the power to act on a complaint. Tomlin endorses Shallmayer's argument that, as the cognomen 'Lucretianus' is uncommon and best attested in Italy, it is most likely that this was his origin, a view probably reinforced by his putting the Italian *Matres* first (ibid.: 830), although in the Roman world Italy must surely always have been seen as pre-eminent! Given that epigraphic dating is not exact, Lucretianus might have had a role in overseeing the layout of the new town, including its unusual defensive circuit which could have been ordered by the Governor because of the significance of the site. Linking back to the burning horizon identified at Oram's Arbour, some shrines (whether Romanized or not) may have required restoration (44).

Probably at this time an aqueduct was constructed, identified at a number of locations outside the walled town (Fasham and Whinney 1991: 5–10, Figs 5–7) before it entered in the north-west corner, ran south and then south-east (Biddulph 2011a: 54–5, Figs 2.10–2.11, Pl. 2.3; Biddulph 2011b, 185–6). Its likely source was in the Itchen Stoke area and its route to *Venta* would have required the construction of a water course of 24 kilometres (Fasham and Whinney 1991: 8–9, Fig. 7), probably to supply the baths and other urban features of the new Romanized town (de la Bédoyère 2013: 144–5). This period also saw works to manage the flow of the River Itchen, and the construction of drainage works to make parts of the lower-lying eastern part of the defended area less liable to flooding (Morris and Biddle 2023: 63). Taken together, these water management projects, and the construction of the defences were major undertakings which might require the posting of a *beneficarius* with the skills outlined above. It is, of course, always tempting to make linkages with known individuals but if it was not Lucretianus, it is likely that another senior military engineer oversaw the layout and building of these substantial projects (de la Bédoyère 2015: 139).

At Lower Brook Street, because of later disturbance, the plans of the first-century rectangular wooden houses laid out along the Roman streets could not be recovered but, from what was found, the excavators argue that they were 'Romanized' in appearance, with glazed windows, plastered walls and mosaic floors (Morris and Biddle 2023: 68). In the south-east corner of the Roman town at Wolvesey, a three-roomed timber structure was discovered aligned with the east side of the north–south street; it had pounded chalk floors, traces of lead waste and iron slag, suggesting a workshop as well as a domestic building. To the south, a large timber house with at least seven rooms, floored with pounded chalk and equipped with verandas, was built in the late first to early second century, replacing an earlier simpler structure (ibid.: 63). These discoveries appear to reinforce the picture of a new town based on the Roman pattern book with some building techniques demanding craftspeople trained in Roman traditions. It seems likely, however, that British carpenters could copy the Roman designs of the timber structures and build using their own established woodworking techniques.

The Roman-era plant remains led Murphy to argue that the absence of carbonized cereals in *Venta*, yet their extremely common presence at contemporary rural sites like Owslebury suggests that grain was being processed rurally in drying ovens to facilitate threshing. Consequently, cereals would have arrived in *Venta* processed as grain for milling and malting or as flour and therefore less likely to be subject to burning leading to carbonization (Murphy 2022: 181). Recent archaeobotanical and isotopic analysis of agricultural practices on the chalk downlands of southern England have suggested continuity with Iron Age farming practices initially, with increasing intensification and changes in manuring practices probably to meet the requirements of the Roman taxation systems. These systems demanded in-kind supplies for the army and, by analogy with other parts of the Empire, to supply urban centres (Lodwick 2023: 445). Maltby's extensive study of animal bones from *Venta* and its environs provides evidence of specialist butchery (ibid.: 177; Ottaway 2017: 154) as well as the careful herd management of cattle, pigs and sheep (Maltby 2010: 144 and 146) as, in the Iron Age, beef was the most common meat although pork and bacon were more prevalent at *Venta* than on rural sites (ibid.: 185). A recent study of lipid residues on pottery from Cirencester shows pigs (and chickens) were fed a mixture of animal and vegetable protein, possibly indicating a 'kitchen scraps'-type diet (Greenwood, Cramp and Hodo 2023: 157–8). Another recent isotopic analysis has shown that some of the animals consumed at the legionary fort of Caerleon were raised on the Wessex downland, possibly in the Winchester area, demonstrating the interconnectedness of *Britannia* along the new Roman roads (Guest et al. 2023: 1).

In the relatively limited areas excavated, Morris and Biddle identify that in late first- to early second-century deposits, metal-working residues were quite common (2023: 69); glass-blowing debris has also been found as well as bone-working waste in the north and western suburbs, although there is no evidence of textile production (Ottaway 2017: 157). There is, though, evidence of the trade in manufactured items from other parts of *Britannia* and further afield (e.g. Lawson 2023). Roman coins have been found dating from this period, but it has been argued that the bronze and brass coins were probably of too high a value for many transactions which may well have continued through exchange and barter (Reece 2023: 648). The items coming from outside *Venta* include pottery, especially greyware cooking pots from the Alice Holt kilns located on the Hampshire/Surrey border (Ottaway 2017: 159); Samian ware from Gaul was also popular as were their British copies (Dannell 2023). There were also considerable quantities of *amphorae* which were used to carry foodstuffs from the Mediterranean (principally olive oil, wine, and fish sauce) (Carreras 2023), as well as fragments of vessel glass, much of which was probably imported from Gaul and the Rhineland (Price and Cottam 2023: 1064). It seems likely therefore that, in the late first and early second century, a proportion of *Venta*'s population had a taste for Romanized food and drink as well as the resources to buy them.

Although water was piped to public buildings, most people would have drawn their water from wells and there is no evidence in Winchester of the sewerage systems known from some other Roman cities (de la Bédoyère 2013: 147). Kennedy (2023: 85) characterized Roman towns as 'filthy, stinking and disease-ridden'; living in close proximity also spread disease and facilitated the succession of plagues across the Roman world (ibid.: 104–5). Several cemeteries seem to have been in use situated along the main roads outside the walls in line with imperial legislation (Morris and Biddle 2023: 70) but the majority of burials from this early period are cremations so it is difficult for osteological research to identify causes of death.

Mid-second to third centuries

During this period, much of what had been established in the early centuries in Winchester continued with some additions and enhancements. As outlined above, *Venta* was unusual in having an early defensive circuit; most Roman towns had these added only in the second century, which some authors have argued was as much about civic prestige as defence (Wacher 1997: 70–81; Esmonde Cleary 2003: 80–4, Table 8.8; Mattingly 2008: 326–33). Nevertheless, there were army mutinies at this time (Russell and Laycock 2011: 132) which would become increasingly frequent later, but it is difficult to know what impact (if any) these had on civilian areas. Whatever the motivation, the decision was made to invest in widening and heightening the existing rampart, and a new rampart was constructed along the bank of the Itchen which Morris and Biddle (2023: 70–1) suggest was previously marked only by an embankment. Only repairs and minor alterations appear to have been made to the *forum*, although a stone building with a tessellated floor and painted wall plaster was built nearby (ibid.: 71). Found re-used in the structure of a Roman oven (dated 100 years later) was a large fragment of an inscription made from Portland limestone, inscribed with letters one Roman foot high – the largest lettering known from Roman Britain. It reads '[. . .]*NTO[*. . .]', presumably ANTONINVS, and was probably an integral part of a large public building erected in the mid- to late second century (Tomlin and Biddle 2023: 832–6). It is not clear how it came to be broken and later re-used in a domestic setting (ibid.: 835).

Construction was going on across the town with the majority of the previous timber buildings being replaced by larger, stone or stone-footed timber-framed houses (Morris and Biddle 2023: 72–3); one had a high-quality mosaic installed in its central hall and another had a central heating system (ibid.: 72). Earlier reference was made to the lack of good quality local building stone hence its regular robbing and reuse (17). The most common origin for *Venta*'s stone is the oolitic limestone known as 'Bath Stone', which is likely to have been mined in the Bath-Box-Corsham area of Somerset (Haywood 2023: 755). It is generally accepted that the Itchen at this time would have been navigable only by very shallow draught boats, so it seems likely that stone was transported by road (ibid.: 764).

Later Roman Winchester

During the mid-third to mid-fourth centuries, *Venta* continued to flourish along with much of southern England, as shown by the large-scale output of the regional pottery industries, the vast quantities of late Roman coins and the large number of luxurious rural villas often with the full trappings of Romanized life (Biddle and Morris 2023: 72–3). For whatever reason, *Venta*'s defences were further enhanced by the addition of a wall and an

FIGURE 4.3 *Roman Winchester by c. 350, including all known observations of significant Roman buildings. Not all buildings shown were necessarily standing c. 350* © WEC.

elaborate stone gatehouse at the southern entrance to the town (ibid.: 75); the size of the circuit now made Winchester the fifth-largest town in Roman Britain (ibid.: 74). It appears that major remodelling of the *forum* buildings took place at this time, including the laying of red tessellated floors (ibid.: 76–7) but the Romano-British temple in the Brook Street area was demolished and built over probably by the mid-fourth century, which Morris and Biddle have associated with the adoption of Christianity (ibid.: 388). Houses continued to be refurbished and more had mosaics and hypocausts; one was roofed with tiles made from Purbeck limestone – another considerable transportation feat (Haywood 2023: 776).

In line with the rest of Britain, there is a peak in coins found in *Venta* dating from the second half of the third century to the middle of the fourth; this indicates an established market economy but also reflects repeated changes of the currency, and to the low value and small size of coins at certain times during this period, in contrast with the relatively stable and good-quality coinage of earlier Roman times (Reece 2023: 645). Imports of pottery from northern Europe appear to have declined at this time, possibly because of a growing instability there, but *Venta* received large quantities of pottery from the New Forest kilns (especially) as well as those in the Oxford region (Ottaway 2017: 160–1).

Fourth-century Winchester and the Germanic transition

Historical context

The Roman soldier turned historian Amminianus Marcellanius reported that in (probably) 367 CE:

> Valentinian was alarmed by serious news which showed that Britain had been reduced to an extreme state of emergency by a barbarian conspiracy ... Theodosius was ordered to go there in haste.
>
> TOMLIN 1974: 308

Theodosius arrived in Britain to find that there were also serious problems with its military forces: some had refused to fight, been away from their posts when the attacks came or simply deserted (Hughes 2013: 119), with the result that the invading groups of *Scotti*, *Attacotti* and *Picti* (and possibly also Franks and Saxons) were able to move where they wished (ibid.: 120). Hughes argues that not only were there fundamental problems with the command structure in Britain (ibid.: 119), but also that the Emperors were prioritizing other parts of the army, with the result that the British garrison may not have been paid regularly (ibid.: 120). In the 369 campaign season, Amminianus records that Theodosius was successful against the usurper Valentinus and the remaining 'barbarians', restored the 'chief towns' and had additional watch towers built on the borders and coasts (Hughes 2015: 137). The details of what happened are not certain, but it does appear that there was a period of disruption caused by both external invaders, the Roman army and possibly also disaffected/opportunistic native people (Russell and Laycock 2013: 157).

Sources record that Magnus Maximus was appointed *Dux Britannianum* in 380 and subsequently made a bid for imperial power which was initially successful, but his invasion of Italy proved a step too far (ibid.: 64–5). Russell and Laycock argue that he may well have taken with him to Europe a substantial number of Britons who they believe made up a significant part of the Roman army in Britain by this time (ibid.: 168). The Emperor Honorius re-established imperial control until 406, when another rebellion again drew military forces from Britain to Europe to engage with Honorius for control of the western empire (ibid.: 173). There has long been considerable debate about whether Honorius' 410 letter telling its recipients to 'look to their own defence' was in fact addressed to Britain, a community in northern Italy (Thompson 1982) or in the province of Raetia (Woods 2012). However, as Fafinski has argued (2021: 91–2) there is little archaeological evidence for any such withdrawal; rather, forts appear to have continued in use into the fifth century. The difficulties of using historical evidence alone to understand what happened over the succeeding centuries was aptly summarized by J. N. L. Myres:

> Between Roman Britain and Saxon England there is a great gulf fixed, a void of confusion whose obscurity remains a standing challenge to historical inquiry; And not least of the dangers which confront those who attempt to bridge the gulf lies in the difficulty of determining the limits of firm ground upon its borders.
>
> MYRES 1936: vii

Town life from the archaeological record

Although not without considerable issues, archaeology can provide some answers about what was happening in the late fourth and fifth centuries, albeit outweighed by the questions still to be fully addressed. Morris and Biddle argue (2023: 80–1; 85) that the mid- and certainly late fourth century onwards saw a decline in the quality of urban life in *Venta* with stone buildings no longer being added and some inhabitants adapting existing buildings as well as erecting more ephemeral timber structures. Nevertheless, the streets continued to be metalled, and Morris and Biddle suggest that bastions may have been added to the defensive circuit (ibid.: 81). Although little clear evidence survives because of later disturbance, it appears that the *forum* remained in use but over time more of it appears to have decayed, with increasing evidence of 'squatter' occupation (ibid.: 84). There are sometimes traces of 'dark earth' above areas that were previously used for settlement (ibid.: 85). The debate about what this sort of deposit this represents continues, but the general view is that it is formed by activity (gardening or middening) rather than abandonment (MacPhail, Galinié and Verhaeghe 2015: 356). Excavations at the south gate show it fell down over its forecourt, but traffic continued over the rubble, wearing smooth the upper surfaces of the fallen masonry). The hollows in the surfaces were roughly filled in and two more surfaces laid before passage was closed at some point in the sixth to eighth centuries (Morris and Biddle 2023: 88). A major difficulty with establishing when and how quickly these changes took place is a lack of the secure dating sequences which characterized earlier Roman periods (Haselgrove 1979: 6, Crabtree 2018: 21). However, it is clear that, as Rogers (2011: 175) has argued, 'Town spaces were evolving and being adapted to the needs and desires of the continuing population'. Morris and

Biddle outline (2023: 93–4) that within *Venta* very few objects were found that are from the period after datable Romanized artefacts fall out of use and before the mid-seventh century, and what was found are mainly from residual (later) contexts or unstratified. Notable amongst these is a fragment of 'claw' beaker probably made in Kent or the Rhineland, dating to the late sixth to mid-seventh century, found near the site of the Old Minster (but in a later medieval context), with two early Anglo-Saxon beads found nearby (ibid.: 94). This area also produced a fragment of hanging bowl; these objects are generally thought to be of British manufacture although frequently found in Germanic contexts as at Sutton Hoo (Bruce Mitford 2005). However, there are some signs of occupation most likely dating to the fifth or sixth century in the Lower Brook Street area, probably reusing the existing earlier buildings and associated with spearheads and what has been identified as Germanic-style pottery (Morris and Biddle 2023: 93).

Rural management and urban links

A number of scholars have made the case that, in the late Roman period, there is a shift at *villa* and other rural sites towards market-orientated cereal production (e.g. Smith et al. 2016; Reddé 2018). Lodwick argues (2017) that this is shown archaeologically by the increased construction of processing structures such as grain-drying ovens and powered mills, as well as above-ground granaries; changes in crop husbandry have also been detected using palaeobotanical analysis. Although rooted in the agricultural systems of previous eras, there was extensification of cereal production that demands very high levels of labour at harvest which was possibly beyond the resources of the permanent rural population (Lodwick 2023: 459). Osteological analysis of Roman rural burials has identified that their joints show degeneration and stress including joint injuries on lower and upper limbs as well as rib fractures and spinal trauma, all linked to the demands of agricultural labour (Rohnbogner 2018: 340–2, 338, 345). Stuckert's analysis of *Venta*'s late Roman inhumation cemeteries revealed that considerable numbers of men suffered limb fractures, and she also noted that osteophytosis in the spine (most frequently in the lumbar vertebrae) was twice as common in males (2016: 128). She suggests that:

> Carrying large loads that over time would have placed heavy stresses on the shoulders, lumbar region, hips, and legs. Superimposed on this pattern shared by men and women was a clear image of male differences that may have been at least partly related to more demanding and stressful activity levels.
>
> ibid.: 129

These similarities strongly suggest that at least some of *Venta*'s male population were participating in agricultural activities, which Taylor has also proposed

(2013a: 417). Such evidence may reinforce the idea of continuing strong links between *Venta* and its rural hinterland, which could have continued from the pre-Conquest period. When the urban economy was flourishing, the town could well have been an attractive place both for individuals and magnates to locate their workforces but once the disruptions intensified, it is possible that there was a shift towards more participation in the rural economy. As noted earlier, even when the urban infrastructure was operating well, Roman towns were not healthy places (49) so once the infrastructure degraded, people may not have regarded *Venta* as a secure place to live. Because of the problems of dating already outlined (see above 53), it is difficult to discern whether the population transferred to rural sites (54) or if there was an overall decline. At Sparsholt, the Romanized *villa* complex apparently fell out of use and a new timber building was erected re-using material from earlier buildings; whether this was done by the original inhabitants or incomers is not certain, as no associated materials were recovered (Johnson and Dicks 2014: 82). Fafinski proposes a radical view of the process:

> The transition of Roman to Medieval as a socio-political and economical process can be seen to start during the crisis of the third century, culminating in the increasing importance of the house of Wessex at the end of the ninth century.
>
> FAFINSKI 2021: 91–2

Germanic presence

Ottaway (2017: 194–203) has documented a number of archaeological finds (mainly from burials) from the Winchester hinterland that seemingly attest to the presence of people whose material culture would identify them as Germanic. Unfortunately, the majority of these discoveries was not found through systematic excavations so there is little detail recorded; Williams argues that in the nineteenth century, growing admiration for the Anglo-Saxons influenced the reporting of the ethnic identities represented in such cemeteries (Williams 2007). Three early 'Anglo-Saxon' cemeteries have been found on the downland to the east of the River Itchen (Ottaway 2017: 196); in this area there was undated settlement evidence which Ottaway dates by analogy to the sixth and seventh centuries (ibid.: 195). At Abbotts Barton, five sunken featured buildings were found on one part of the site and three post-built structures in another. Cattle, sheep and pig bones were found, as were charred grains (predominately of barley) and pottery that the excavator dates as no earlier than the sixth century (Powell 2015). The structures are aligned to the Roman road from Silchester, suggesting this was still in use (Ottaway 2017: 196). Later excavations nearby also revealed two buildings dating to the 'Anglo-Saxon' period, but they are not yet published fully (McCulloch and Osgood 2018: 20).

In 2022, Gretzinger and collaborators published alongside archaeological data a major study of genome-wide ancient DNA samples from 460 medieval north-western Europeans (including 278 individuals from England). For the eastern part of England, their analysis demonstrated that 76 per cent of their ancestry was from the continental North Sea zone (Gretzinger et al. 2022: 112). Moving west, the proportions reduced considerably and there was more evidence of ancestry from both the pre-existing gene pool and that from the North Sea zone (ibid.: 114). When grave goods were matched to DNA evidence, women with immigrant ancestry were more often furnished with grave goods than women with local ancestry, whereas men with weapons were both 'native' and immigrant. The authors take these findings as evidence that in some parts of England there were substantial numbers of Germanic people coming from mainland Europe (ibid.: 118), and not supporting the prevailing idea of a more limited elite migration (e.g. Oosthuizen 2019). This view is also reinforced by the recent 'Twigstats' analysis of the ancient DNA of British populations (Spiedal et al. 2025: 123).

Unfortunately, DNA results for burials from Winchester and the surrounding areas are not yet available, although there have been isotope analyses from a number of individuals from the Lankhills cemetery: they appear to have been brought up in Europe either within or outside the Roman Empire (Clarke 2023) and further scientific studies are underway (Clarke pers. comm.). Archaeologically the Lankhills group of sixteen burials was dated to the mid-fourth century, with distinctive bronze belt buckles and other personal ornaments identified as military; a number of female graves had distinctive grave goods (ibid.: 1223–4). Also unusual was the discovery of more than thirty cremation burials within the cemetery which are dated to 350 CE or later, at a time when the Romano-British burial rite was predominately inhumation (ibid.: 1235–6). A further group of eight burials in the 1967–72 excavations were late in date, did not share a common layout nor clear parallels elsewhere, but showed features not seen previously at the site, and are identified by Clarke as dating from 390 CE onwards (ibid.: 1240–2); Clarke also includes in this group two graves excavated later. One burial was of a child with a spearhead which Clarke notes has parallels in graves identified as 'Anglo-Saxon' (ibid.: 1242), as was a zoomorphic strap end from another grave at the site (ibid.: 1241). Another buckle is comparable with one found in Gloucester – from the grave of an individual identified from the grave goods as a 'Goth' – which has strong European parallels; in other graves at Lankhills, what appear to be decorated headbands were found that have parallels in Gaul, the Rhineland and the Danube provinces (ibid.: 1242).

As outlined above (52), the fourth century became progressively more turbulent, with various military commanders vying for control of the western Roman Empire and taking more troops from Britain to support their campaigns (de la Bédoyère 2013: 257). Against this background, hiring additional military support might have seemed attractive to those who held power in *Venta*; it was being done increasingly by the Empire itself (Russell and Laycock 2011: 164). Who did the hiring, and how this 'militia' fitted in to the 'mainstream' of provincial government or military structures, is unlikely to be resolved, but their presence is the first evidence in *Venta* of Germanic peoples whose cultural identities appear to have mixed their ancestral traditions with those of Rome as well as with British and other religious traditions they encountered in Winchester.

Epilogue

The preceding discussions of *Venta*'s development have sought to build a picture of life within the town and its hinterland during the period when its inhabitants were part of the Roman Empire, whether as citizens or enslaved people. *Venta* differs from many other Roman towns in having been apparently a new creation on a site without chronologically direct antecedents. It was equipped with many of the outward and visible signs of what any visiting Roman would expect to see and there is clear evidence of its inhabitants accessing (and in some cases creating) the full range of material culture that participation in the Roman Empire enabled, supported by the agricultural surpluses that its hinterland generated. It seems plausible that local elites played a continuing role in *Venta*'s creation, development and management, possibly alongside people from other parts of the Empire; this may have included hiring a foreign-born militia in the fourth century. It is probable that these magnate dynasties had the rights and privileges of Roman citizenship very early on and were keen to demonstrate their *Romanitas* to fellow members of the elites by, for example, installing mosaics in Romanized *villas* (as at Sparsholt). Equally, if their traditional overlordships continued, the likely involvement of *Venta* men in the magnates' agricultural production (as evidenced by the osteological evidence) would suggest that at least some of the town's inhabitants had continuing obligations to these elites. Once political and economic circumstances changed, conspicuous Romanized consumption may no longer have been possible or indeed attractive. It is very possible that there was a change in emphasis in how elites maintained their power and influence, the alliances they entered into and the material culture they adopted. *Venta*'s success was, however, rooted in being the nexus of an economic web that enabled dense settlement within an enclosed circuit; once that began to be disrupted, life within the town became less viable. When the infrastructure collapsed, more people probably succumbed to disease and others may have moved out to the rural hinterlands, relatives and social networks. The archaeological remains indicate that there was activity within the defended circuit but in essence *Venta* had lost its reason to exist so apparently did not continue as the urban centre it had been created to be.

5

The Golden Age of Early Medieval Winchester

The early medieval context

As explored in the last chapter, it is clear that *Venta* ceased to function as the urban centre that it had been, although there was some activity within the walled circuit (54) into the fifth century. As Morris and Biddle have identified:

> this long mysterious period comes to an end with the building in Winchester by Cenwalh, king of Wessex 642–72, of the church later known as Old Minster. The exact date is unknown but was presumably in the fourteen or so years between Cenwalh's conversion to Christianity *c.*646 and the date, probably between 660 and 663, when the king appointed Wine as the first bishop of Winchester.
>
> 2023: 94–5

Morris and Biddle suggest that there was a shift in focus further south and west for the emerging kingdom of Wessex, possibly in some way connected with the growing importance of the trading centre of *Hamwic* on the Solent (Biddle and Kjølbye-Biddle 2007). This view is reinforced by the discovery by Wessex Archaeology at St Mary's Stadium in Southampton of late seventh-century burials with high-status grave goods (Birkbeck 2005: 75–6).

Documentary evidence

Unfortunately, most of the documentary sources for the earliest medieval period date from later periods and have their own agendas (15). The general consensus is that the *Anglo-Saxon Chronicle* was written at King Alfred's court in the ninth century to create a common national identity for the English, drawing on the recent past but also selecting from other, earlier

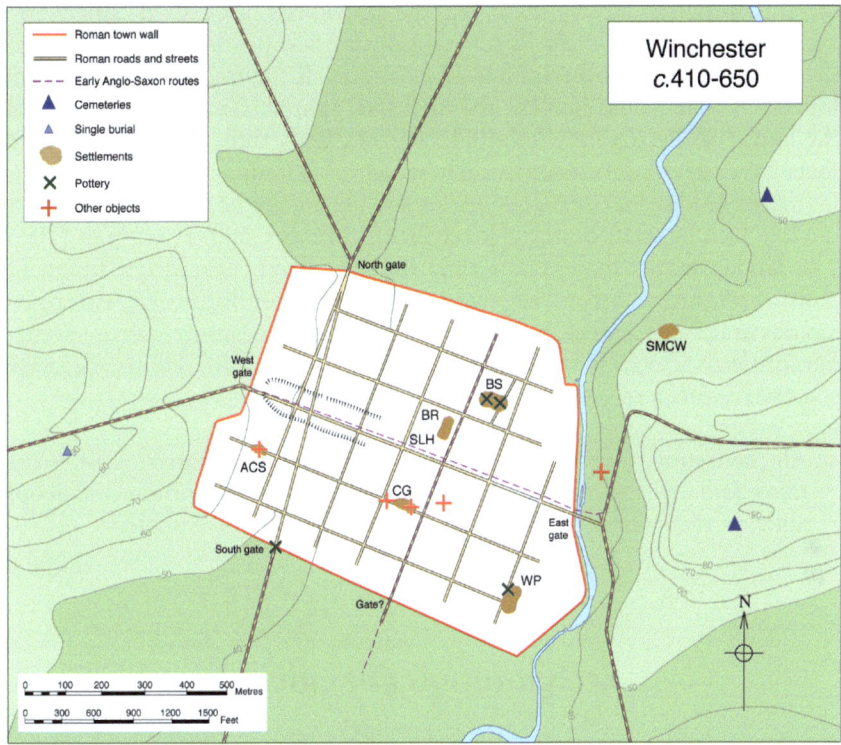

FIGURE 5.1 *Winchester c. 410–650* © WEC.

ACS, Assize Courts South 1963–5; BR, The Brooks, Middle Brook Street, 1987–8; BS, Lower Brook Street 1965–71; CG, Cathedral Green 1962–70; SLH, The Slaughter House, St George's Street, 1957; SMCW, St Martin's Close, Winnall, 1986; WP, Wolvesey Palace, 1963–71.

sources to reinforce the thread from the fifth and sixth centuries onwards (Keynes 1986: 198; Konshuh 2020). Konshuh emphasizes (2020: 154–5) that it selected, organized and inflated a range of material: Roman legacy, Christian history and mythical accounts of the Germanic tribes' arrival in England, from sources like Bede, Orosius, Gildas, recent memory and oral tradition, in order to legitimize the Cerdic dynasty (Alfred's ancestors) and therefore confer authority on Alfred. Following Bede, the *Chronicle* states that in 449 Hengest and Horsa were invited to assist the Britons, and emphasis is put on the legitimacy of their presence and therefore the warfare in which they subsequently engaged (ibid.: 166). Although there are brief mentions of the other dynasties throughout the early annals, emphasis is put on West Saxon conquests prefiguring those of King Ecgberht's, and then on Alfred's own successes as the only ruler to have defended his lands and decisively defeated (and Christianized) the Vikings (ibid.: 170). In addition, there is a particular emphasis on the previously little used *'Angelcynn'* identity that the *Chronicle* defines as opposing first Britons and then Vikings, thereby creating an over-arching identity for all the previous Anglo-Saxon kingdoms that would become the inclusive, shared, Germanic identity that the house of Wessex now led (ibid.: 157–8). Only three identifiable insular texts have survived to describe early medieval Britain and the most detailed is that of Gildas – *De excidio Britanniae* (The Ruin of Britain), describing the late fifth or sixth century (Joyce 2022: 14): as Coumert outlines (2019: 19), Gildas writes that he has only limited sources for earlier times. He paints a picture of a troubled island where Christian Britons vie with pagan Saxons and Picts; a weak British church is failing to censure corrupt secular authorities/warlords whom Gildas calls 'kings' (ibid.: 150). He also describes successive warfare:

> All the major towns were laid low by the repeated battering of enemy rams; laid low, too, all the inhabitants – church leaders, priests and people alike, as the swords glinted all around and the flames crackled.
>
> ibid.: 28

Archaeological evidence

For their own reasons, therefore, these documentary sources paint a picture of serious armed struggle between the Germanic peoples and the Britons, but what can the archaeological record reveal? As the last chapter outlined, there appears to be evidence of people with Germanic material culture settling in the environs of Winchester from the fifth (and possibly) the fourth century (54). Laycock has explored (2008: 202) the extent to which material culture equates with ethnicity; locally Mees (2019: 8–10) has assembled a database of cemeteries dating between 450 and 850 CE, from what she believes became the territory of the *Gwisse*, the rulers for Bede (but not the *Anglo-Saxon Chronicle*!) of the area that became Wessex. Relevant to the Winchester hinterland is the *'pays'* she identifies as 'The Hampshire Downs', made up of the band of high downland in the north and east, and the lower downland to its west, cut through by the principal river valleys. Acknowledging some sampling effects, although there are isolated burials on higher ground, Mees draws attention to the predominant location of cemetery sites in the major river valleys (ibid.: 120). Close to Winchester, at Itchen Abbas rescue excavations revealed a mix of cremation and inhumation burials dated by their excavators to the mid- to late fifth century. They include some with hobnails, perhaps a continuation of a Roman burial rite (ibid.: 125) found, for example, at Lankhills (Clarke 1979: 322–5), and the burial of a young man with a more 'Germanic assemblage' of spearhead, sword, knife, chape and two belt fittings. Subsequently a Wessex Archaeology evaluation nearby (presumably part of the same cemetery) revealed a rare east Wessex example of a prehistoric pond barrow that appears to have been the later focus for both cremation and inhumation burials; these were not accompanied by any finds (Mees 2021: 125). South of Winchester at Twyford Down and at the Winchester South Park and Ride sites, two further 'mixed' sixth- and seventh-century cemeteries were found, where burials appear to be orientated towards pre-existing earthworks and the Roman road (ibid.: 126). Overall, Mees concurs with the view that:

> by the seventh century, the Wessex landscape can perhaps be characterised as a 'patchwork' of separate regions, some at least of which were dominated by Britons, held together by the overall supremacy of an English redistributive chieftaincy.
>
> WOOLF 2007: 128

Once again, more extensive DNA analysis will enable a testing of these hypotheses and more generally clarify the Germanic/Romano-British relationships (Higham 2007b). It appears that the 'Twigstats' methodology has considerable potential in enabling a more detailed understanding of the population derivation of early medieval individuals (Spiedal et al. 2025).

Surviving Britons

There is another perspective on the position of people identified as British within the emerging Kingdom of Wessex. Grimmer (2007: 102–3) analysed the law code of King Ine (usually dated 688–93) which survives as an appendix to the laws of Alfred and contains eight laws relating to Britons (ibid.: 104). For free Britons, the law defines the *wergild* (compensation if they were killed), with a range from 600 shillings for a Briton who held 500 hides, 200 for a horse rider for the king, 120 for one with one hide of land and for a tax/tribute tax/tribute-payer, 100 for the son of tax/tribute payer, 80 shillings for a Briton with half a hide of land and 60 for someone with no land (ibid.: 104–5). For someone defined as *Englisc* or *Engliscmon*, there is not such a precise series of definitions, but the range is from 200 to 1,200 shillings (ibid.: 105). As far as enslaved people were concerned, an oath of twelve hides was required to compel the public whipping of a British slave, whereas thirty-four were required for a Germanic one (ibid.: 106). These laws reveal that, although clearly less valued than their Germanic neighbours, there were a number of Britons who had considerable landholdings, but the absence of intermediate amounts of compensation suggests that most Britons had much less wealth. It also suggests that a few identifiable Britons still had some status within the Wessex royal court (ibid.: 103). It could be that tax/tribute payers were town dwellers in reviving urban centres such as Winchester.

Alfred chose a Welshman, Asser, to be his biographer and Thomas has argued that:

> In the Life of King Alfred, the Welsh are territorially and linguistically defined as distinct from the Angelcynn. But in Asser's view what they share is more important. They are all Christians and members of Alfred's political community, and this group identity transcends all others. According to Asser, being Welsh at Alfred's court is altogether unimportant; there are peoples there from all sorts of different places, and their origins do not matter, because Alfred's kingdom welcomes all.
>
> THOMAS 2022: 172

Karasawa has also argued that the extent of 'replacement' of the indigenous population by incoming Germanic people was emphasized by the late tenth-century chronicler, Aethelweard's interpretation of Gildas and Bede, which was then adopted by later medieval and early modern writers (2022: 179–89). He proposes that 'the myth provided a 'historical' basis to the 'Anglo-Saxonism' with racial emphases when it began to flourish and spread by the mid-nineteenth century, influencing the interpretation of this period (ibid.: 189).

Bede's *Uintancaestir* ('Walled place of *Venta*')

As outlined above (58), the documentary sources do not reveal why a new church was built in Winchester and there has been considerable debate about whether this was a royal or ecclesiastical project (Yorke 1982: 79; Biddle and Kjølbye-Biddle 2007: 205). The publication of the major excavations on the sites of the Old and New Minsters is imminent – WS 4.i *The Anglo-Saxon Minsters of Winchester* (Kjølbye-Biddle and Biddle forthcoming) and this is the major source for the following sections on the Old and New Minsters. Given the complexities of the written sources explored above, it can be no surprise that there are some uncertainties about the date of its foundation, but the excavators' view is that a church dedicated to St Peter and St Paul was probably in existence by *c*. 663, when the see of the West Saxons was divided and Bishop Wine was appointed to Winchester, or shortly afterwards. This agrees with the evidence of the *Anglo-Saxon Chronicle* that Cenwalh had the church built at some unspecified point in his reign.

Archaeological excavations outside the Norman cathedral revealed that the church that became known as Old Minster was situated at the site of the Roman *forum*, from whose ruins much of the stone to build the church was robbed. As WS 4.1 describes, four-fifths of the church was excavated including following the later robber trenches, to reveal the first church as a simple cruciform structure with north and south porticos off the nave, and an elevated eastern arm to which an apse was added in the eighth century (Kjølbye-Biddle and Biddle forthcoming). The walls of the first church

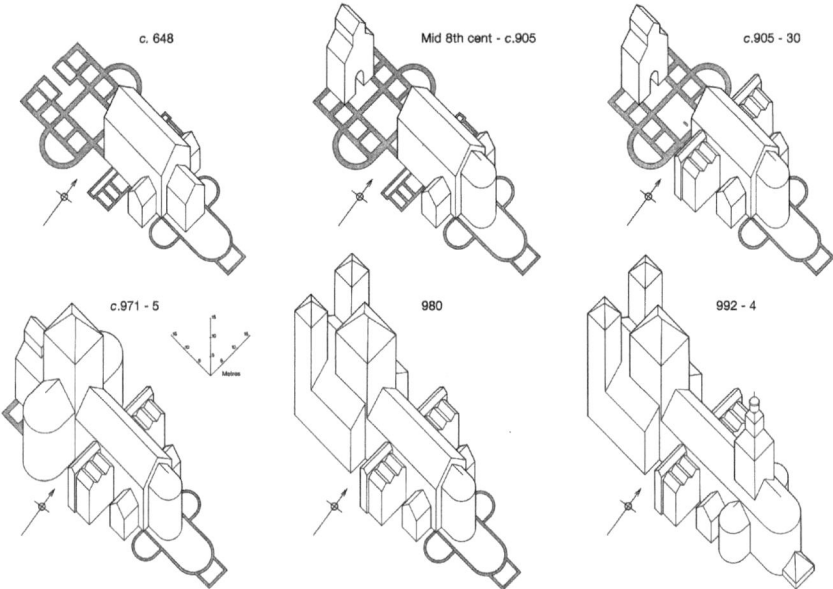

FIGURE 5.2 *Three-dimensional views of the development of Old Minster from c. 648 to 992–4, seen from the south-east, each phase set in the context of the full final plan (stippled)* © WEC.

appear to have been plastered, flagstones made up the floor and windows were glazed with clear blue, turquoise and transparent glass. It is important to recollect that in the mid-seventh century, there was no surviving indigenous tradition of monumental building in stone (Taylor 1984: 736) Similarly Bede records that glaziers had to be summoned from abroad to install the windows at Monkwearmouth and other early church sites (Cramp 2001). The excavators argue that the design of the church has a north Italian inspiration and therefore may well be linked to the 'Roman' Birinus who was responsible for the conversion of Cenwalh, and they believe that the archaeological evidence confirms a construction date of 648 (Kjølbye-Biddle and Biddle forthcoming). Whether Birinus was accompanied by someone who could accomplish the build or had the contacts to recruit someone later is not certain. The authors argue that the separate St Martin's Tower, added *c.* 750, marked the entrance to Old Minster's precinct, and soon this became a focus for burial. Within the church was at least one high-status inhumation, furnished with a gold braided cap and at his knees two niello-decorated silver garter-hooks. The authors concur with the view that Yorke (2021b: 65) proposed that the strongest candidate in the likely timeframe is Athelstan, the eldest son of King Aethelwulf (839–58). Osteological studies of the early medieval burials discovered at both the Old and New Minster excavations were published in WS 9.i (Molleson et al. 2017). Evidence of sword cuts and cranial fractures were found on a number of early medieval male bodies, mostly dating to 870–90 (Stuckert 2016: 410) but the majority appear to have died of natural causes, although plagues and epidemics are not easily detectable in skeletal remains (ibid.: 402–3).

The next phase of Old Minster's development will be discussed after reviewing what is known of the rest of Winchester at this time. At the Lower Brook Street site discussed above (54), a small cemetery of five burials was found, dated to the seventh century; three had grave goods, including one with an elaborate necklace consisting of three gold and garnet pendants, two other gold objects, two silver pendants and twenty-seven silver rings (Hawkes 1990). Biddle suggests that this cemetery belonged to a high-status community probably living within the walls and possibly associated with the royal court (Biddle 1983: 118). A timber building complex was built subsequently, which was itself replaced by a possibly two-storey stone building, with flint walls and quoins of reused Roman tiles, ashlar blocks and column drums, and a doorway with through-stone jambs. This building had a radiocarbon date of 700+/–70 CE, and a dendrochronology date of 790 +/– 60 CE from an associated well (Biddle 1975: 309–10).

Below the first phase of the Nunnaminster complex, iron working debris was found; the deposit was radiocarbon dated to 710–940 CE (ibid.: 202). Morris and Biddle identify a further site probably dated to this period immediately west of the Roman *forum*: in a timber building there is evidence for metalworking, including recycling quantities of late Roman metalwork, with 150 fourth-century coins. The deposit was dated by an Anglo-Saxon silver penny of *c.* 710–25 (Morris and Biddle 2023: 101). Generally, however, few coins of the period have been found suggesting that barter predominated, although trade and exchange was flourishing at *Hamwic* before the mid-eighth century (Hodges 2025). It is likely that Winchester served as a market for agricultural crops produced by estates in its hinterland, which a number of authors have suggested were becoming more formalized at this time, not least because of being given as endowments to the new Christian foundations (Rippon 2010: 62–3; Brookes 2020).

Late eighth and ninth centuries

For 789, the *Anglo-Saxon Chronicle* records the arrival of three ships (probably at Portland): the 'first ships of the Danish men which sought out the land of the English race'; this encounter also resulted in the death of the royal reeve (Price 2020: 279). The *Anglo-Saxon Chronicle* makes no mention, however, of the raids going on elsewhere that are documented in other sources but identifies an increase in raiding from the 830s; Price suggests that this may be an example of the *Chronicle* omitting occasions when Wessex was less successful against the Vikings (ibid.: 283). Although it has not been shown archaeologically, at the beginning of the reign of Aethelbert (860–5) both the *Anglo-Saxon Chronicle* and Asser's *Life of*

King Alfred record a Viking raid on Winchester, with the longer account being given in Asser – 'a great Viking army, arriving from the sea, aggressively attacked and laid waste the city of Winchester' (Keynes and Lapidge 1983: 73). What the *Chronicle* entry *does* imply, however, is that there was something worth raiding at Winchester, possibly at the bishop's palace or Old Minster; monasteries and churches were popular targets for Viking raids (Price 2020: 280–3).

The mid-ninth century is marked by the appearance of the historical icon who became synonymous with the town as its key pilgrimage draw – St Swithun. As Lapidge points out in his account of the saint's cult:

> In the centuries following the translation of his remains into the Old Minster, Winchester on 15th July 971, St Swithun became one of the best known and widest culted Anglo-Saxon saints both in England and on the Continent. But of the saint's career on this earth, by contrast, very little is known.
>
> LAPIDGE 2003: 3

Later sections will explore how this tenth-century event formed a central part of religious re-shaping of later Anglo-Saxon Christianity, and monastic life in particular, as well as the importance of St Swithun in the medieval life of the town (see 73). From charter evidence, it seems probable that Swithun was Bishop of Winchester from 852–63 (ibid.: 4); he appears in the so-called '*Second Decimation*' charters which in 854 record King Aethelwulf (839–58) assigning property to various people who would then say prayers and masses for the king (ibid.: 6). Swithun's final appearance is in a poem (probably dating to the tenth century) in which he is recorded in 859 as building a bridge at the east gate of the town (ibid.: 7).

At some point in the late ninth century, a new grid of streets was laid out in Winchester; it did not follow its Roman predecessors and included a new road enabling access to the Roman defensive circuit (Biddle 2020). These remnants were presumably refurbished, possibly with the addition of an additional ditch, but no clear archaeological evidence of when this took place has been found (Biddle 1975: 120–1; Qualmann 2025). Certainly, the early tenth-century *Burghal Hidage* provides a length for Winchester's defences which corresponds almost exactly to the estimated length of the Roman circuit (Biddle 2017: 26). What hand King Alfred (871–99) had in the developments in Winchester is not certain; the only time he is recorded as being in the town is in 896, when he ordered the hanging of some Viking raiders (Levelle 2020: 319); there is, however, evidence of his coins being minted in Winchester with 'vIN' appearing on their obverse (Lyon 2012: 3). Of course, the court of Wessex would have been peripatetic and the kingdom was extremely extensive at this time, covering most of southern England (including London, but not Cornwall) and the midland kingdom of Mercia (Konshuh 2020: 159); kings had to maintain relationships with all the local

FIGURE 5.3 *Winchester's Roman street plan overlain by the Anglo-Saxon street-plan of the mid- to late ninth century* © WEC.

aristocrats who provided the kingdom's military support (Crabtree 2018: 139; Scull 2011: 850) and the nobles of the 'witan' also had a key role in determining the royal succession (Roach 2013: 236; Wood 2020a: 142). Documentary evidence suggests that Alfred's widow, Ealswith, was the likely sponsor of the new Nunnaminster foundation in Winchester (Ottaway 2017: 227); although she was originally from Mercia, it could well be that she remained in Winchester after Alfred's death (Wood 2020a: 168), suggesting strongly that the town was a key site for the royal house of Wessex by this time, if not before.

Whether or not Alfred instigated the idea of a fortified centre that became the *burh*, he was certainly responsible for its extension to a network of strongholds which crucially were not just refuges but, as the *Burghal Hidage* documents, were to be defended by men assigned by their local lords on a unified system of staffing; as Morris points out, this extended the military capacity of the realm beyond the traditional military elite (Morris 2021: 227–8; Scull 2011: 860). The *burhs* also provided more secure spaces for markets and trading; the growth of Winchester as a trading centre may have benefitted from the decline of *Hamwic* with the threats to its maritime trade from increasing Viking raiding (Crabtree 2018: 1). Haslam (2015: 176) argues that the *burh* network was Alfred's concept, as part of the process of the wider creation of a unified '*Angelcynn*' realm discussed earlier (60) (Konshuh 2020: 157–8). Haslam's summary highlights the web of strategic, local inter-connection and reciprocity linking the *burhs* with their rural hinterlands, that under-pinned Alfred's new concept of how to unify and rule his extensive territories as well as ensuring a secure military force to repel any new Viking threat through:

> the formation by the king of a connection between the rural manor of the *thegn* ... and a new tenement within the *burh* ... This arrangement would have served to facilitate and consolidate the support and upkeep of *burhs*, through the establishment and reinforcement of lordship bonds which arose out of obligations derived from the holding of land. This would have involved all the thegns of the burghal territory in taking oaths of submission ... to the king at each of the *burhs*. As a system, therefore, the *burhs* must have been instrumental in consolidating the king's control over the whole kingdom.
>
> 2015: 176

Leaving aside scepticism about Asser's description of his patron's panoply of virtues (Thomas 2022: 155), there is no doubt that Alfred must have had a range of personal qualities that at first enabled him to regain Wessex from the Vikings, recovering from the low point of his guerilla band in Athelney (Morris 2021: 215–16). Later he delivered a strategic vision that bound together the Germanic peoples of Wessex and Mercia (as well as the Welsh of Gwynedd) into a complex entity of social, political, economic and military systems (Karkov 2004: 36; Thomas 2022: 172). Alfred's Wessex was the first united realm since the days of *Britannia* and also delivered a *modus vivendi* with Guthrum, the most powerful Viking ruler, bringing about his conversion to Christianity along with significant numbers of his followers (Morris 2021: 219). In addition, Alfred was a patron of learning, both promoting the translation of a large number of significant texts (Karkov 2004: 24) and being an artistic patron (Ramirez 2015: 264–6) with his likely commissioning of *aestels* like the Alfred Jewel (ibid.: 266–7; Hinton 2008: 27–9), which Karkov (2004: 32) suggests may incorporate an image of Alfred himself. Part of Alfred's campaign to promote greater learning within the Church was the recruitment to his court of a number of learned churchmen including, in 866, Grimbald, a priest and monk from the monastery of Saint-Bertin, in the Pas-de-Calais, for whom Alfred established a *monasteriolum* in Winchester (ibid. 2015: 269–70). This seems to have been a small monastery with chapels and living quarters, although no archaeological trace of it has yet been found; knowledge of it comes primarily from the account of land acquired for his New Minster by Alfred's son Edward the Elder (899–924) (Rumble 2002:

52). When Alfred died in 899, he was first buried in Old Minster but once New Minster was complete, his son had his 'bones and ashes' translated there (Albert and Tucker 2015: 209).

Tenth century

Despite all that he had achieved, Alfred could not secure the automatic succession of his son, Edward, who had to win a civil war against his cousin with his Viking allies before securing his kingship (Holland 2016: 25–6). Once his crown was secure Edward – with his sister, the Mercian ruler, Aethelflaed – pursued their father's vision of a united kingdom of England (Morris 2021: 254–9). Symbolically reinforcing the primacy of the royal house of Wessex may well have been part of Edward's motivation for commissioning what became known as New Minster. In WS 4.1 it is argued that the Carolingian royal church of St Denis (Metropolitan Paris), which housed the burials of many members of the Carolingian dynasty, may well have been its model as the two churches have the same proportions, and this church would have been known in the cosmopolitan Wessex court (Kjølbye-Biddle and Biddle forthcoming).

From the *Anglo-Saxon Chronicle*, the foundation of New Minster is usually dated to 901–3; once it was consecrated, Edward had his father's body transferred into 'a tomb monument of special construction' along with that of his mother, Ealswith. Based on documentary evidence, when Edward himself died in 924, he was brought to Winchester where his body was 'buried royally in New Minster' and when – within days – Edward's son Aelfweard, died in Oxford, he too was buried 'where his father lies'. Only 6 per cent of the original extent of New Minster has been excavated so limited detail is known, although much has been deduced from material recovered from the later robber trenches. There is evidence that the first church was a *basilica* type with a 20-metre-wide aisled nave probably accessed through an arcade, with walls covered in yellow mortar, painted window glass, and adorned with dressed stone features from a number of sources. Flints set in bright yellow mortar with a mixture of chalk made up the walls, which were covered in a yellow plaster and generally whitewashed, with red paint in at least some places (Kjølbye-Biddle and Biddle forthcoming).

Following the construction of New Minster, a new façade (*c.* 30 m wide and faced with pink plaster) was added to Old Minster, in two stages between *c.* 910 and 930. At some point after the construction of the façade, chapels probably of two storeys were added to the east side of the façade in such a way that the three latest graves in the area lay in the centre of each of the three chapels (again with pink wall plaster); new flooring was added. The authors suggest that these architectural additions may reflect changes in liturgical practice manifested too by the installations of more altars. In addition, they argue that the line of the main route of access to Old Minster from the west through St Martin's Tower became increasingly encroached upon by high-ranking burials (some with exceptional grave goods). The documentary sources record that King Eadred (923–55) specified that he too should be buried in Old Minster, which he had previously endowed with land and treasure, as well as apparently wishing to decorate its eastern portico with gilded tiles (Morris 2021: 292); this might have been a figurative mosaic of Continental type (Kjølbye-Biddle and Biddle forthcoming).

The archaeological evidence for the third major foundation of the early tenth century – Nunnaminster – is very sparse; most of it has been observed only in rescue contexts. Although some limited controlled excavation was undertaken, the earliest levels were damaged by later rebuilding and the presumed main area of the church lay beyond the excavation (Ottaway 2017: 221). Two lateral apses which the excavators suggest, by analogy with Old Minster, may date to the 970s and be additions to the original church formed the west front and main ceremonial entrance to a 6.5-metre-wide nave (ibid.). A masonry tomb was found in the southern apse; its prominent position and its removal before the construction of the later church led the excavators to suggest that it might be the original resting place of St Eadburgh (ibid.). Yorke has summarized the various documentary sources for Nunnaminster in WS 4i (Yorke forthcoming) and the following section draws on that work. As noted above (67), in Hyde Abbey's *Liber Vitae*, Queen Ealswith was recorded as the founder (*aedificatrix*) of Nunnaminster, and Yorke proposes that the use of the present tense in that document implies that the foundation was made in Ealswith's lifetime. The most complete account of the life of Nunnaminster's patron saint, Eadburgh, the daughter of King Edward and his third wife Eadgifu, was compiled by the twelfth-century Dean of Westminster, Osbert of Clare, probably drawing on a range of earlier sources. Yorke explains that usually the royal sponsors of such foundations would become their patron saint but, as Ealswith was already part of the New Minster dynastic array, someone else suitable was required: fortunately, a royal daughter was available. Yorke outlines that when Eadburgh was three:

> the infant princess is said to have been placed in front of religious and secular objects, and her choice of a bible, chalice and patten rather than gold, silver and jewels dictated the future course of her life.

Eadburgh died at the age of thirty, probably about 953, and appears to have become recognized as a saint relatively soon; her cult was well established by the time of the reforms instigated by Aethelwold after he became bishop in 963 (Ridyard 1989: 106).

In the wider world, the royal house of Wessex continued its mission to create a united kingdom with mixed fortunes, especially in relationships with the growing Scandinavian communities. The reign of Alfred's grandson Athelstan (894–939) – raised at the Mercian royal court – marked the next stage of the mission (Holland 2016: 34) and it appears from the documentary sources that he faced hostility from the Bishop of Winchester and other key Wessex powerbrokers who had initially favoured his rival to the throne, Aelfweard, who had grown up in Wessex (ibid.: 48; Roach 2013: 57). After Aelfweard's death, however, Athelstan was recognized as king although it seems some resentment persisted; the monks of New Minster omitted Athelstan from the list of West Saxon kings, and stories were told of a plot in Winchester to capture and blind him (Holland 2016: 48). So, it is perhaps unsurprising that Athelstan's elaborate ceremony of royal coronation took place in Kingston rather than in Winchester, possibly also to signal a less Wessex-centric focus for the united kingdom that encompassed Mercia as well as Wessex (Roach 2013: 57, Wood 2022a: 191–3). Throughout his reign, Athelstan's attention was on the whole island of Britain where he campaigned to conquer and build alliances with Scottish, Scandinavian and Welsh rulers; in Cumbria in 927, he named himself *rex totius Britanniae* (Holland 2016: 59). However, Winchester still figured in the displays of royal power, with a large-scale celebration of the feast of Pentecost there in 934, at which kings from Wales and Scandinavian rulers were present (ibid.: 62).

As well as undertaking these political and military activities, Athelstan sought to signal the unity of the new kingdom. He called regular assemblies of the powerful secular and religious leaders at different sites across the new kingdom of *Angelyn* (Wood 2022a: 199–202) and introduced a number of key legal, economic and religious measures (ibid.: 197–202). A new set of unified law codes was promulgated at Grateley (Hampshire) (ibid.: 198) including the first English laws to control the minting of coinage, as well as trade controls promoting the economic growth of *burhs* (ibid.: 198–9). He also restored ecclesiastical foundations, especially in the northern areas which had suffered particularly from earlier Viking raids (ibid.: 199). In 934, Athelstan staged his next public manifestation of the creation of the new realm (ibid.: 205–6), at Cirencester where he was proclaimed '*basileus and curaglas* of the whole world of *Britannia*' (ibid.: 206). Athelstan's success had already been recognized in Europe where he secured a number of key dynastic marriages for his half-sisters (ibid.: 79). Clergy on these visits to the Frankish kingdoms also saw the newly reformed monasteries like Fleury in action and brought news back to the royal court where reform was already in the air (Morris 2021: 284). The final challenge to Athelstan came in 937 at the great northern battle of *Brunnaburh* where his united army defeated a coalition of Scandinavian and Scottish forces, though with heavy losses on both sides (ibid.: 10).

Morris writes:

> Dunstan and his episcopal colleagues were more important and influential than any of the kings they served. In the forty years after Aethelstan's death in 939, the united kingdom he had forged was ruled by five

consecutive monarchs, none of whom made it past their early thirties ... The leading reformers, by contrast, all lived to be old men ... In addition, the lives of the reformers are far better documented than those of their royal masters.

MORRIS 2021: 278

Unfortunately, space precludes a discussion of Dunstan (909–88) except in relation to his protégé Aethelwold (904/9–84), who was to play a crucial role in the next stage of Winchester's development (ibid.: 290). Aethelwold's life is documented in accounts written by two of his students – Alcuin and Wulfstan – who, naturally, record events through the prism of their admiration for him (Ramirez 2015: 275). In 909 a new monastery was founded at Cluny by William, Duke of Aquitaine, starting a major change in how monasteries operated which meant that they were no longer the objects of aristocratic patronage but would be answerable only to the Pope. Monks were expected to follow closely the rule of St Benedict by being celibate, owning no private property and abstaining from meat (Morris 2021: 282). The second Abbot, Odo, began to reform other Frankish monasteries, including Fleury that an earlier section (70) noted was visited by a bishop from Athelstan's court. After periods of success and unpopularity as a royal advisor, Dunstan became Abbott of Glastonbury (ibid.: 286–7) and as part of his rebuilding the Abbey, surrounded it with a wall 'so he could pen in the sheep of the Lord', beginning a trend towards monastic segregation (ibid.: 287) that Aethelwold would have seen when he joined the community there, and which he implemented in his own reforms in Winchester (73). Aethelwold's biographers state that he came from a noble family in Winchester and was first a clerk in Aethelstan's court (Ramirez 2015: 272) before joining in the 930s the household of the Bishop of Winchester, Aelfheah, where Dunstan was also based (ibid.: 290). Apparently both men were ordained on the same day (ibid.: 291) and Aethelwold soon joined Dunstan's Glastonbury community where he took the tonsure and stayed for a decade, studying grammar, rhetoric and patristics (Ramirez 2015:273) as well as becoming Dunstan's deputy (Morris 2021: 29).

After his ten years at Glastonbury, Aethelwold expressed the desire to travel to Europe 'to receive a more perfect grounding in the monk's religious life' but was persuaded to stay by King Eadred (946–53) and his mother, Queen Eadgifu, who granted him the former royal abbey of Abingdon as well as funds to rebuild it (ibid.: 291). Aethelwold brought other monks from Glastonbury and promoted learning at Abingdon, including educating his later patron, Edgar (959–75), as well as his two biographers (Ramirez 2015: 274–5). As outlined above, Eadred was buried in Old Minster; his successor Eadwig (940–59) was buried in New Minster in 959, his death enabling his co-ruler and younger brother, Edgar to take the throne of a restored single kingdom (ibid.: 297) and in 963 the new king appointed Aethelwold to be Bishop of Winchester (ibid.: 298). Edgar chose Bath, however, for his spectacular coronation in 973, possibly because of its heritage or its Mercian links (Keynes 2008: 48–50). Edgar consolidated Athelstan's work by ensuring that there were common systems of both landholding and justice administered through the shire and its courts (Jarman 2023: 156). Other laws attempted the standardization of weights and measures, the promotion of a common currency and the control of the number of moneyers (Lyon 2012: 6; 23). Central also to the process of unification was his explicit support for the sometime radical steps that Aethelwold would take to impose the stricter rule of St Benedict on monastic houses.

New Minster's Refoundation Charter (Cotton MS Vespasian A VIII), Wulfstan's *Vita S. Æthelwoldi*. and a near-contemporary entry in the *Anglo-Saxon Chronicle*, all record Aethelwold's unprecedented approach to what he found in Winchester. He demanded that the resident clerics of the Old and New Minsters adopt the Benedictine rule; when they refused, with the help of the nobleman Wulfstan, he had them forcibly removed and replaced them with monks from Abingdon (Hudson 2022: 94–5). As the 966 charter for New Minster sets out, Aethelwold commissioned new precinct boundaries for all three Winchester minsters (ibid.: 161). These new barriers separated the minsters both symbolically and physically from the growing town, as well as reinforcing the focus of the monks and nuns on the monastic life; the new boundaries also ensured that the church authorities managed the communities' interactions with the laity (ibid.: 163). It was about this time that the site of what became the great medieval Bishop's Palace at Wolvesey had its first post-Roman occupation. It may be that Aethelwold constructed an episcopal complex where he could sometimes be distant from the court and practice the seclusion advocated by the Benedictine rule; certainly, there is mention of a Bishop's *aula* (hall) at Wolvesey by 1000 (Biddle and Keen 1976a: 323–4).

As outlined above (71), Edgar was a key supporter of Aethelwold's schemes: he authorized the necessary land acquisition and modifications as well as exchanges of land between the various minsters to facilitate the new arrangements. That the forcible ejection of the monks was an exceptional act is shown in the attention it is given in the New Minster's refoundation charter, with claims that the clerics' prayers were ineffectual compared with those of monks, as well as comparing their expulsion to those of Satan and Adam (Rumble 2002: 68). However, it is clear that there were concerns that the ejection might set a precedent, as the Charter records severe penalties for anyone helping clerics to evict the new monks (Hudson 2022: 95–6). This ornate, sixty-page charter is unique, being the only illuminated manuscript written entirely in gold to have survived in England from the early medieval period (Karkov 2008: 224). The frontispiece is divided into two unequal levels, the uppermost being devoted to the image of Christ in Majesty, surrounded by a *mandorla* supported by four angels. Below, King Edgar is depicted offering the golden charter to Christ and he is flanked by the two patron saints of New Minster – Mary and Peter (ibid.: 225). In Karkov's view, Edgar's position and relative size depict him as the bridge between God and the New Minster congregation (ibid.: 240). As will be discussed below, the close association between King and Church is also a feature of another key plank of Aethelwold's reform agenda for the world beyond Winchester – the *Regularis concordia* (76).

Lapidge (2003: 36) suggested that Aethelwold, through his interactions with Continental monks with whom he was consulting in drawing up the *Regularis concordia*, may have been made aware of the European practices of the translation of saints' relics and the miracles that then ensued. In her review of how Aethelwold and his 'circle' pursued their reform project, Hudson stresses how central the veneration of saints was, both through their own practice and by persuading royal patrons to provide very lavish reliquaries and invest in building works, as well as endowing their monasteries (2022: 222). She also suggests that promoting saints who already had a following could have helped to defuse the opposition of the displaced clerics; Eadsige, who reported Swithun's first miracle, had been expelled from Old Minster yet he not only returned to the fold but also was made sacristan, controlling access to the Saint's relics (ibid.: 102). Gretsch has argued:

> Swithun was 'revealed' as a saint . . . in the early 970s, that is, during the years which witnessed King Edgar's coronation at Bath, his reform of coinage, and the promulgation of the *Regularis concordia*. These events signal the apogee of the monastic reform movement, but they also signal that the 'Kingdom of the English' had become an undisputed reality. Swithun's 'revelation' confirmed to Winchester and to all England that these recent political and ecclesiastical developments had indeed been pleasing to God.
>
> 2006: 193

Documentary sources relate that in 971 Aethelwold presided over the translation of the bones of St Swithun from his previous tomb outside into Old Minster, in an extremely elaborate ceremony (Lapidge 2003: 18). According to Wulfstan's account, soon afterwards King Edgar commissioned a magnificent reliquary for the saints' remains, assigning three hundred pounds' weight of silver, rubies and gold to its construction. This was apparently undertaken on his own estate at (probably) King's Somborne from where, in another elaborate ceremony, the reliquary was carried in procession to Old Minster where Aethelwold installed it on the high altar.

The next task was to extend the Old Minster to be a fitting home for the saint (Lapidge 2003: 19). Excavation evidence again contributes to understanding what happened to all three of Winchester's Minsters under Aethelwold's leadership (Kjølbye-Biddle and Biddle forthcoming). A

FIGURE 5.4 *Excavation in 1968 at Old Minster: the north apse and northern half of the central space of the double-apsed link-building or* martyrium *built c. 971–5 around the grave of Swithun (d. 863), looking north* © WEC.

The chalk foundation (on which the scale lies) of the N. wall of the central space butts the N-W corner of the seventh-century nave to the E (right) and the N-W corner of the eighth-century St Martin's Tower to the W (left). The flooded robber-trench of the north wall of the westwork which replaced the double-apsed martyrium cuts across the apse from west to east, to where the east wall of the apse was retained as the east wall of the westwork. The robbed shrine/cenotaph of Swithun is in the foreground, on the axis of the building, with the south wall of the thirteenth-century chapel of St Swithun to this side

martyrium was constructed outside Old Minster that both linked the seventh-century nave to St Martin's Tower and provided a structure over the site of Swithun's original tomb (marked by a stone coffin), with deep apses south and north, and covered by a tall central tower. This structure did not remain for long, however, for when Aethelwold held a powerful position in the court of the new young king, Aethelred (978–1013, 1014–16), Old Minster was remodelled and, in 980, rededicated. Wulfstan's account of this rebuilding of Old Minster has been summarized thus:

> Æthelwold strengthened an earlier work to south and north by the addition of 'solid porticus and various arches'. Second, that he added, perhaps but not necessarily as part of this work, numerous chapels with

altars. Third, that the effect of the addition of the chapels was to make the interior of the building so confusing with its many openings that it might (as least by way of poetic licence) be possible for a stranger to lose his way out.

KJØLBYE-BIDDLE and BIDDLE forthcoming

From a combination of evidence, the Biddles believe that the new Westwork was a massive construction forming a square with sides 22 metres long enclosing St Martin's Tower and the central parts of the former link-building, with four compartments or chapels to north and south. Their calculations suggest that either side of St Martin's Tower there were two towers each 30 metres high, with the rest of the structure at the same height as the existing nave; and that it was this Westwork that was the main focus of the 980 remodelling. The archaeological evidence indicates that within the newly expanded church the original grave site of St Swithun was marked by a further structure above the stone coffin as part of key message:

Lantfred's *'Translatio'*, establishing and locating Swithun's miracle cult, combines forces with the production of new books, new shrines and new images to inscribe a holy space around the physical location of the relics and the original tomb, and the Reform community that allowed these things to be revealed. The newly established cult of Swithun was intricately connected with Æthelwold's ideals for reform at the Old Minster.

LORDEN 2016: 309

Because of the limited archaeological exploration, most evidence of what probably happened at Nunnaminster as part of Aethelwold's reforms is from the documentary reviews that Ridyard (1989) and more recently Yorke (forthcoming) have undertaken and to which reference has been made earlier (70). The excavations produced no evidence that can be associated directly with the reformation process but do suggest that some additions were made to the original church, possibly *c.* 970, and that a second church was built, probably in the late tenth century; this church had Greensand ashlar walls faced with white plaster decorated in red. The excavators interpret a flint-built rectangular structure as a double-celled tomb (Ottaway 2017: 229). Osbert of Clare records that Bishop Aethelwold:

witnessing Edburga's miracles, recognising her glory and encouraged by visions, determined that her relics should be translated to a silver shrine. The abbess and community of Nunnaminster were duly consulted and with their support, in the presence of the conventional crowd of clergy and people, the saint was raised from her tomb and laid to rest in a richly decorated shrine.

RIDYARD 1989: 106

Although (as will be explored later) Nunnaminster continued successfully into the post-Conquest period, Ridyard draws attention to the fact that, in contrast to the Old and New Minsters (and Nunnaminster's own apparent earlier history), the nunnery received very little royal patronage at the time of her translation or later, despite its founder and saint themselves being royal. The few miracles that are recorded are also for ordinary (mainly local) people (ibid.: 119–20).

While his major building projects were clearly important to Aethelwold in ensuring that the monastic foundations operated in line with his perceptions of the proper approach to the monastic life, his central concern was the widespread adherence to the Rule of Saint Benedict. As more monasteries were founded and reformed therefore, in 970, after King Edgar's and Queen Ailfthryth's coronations he called a congress in Winchester to agree the rule to be followed known as the *Regularis concordia* (Kornexl 2013). It has been argued that this document is clear evidence that 'the links between Church and State were now being put down formally', with the king being identified in the Rule as the animator of monastic reform and both the king and the queen having formal responsibility for the new, reformed monastic communities (Ramirez 2015: 276, White and Conybeare 2024: 372). Stafford argues that the church was now distanced both from the laity to whom the old priests were deemed to have been too close, and from the nobles who had been the previous patrons of monastic houses (1999: 20–2). The eleventh-century copy of the *Regularis* from Christchurch, Canterbury (British Library, Cotton Tiberius A. iii) shows King Edgar, Dunstan and Aethelwold tied together by a copy of the *Rule,* with a monk depicted below them but also bound into it (Ramirez 2015: 275–6; Karkov 2008: 239). Although written in Latin, the *Regularis* was 'glossed' into English to ensure its widest dissemination and understanding (Stafford 1999: 11): in addition to showing the doctrinal control that Aethelwold sought to exert, textual analysis suggests that the vocabulary and linguistic style used in the Winchester *scriptorium* was highly influential in the wider monastic construction of texts, especially in south-east England (Hoffstetter 1988).

Further evidence of the skills of the Winchester *scriptorium* is seen in the exceptional design and illumination of the *Benedictional of St Aethelwold* (Deshman 1995); this contains the various pontifical blessings used during Mass on each of the days of the ecclesiastical year, and a form for blessing the candles used during the Feast of the Purification. The text states that the *Benedictional* was produced by the scribe Godeman, at the behest of the Bishop himself who was specific in what he wanted – 'He commanded also to be made in this book many frames well adorned and filled with various figures decorated with many beautiful colours and with gold'. In addition to the text there are twenty-eight full-page miniatures, nineteen other framed pages, and two full-page historiated initials, one framed; there were probably intended to be a further fifteen full-page miniatures and more framed pages. Wilson identifies a range of influences for the iconography of the

Benedictional – Insular, early Eastern Christian and styles paralleled in the Carolingian ivories from Metz (Wilson 1984: 169).

Early in the twentieth century, art historical analyses of this and other manuscripts identified the 'Winchester School', influenced by Carolingian art (Saunders 1928) and characterized by elaborate foliate frames in which acanthus leaves were extended to cover partly and envelop the framework around expertly drawn, colourful figures (Backhouse, Turner and Webster 1984: plate XV). Further features include outline drawing as well as elaborate initials decorated with foliage, interlacing stems and biting animal heads (Saunders 1928: 20). By the mid-1950s, it was generally accepted that the Winchester School spread from Winchester to other centres of manuscript production, particularly Canterbury (Brownrigg 1978: 249). More recently there has been more debate about whether this artistic movement emanated from Winchester alone, although there seems to be consensus that the Winchester *scriptorium* was a major source of artistic inspiration (Kershaw 2008: 254–5), as well as the religious and linguistic inspiration explored above (77). Art historians have also identified the influence of the Winchester School in items produced in other media including walrus ivory the most notable of which is a triangular panel from Winchester depicting two addorsed angels with enlarged hands and fluttering drapery which are closely paralleled in the decoration of the Charter of the New Minster (Wilson 1984: 190–5). In the twenty-first century, metal-detecting increased

FIGURE 5.5 *Old Minster at 992–4 from the S-W with New Minster in the background. Artist's impression by Simon Hayfield* © WEC.

the corpus of Winchester School metalwork as well as demonstrating its wider distribution into the Danelaw; Kershaw (2008: 256–7) argues these items display the full range of Winchester School motifs and there is also evidence of their manufacture within the Danelaw (ibid.: 262–3). Some strap ends have close parallels in ornament: a clearly defined central stem springing from an inverse animal mask or plain trefoil feature, and off-shooting tendrils ending in scrolled terminals, visible on the strap end found in one of the New Minster burials (Hinton 1990: fig. 125). Others are much simpler and there is evidence, too, of blending with motifs derived from both Carolingian and Scandinavian traditions (Kershaw 2006: 266).

Returning to the hub of these artistic traditions in Winchester, as WS 4.i will describe, the next phase of Old Minster entailed a remodelling of the east end, the digging of two crypts, and possibly the creation of a baptistry that may have been started at Aethelwold's order but was completed by his successor, Aelfheah (944–75), with a rededication in 980. The authors of WS 4.i note that as well as having the archaeological evidence, unusually, the interpretation of this phase is informed by Lanfranc's contemporary account and by the depiction of Old Minster in the *Benedictional of St Aethelwold*. Bringing these sources together, they argue that the east end had triple stilted apses; an eastern external crypt probably added to accommodate high-status burials; and a new central tower which the Benedictional image suggests may have been staged. The function of the new central crypt cannot be ascertained with any certainty, however, because of the extent of the robbing of its stone in the Norman period. The excavators believe there is evidence (certainly by the mid-ninth century) for the existence of staged timber towers of sophisticated form in the part of northern France closest to south-east England, and at monasteries that had links with Winchester. Based on analogy with a range of representations and artefacts from a number of European sites, as well as depictions in English manuscripts, they propose that the tower's main purpose was to represent the tomb of Christ, linking it to the liturgy of the Eucharist. They suggest that the inspiration for the Old Minster design may have come from the monastery of Fleury with which, as earlier sections explored, there appear to have been established connections (71). The *Benedictional*, and Continental manuscript descriptions, show these towers with complex arrays of bells; further weight is added to this interpretation by the discovery during the excavations of a tenth-century bell-casting pit.

Documentary sources record modifications to New Minster, commissioned by Edmund in 939–46 and completed by Edgar in 972 (linked to the issuing of a new charter as part of the monastic reforms); and the construction of a tower for Aethelred in the 980s. The highly decorated six-storey structure positioned at the western end of the New Minster was probably intended to match and surpass Old Minster's Westwork (Quirk 1961).

Looking more widely WS4.iiii *Property and Piety in Early Medieval Winchester* (Rumble 2002) is an edition and translation of thirty-three Anglo-Saxon and Norman documents relating to the topography and minsters of early medieval Winchester; Rumble's extensive commentary elicits information on what was happening in the town at the same time as the church building. In 900, *Document XXV* records that Aethelred granted his thegn, Athelweard, nine properties on Tanner Street (later Lower Brook Street); it highlights that leather preparation was most likely already underway there) (ibid.: 200–6). Near the High Street there are records of at least three large properties, which were later subdivided to increase their rent revenue (Biddle and Keene 1976a: 340). Unlike churches, domestic buildings were generally made of timber, and only limited evidence of their construction survives; they are most often represented by successive spreads of flooring. The majority seem to have been rectangular with their gable end facing the street frontage (Ottaway 2017: 24), one excavated at the Brooks (Building B1) started in the late ninth to early tenth century as a rectangle (6.3 m wide and extending about 10 m from the street), and was later replaced by a multi-room, L-shaped building (Scobie, Zant and Whinney 1991: 37–8). Evidence has also been found of wattle walls, and of substantial post-holes that Ottaway suggests could have supported a second storey; other houses seem to have had cellars added (2017: 244). Environmental evidence suggests that at least some of these dwellings had small holdings attached (Crabtree 2018: 145). Although pollen analysis shows that there was an extensive marsh landscape stretching along the River Itchen, the very high occurrence of cereal pollen indicates that agriculture was practised in nearby areas (Iverson and Renfrew 2022: 142–3) and processing of cereal crops probably took place within or very close to the walled town (ibid.: 156–7).

Plant remains were discovered in a number of anaerobic pits and wells, providing evidence of what was being grown and how it was being processed, although it must always be remembered that conditions affect the survival of plant remains differentially (Monk 2022: 183–5). The most numerous finds from Lower Brook Street were fruit stones and pips, which Monk interprets as evidence for the beginnings of organized, wide-scale orchard or hedgerow husbandry (ibid.: 196–203); these fruit species included plums, although sloes, apples and pears were also present, and a few hazelnuts and blackberries (ibid.: 203–4). The majority of the other plant remains were either from plants of disturbed or cultivated ground, or from waste-ground (segetals and ruderals), some of which may have been deposited as waste from animal byres where it had been used as bedding (ibid.: 217). At the Cathedral Green site (near Old Minster), in addition to plant remains from pits and waterlogged deposits, an important group of material was recovered from bell-casting pits: carbonized remains of plants and seed impressions were preserved in the fired-clay fragments of the bell-moulds (ibid.: 217) These discoveries indicate that previously popular hulled wheats – emmer and spelt – were replaced by free-threshing species of bread wheat; Monk links the transition to the cultivation of the heavier clay soils in the valleys, which followed the introduction at this time of the mould-board plough (ibid.: 224). In addition to the same sort of fruit remains found at Lower

Brook Street, the Cathedral Green site also produced examples of immature grape pips: a vineyard in the vicinity would fit well with the need to supply wine for liturgical purposes (ibid.); there is documentary evidence of substantial vineyards in the later medieval period (93). Plant remains from a ditch on the Castle Yard site again provided evidence of cereal cultivation and orchard/hedgerow plants but also examples of legumes – broad beans and field peas – which were not found elsewhere in Winchester, but which were found carbonized at *Hamwic*. Monk identifies that there are place names and charter references to legume cultivation (e.g. 'beanland') and suggests that legume structure mitigates against their preservation in the archaeological record; legumes therefore may have contributed more to people's diet than the recovered remains suggest (ibid.: 232).

The three major Minsters were deriving considerable benefits from the very extensive estates granted to them and Winchester is likely to have acted as major market for a range of agricultural products including wool (Crabtree 2018: 145). Banham and Faith (2014: 238) suggest that the rise of Winchester as a commercial centre may have been accompanied by an intensification of production on these estates through a more coordinated approach to their management and possibly the introduction of new crops and farming methods. It is likely that sheep and cattle would have been kept on these rural estates and the animal bone evidence published to date suggests that these animals were kept for dairying and wool production; pigs seem to have been kept in the town itself as in Roman times (Coy 2009: 39–40). The range of craft-production in the town is attested by both street name and archaeological evidence; given the presence of the court and its elites, it is not surprising that in addition to the tanners referred to above, there was also a street of shield-makers (Biddle and Keene 1976b) as well as evidence of sophisticated blacksmithing that produced hardened blades (Tylecote and Gilmour 1986: 2–3). In addition to supporting the *scriptorium* discussed earlier (77), the metalworkers of precious metals and copper also had clients amongst the elites of court (Ottaway 2017: 246–7). More mundanely, pottery finds are common from late Saxon contexts although no local kilns have been yet discovered (ibid.: 248–9) and there is evidence for the more domestically based crafts of spinning and weaving as well as bone- and horn-working (ibid.: 251).

At this period, Winchester had a significant mint with (at the time of *Winchester Studies* 8's publication) silver coins minted there being the fourth most frequent of those surviving from the time of Edgar's reforms until the Norman Conquest (Lyon 2012: 5). Documentary sources record six moneyers in Winchester in the time of King Alfred, which rose to eight by Edgar's time and increased further to cope with the requirements of producing the *Danegeld* in the 990s (ibid.: 6). From Edgar's reform of *c.* 973 until at least the end of Aethelred's reign, the Winchester moneyers were responsible for new coinage designs (ibid.: 10–11). Biddle and Keene identify that the mint workshops were located on the south side of High Street (1976b: 398). One of the functions of silver coinage was the facilitation of long-distance trade that the more localized forms of barter and exchange could not accommodate, and the presence of secular and ecclesiastical elites would have provided a market for more exotic goods. In addition to the evidence of the precious metals needed for the production of manuscripts discussed earlier, pottery finds suggest wine being brought in from the Rhineland (Dunning 1964) and silk items, even more exotic, from the Near East and China also arrived in Winchester from at least the tenth century (Crowfoot 1990: 473–4). Jarman's research into long distance trade and exchange emphasises the interconnections stretching from northern Europe along the great rivers of central and eastern Europe, to Constantinople and the wider Middle East and beyond, following what would later become known as the Silk Roads (Jarman 2021).

Beyond the walled area of Winchester, excavations have revealed suburban development outside the northern, eastern and western gates of the town (Ottaway and Qualmann 2018: 26–7; 331–2). In the western suburb from the bottom of a rubbish pit (dated late ninth to tenth century) was recovered a *burse* reliquary of gilded copper sheets on a wooden base now known as the 'Winchester Reliquary' (ibid.: 161; Hinton, Keene and Qualmann 1981). The front of the reliquary has a figure of Christ with features that in inspiration could be traced back to the seventh century, while the depiction of the face, hand gesture and robes all have parallels in tenth-century works produced by the Winchester School. However, they suggest that the acanthus decoration on the other sides more directly reflect the acanthus design visible in the ivories produced in Metz rather than those of the Winchester School; it is not certain, therefore, where the reliquary was made (ibid.: 72).

In many ways, the rededication ceremony for Old Minster can be seen as a moment of transition both for Winchester and England as a whole. The *Life of St Aethelwold* records the bishop organizing in 980 a magnificent two-day ceremony at which all the great and the good were present, including Aethelred; it depicts a public ceremony very different from the zenith of reform that had characterized Edgar and Aethelwold's previous celebrations at Winchester:

> All who had previously seemed his enemies, standing in God's path, were suddenly made, as it were, sheep instead of wolves: they revered him with extraordinary affection, and lowering their necks to his knee and humbly kissing his hand, commended themselves in all things to the man of God.
>
> MORRIS 2021: 320

Aethelwold clearly had encountered some opposition to his reforms from 'his enemies' but by some means they had been overcome and a public demonstration of their acquiescence was apparently needed. What started this change was Edgar's death in 975:

> At his death the whole kingdom was shaken. Bishops were disturbed, ealdorman were angry, monks were struck with fear, the people were terrified.
>
> ibid.: 310

One major reason was that there was no clear heir. Edgar had left two sons – Edward, who was a teenager, and Aethelred, who was still a child; after two days of argument Edward was chosen, and crowned shortly after by Dunstan, now Archbishop of Canterbury (Roach 2016: 61–3). At Edgar's death, the magnates who had been forced to cede lands to the control of the reformed monasteries are recorded as attacking them, driving out the monks and abbots who, in some cases were replaced by the previous clerics (ibid.: 102; Wood 2022a: 277). This proved a catalyst for armed conflict between the two brothers' factions which culminated in Edward's murder in 978 (Morris 2022: 278), and in Aethelred's accession, with his mother, Bishop Aethelwold and a Mercian ealdorman acting as his regents.

Aethelred and the eleventh century

As Wood wrote, 'Ethelred the Unready has acquired the poorest reputation of any English king' (Wood 2022a: 273), but as early as 1986 Keynes identified that the main account of his reign was composed after his death and with full knowledge of the eventual outcome (1986: 201). Crucially as Morris (2022: 328) and Wood (2022a: 282) have argued more recently, the scale of the Scandinavian raids was much larger and more co-ordinated than previously, possibly because of the prosperity that Edgar's reign had brought about (Morris 2022: 324). A number of authors have also argued from analysis of the make-up of coin hoards in Scandinavia that at this time there may have been a diminution of trade with the east (e.g. Moroney 2019; Jarman 2023: 203). Nevertheless, there can be no arguing that the range of strategies that Aethelred employed – bribery, diplomacy, employing mercenaries, church reparations, purges of advisors, genocide and military conflict (Wood 2022a: 276–97) – all failed to stem the tide of eventual Scandinavian takeover (ibid.: 297). Although his son Edmund Ironside briefly reached an accommodation with the young Scandinavian ruler Cnut (996–1035), whereby Edmund controlled his ancestral lands of Wessex, after Edmund's death in 1016 Cnut became the undisputed ruler of England (Morris 2022: 357). Winchester was the scene of some major events in Aethelred's reign, but much more of significance happened in London, probably because of its wealth and strategic importance in a nationwide series of conflicts (Naismith 2018: 180–1). Foreshadowing Henry Tudor's interest in using Winchester's history to emphasize the legitimacy of his rule (114), Cnut invested both time and resources in the town (Karkov 2004: 123; Yorke 2021a: 63), probably as part of his overall strategy of promoting continuity rather than change; this is shown also by the assembly he called at Oxford, at which both the Scandinavians and English agreed to observe Edgar's laws (Wood 2022a: 301).

As outlined earlier (82), one of the strategies that Aethelred employed in his efforts to combat the Scandinavian incursions was diplomacy, and in 1002 he established an alliance with the Duke of Normandy to deny his ports to the Scandinavians. As part of the alliance, Aethelred married the Duke's sixteen-year-old daughter known then as Emma (Wood 2022a: 284); one of the properties with which he presented her was what became known as 'Godbegot' in Winchester's High Street (Barlow et al. 1976: 37–8). The general under-representation of women in the historical record has already been noted (15) but this cannot be said of Emma, who became known as Ælfgifu while married to Aethelred (Ramirez 2023: 158) and appears to have used both names subsequently depending on circumstances (Karkov 2004: 121). From all that is known of her later life, it seems likely that as Aethelred's widow, she would have recognized the possibilities of a marriage with Cnut, but it is not clear how much choice Emma had in reality (Morris 2021: 364). That said, it appears to have been a successful partnership in which she had considerable agency (Karkov 2008: 119).

The first depiction of Emma and Cnut is in the frontispiece of the New Minster *Liber Vitae,* which was used each day at mass to commemorate the dead who had special significance for the Winchester community. Whilst it is Cnut's hand that is shown actually around the great golden cross that he is presenting, there is no doubt that Emma is very much part of the ceremony (ibid.: 126–7). Iconographically, this image – that also includes Christ in Majesty flanked by the Virgin Mary and St Peter – clearly links back to that of Edgar discussed above (73). However, in this later depiction the royal couple are shown standing on a mound on either side of the altar and peering out of the arches are a collection of monks, again signalling the interconnection with the church and its support (Ramirez 2023: 163). In the spirit of continuity, the following pages of the *Liber* set out the earlier history of the New Minster, from King Alfred's death to the construction of Aethelred's great tower that was later dedicated by Dunston. The names of those who made significant contributions to or were buried in New Minster were picked out in gold (ibid.: 143). Karkov summarizes the role of the *Liber*:

> The list of saints is followed by the West Saxon regnal list beginning with Ine and ending with Cnut (fol. 39rv). In all these texts names matter . . . and the historical continuum that linked the community in 1031 to the past communities of both church and court.
>
> ibid.: 145

This idea of continuity was further emphasized by the law code that Cnut issued in Winchester at Christmas 1020 or 1021 summarizing the major legislative statements of his predecessors from Aethelbert to Aethelred (ibid.: 139); notably Cnut also initially kept direct rule over Wessex when he divided his new kingdom into four major earldoms, although this was subsequently passed in 1020 to the man who had become one of his strongest allies, Godwine, who Cnut also married to the sister of his brother-in-law (Morris 2021: 366–7). It appears that Cnut became increasingly reliant on Godwine to manage English affairs as the king also had to pay attention to his Scandinavian possessions: he sent Harthacnut, one of his sons with Emma, to rule Denmark (ibid.: 369). As has been discussed above (70), when a strong and charismatic king dies, the complications of multiple potential heirs lead to periods of instability and conflict (82), and this was the case after Cnut died (and was buried in New Minster) (ibid.: 371). Another of the great assemblies was held in Oxford with again no consensus: Godwine and his allies (with Emma) supported Harthacnut, whereas the thegns north of the Thames favoured Harald (Harefoot) (1035–40), who – unlike Harthacnut – was in England (ibid.: 371). The northern group appear to have got the upper hand by proposing that Harald should be regent until Harthacnut returned, although Godwine won the concession that Wessex would remain under the direct control of Emma, who was to reside in Winchester supported by Cnut's household guard (ibid.). In the Cathedral Green excavations, a 'hogback' tombstone of Scandinavian form, inscribed to 'Gunni, the earl's companion', was found (Biddle and Kjølbye-Biddle 1995: 278–80; Jarman 2023: 250–3) and a stone with an eleventh-century runic inscription is incorporated into the later tower of St Maurice (ibid.: 327–8). The sculptures could be connected with the Scandinavians of Cnut's household guard who remained with Emma. A piece of decorated stone from New Minster's destruction levels is widely interpreted as part of the story of Sigmund in the *Volsunga* saga, which the excavators argue would have had a shared resonance for the Wessex and Scandinavian communities and might be part of a decorative freeze added to the church (ibid.: 314–22; Jarman 2023: 249–50 and will be discussed in WS 4.i (Kjølbye-Biddle and Biddle forthcoming).

Possibly because he recognized that his success had been gained through his alliance with Cnut, Godwine saw his best chance of keeping his position as the most powerful earl in England would lie in supporting Cnut's sons rather than Aethelred's – Edward and Alfred – and so he opposed both the expeditions they led from Normandy (Morris 2021: 372). Edward sailed back to Normandy after his forces were defeated; Godwine initially pledged loyalty to Alfred but then betrayed him to Harald, who ordered his half-brother to be blinded, which appears to have led to his death (Karkov 2004: 149–50). Whilst this move secured Godwine's position, Emma was banished, and Harald reigned as king; nothing is known of his reign as no charters survive and there are no records in the extant versions of the *Anglo-Saxon Chronicle* (Morris 2021: 374–5). Possibly this may be because of the vengeful attitude of Harthacnut (and probably Emma) when he became king in 1040, upon Harald's death: soon after, Harald was exhumed from Westminster Abbey and 'flung in a fen' (ibid.). In this atmosphere, the destruction of records seems entirely possible. However, Harthacnut's harsh taxation and general behaviour do not seem to have endeared him to the magnates of the court, and in 1041 Edward was invited back from Normandy to share the rule of England (ibid.: 375). It was at this time that Emma commissioned the *Enconium Emma Reginae* (Campbell and Keynes 1998), probably produced by a monk at or from the monastery of Saint-Bertin in Saint-Omer in Flanders (Karkov 2004: 146). The text of the *Enconium* begins with an account of the period of success and peace that Cnut's rule brought to England in contrast to the havoc that resulted after his death (ibid.: 146–7). Scorn is poured on Harald's legitimacy, and the horror of Alfred's death receives special mention (ibid.: 150) as do the miracles that had taken place at his tomb, thereby raising his status as a martyr (ibid.: 151). The 'dual kingship' of Harthacnut and Edward characterizes their rule (with her) as comparable with the Holy Trinity with 'no disagreement between them' (Morris 2021: 376). It appears that Emma did indeed have an important role in the kingdom as she is recorded as *mater regi*s in charter witness lists (Jarman 2023: 269).

Only a year after Edward's return, Harthacnut died suddenly in London (Morris 2021: 376) but was returned to Winchester to be buried in Old Minster (Yorke 2021a: 70); Edward became king in 1042 and was crowned in Winchester at Easter 1043. What happened shortly afterwards suggests that the picture Emma painted in the *Encomium* may have been far from the truth, as Mortimer has summarized, drawing on the various versions of the *Anglo-Saxon Chronicle*:

> The three versions diverge a little more interestingly later that year when dealing with Edward's first recorded action as king, his deprivation of Queen Emma, his mother, of her possessions. C and E tell how Edward took into his own hands all his mother's land and everything she had in gold and silver beyond description, 'because she had withheld it too firmly from him'. D adds further details: the king acted on advice, rode from Gloucester with earls Leofric, Godwine and Siward and came unexpectedly on the Lady and deprived her of all her uncountable treasures, 'because she had formerly been very hard to the king her son, in that she did less for him than he wished before he became king and also since' and they allowed her to stay there afterwards.
>
> MORTIMER 2009: 7

However, there is no detail of what happened subsequently, until Emma's death and burial are recorded in 1052 (Jarman 2023: 269). The Latin inscription on one of the six Renaissance mortuary chests in Winchester Cathedral records Emma's name (Crook 2022: 134). The 2012 renovations necessitated the removal of the chests from their traditional location in the

Choir, and the opportunity was taken to examine their contents (Yorke 2021a: 61): 1,300 bone fragments from twenty-three individuals were found (Jarman 2023: 310). The full results of their investigations are yet to be published but in 2019 the team announced that they had identified one female skeleton aged fifty or above and, from radiocarbon dating, of early medieval date; they believe these are the remains of Emma (Crook 2022: 136). Although crowned in Winchester, Edward's focus appears to have been on London, where began his great project to build what became Westminster Abbey (Mason 1991: 58–9); Morris (2021: 386) has suggested that this was because Winchester had become too closely associated with Cnut's dynasty. Nevertheless, Winchester still held the royal treasury and was clearly prosperous, as attested by the survey of rents and services due to the king carried out in Edward's reign (Ottaway 2017: 210).

As is the case with many significant historical moments, the end of Anglo-Saxon Winchester was not marked by any spectacular battle or cataclysm but by pragmatism, when (apparently on the advice of Edward's widow, Edith) the citizens surrendered the town to William of Normandy after the Battle of Hastings (Bates 2020: 519)

6

Medieval Winchester

Introduction

The previous chapter indicated that, for whatever reason, Edward the Confessor had chosen to invest in London for his flagship project – Westminster Abbey. Once William I (1066–87) took the crown, showing continuity with Edward's legacy was key and he signalled this by being crowned in his new Abbey. However, William is also recorded as greatly expanding the Royal Palace in Winchester and having the very substantial castle built to dominate the town, as well as commissioning the building of the great new Cathedral that survives today (Bates 2020: 521–2); moreover, the Treasury remained at Winchester. As later sections will explore, some major royal events still happened in Winchester and its bishop was the richest prelate in England. Nevertheless, Winchester was never as central to national life as it had been in its early medieval heyday including being absent from the 1086 Domesday Book.

The *Liber Winton*, or Winton Domesday, is a record of two major surveys of medieval Winchester. In *c*. 1110, a survey recorded a list of the 300 properties that were regarded as being part of the royal *demesne* (Barlow et al. 1976). A second survey was carried out in 1148 for the Bishop of Winchester, the town's largest landlord; it was designed to ensure that he had a full record of his holdings and the revenues due (ibid.: 18). Combined with archaeological evidence, these records provide a rich picture of the lives of a much greater range of people than was possible for the early medieval period, so this chapter will first review what we know of the citizens of Winchester before considering the activities and impact of the royal and ecclesiastical elites.

The citizens of Winchester

Using evidence from Exeter, Mortimer has described what a visitor would encounter on arrival at a medieval town with much in common with Winchester:

> It is the cathedral which you will see first ... it is hundreds of times bigger than every other building around it and dwarfs the walls that surround the city ... When you draw closer to the city walls you see the great gatehouse ... it leaves you in no doubt about the civic pride of the city nor its authority. Here resides the king's officers in the castle ... Here is place of rule and order. And then you notice the smell ... The road crosses a brook. As you look along the banks you see piles of refuse, broken crockery, animal bones, entrails, human faeces, and rotting meat strewn in and around the bushes. In some places the muddy banks slide into thick quagmires where townsmen have hauled their refuse and pitched it into the stream. In others, rich green grasses, reeds and undergrowth spring from the highly fertilised earth ... You have come face to face with the contrasts of the medieval city. It is so proud, so grand, and in places so beautiful ... Welcome to a place of pride, wealth, authority, crime, justice, high art, stench and beggary.
>
> MORTIMER 2009: 7–8

The medieval period produced a greater range of documentary sources, but they still cannot present a full picture of the whole population, especially of ordinary people – the majority of whom were not literate (Bartlett 2009: 5–10; Carr 2018: 6). Similarly, surviving archaeological evidence is affected by environmental conditions, subsequent activity and the context of discovery (Carver 1987: 14, Ottaway 1992: 11–12). Dempsey has argued there also needs to be an attitudinal change in not only how archaeological evidence is studied, but also in the narrative it presents:

> Our discourses must create multi-vocal narratives that reveal the social complexities and diversity of the world. In an era of global feminist activism, it is no longer acceptable to portray the past through one master narrative that consistently ignores the lives and experiences of othered people, especially women and those who do not conform to the heteronormative or white Eurocentric 'ideal'.
>
> DEMPSEY 2019: 783

In this spirit, consideration of life in medieval Winchester will begin by exploring what is known of two women whose stories provide insights into how they were able to exercise agency and play a significant role in the lives of the wider community. As mentioned above (15), unusually we hear of an ordinary woman. Juliana de la Floude (as she became known) is recorded in 1299 as having a dispute with one of her wealthy neighbours in the Brooks area – John de Tyting – who had reportedly cut off the water supply to her property, which was vital to her business as a laundress (Keene 1985: 715). Having not received satisfaction, Juliana appealed to Edward I (1272–1307), who appointed a commission of local residents to investigate and as a result of their findings, the king ruled that 'water has always been common', i.e.

everyone had the right to access water supplies. This decision then passed into statute. In 2010, The *Concorde de Juliana* was adopted by the United Nations General Assembly in recognition of the human right to water and sanitation; its achievement became one of the UN's Sustainable Development Goals (World Water Day 2022).

Another notable medieval citizen was the Jewish entrepreneur, Licoricia (Keene 1985: 385, 1365; Brown and McCartney 2004; Bartlett 2009; Abrams 2022), whose life is of considerable interest in its own right as well as providing insights into the position of the Jewish community in Winchester and more widely (Griffiths 2021). The earliest reference to Jews at Winchester is in the Winton Domesday survey of 1148 when two Jews – Urselin and Deulecreise – are recorded with properties in *Scowrtenestret* (now Jewry Street) (Biddle 1976: 101). This area appears to have been the hub of Jewish settlement in the town, probably because of its proximity to the Castle, to which the Jewish community could go for the royal protection to which they were entitled (Bartlett 2009: 37). A 'Jews' Tower' at the Castle is also noted: it seems to have served as both a refuge and a prison when local Jewish men were accused of various crimes (Griffiths 2021: 229). In 1177, the community took advantage of Henry II's edict permitting them to establish their own burial grounds and rented a large plot of land from St Swithun's Priory (Keene 1985: 1034), just outside Winchester's Westgate and near the Castle (Griffiths 2021: 228).

It was into a well-established community then, that the widow Licoricia arrived in 1234; initially she appears to have been in partnership with another Jewish woman but was soon lending substantial amounts of money on her own account (Brown and McCartney 2004: 15). In 1242 she married David of Oxford, an extremely wealthy businessman (Bartlett 2009: 53); he lent extensively in Oxford to local magnates (Brown and McCartney 2004: 11–12) as well as to Henry III and the court (Bartlett 2009: 54). Licoricia moved to Oxford, and it appears that she and David had a son before David's death less than two years later (Brown and McCartney 2004: 16). The Crown took possession of all David's records and Licoricia was confined in the Tower of London while the settlement was worked out. Henry III's share was fixed at 5,000 marks, 4,000 of which he assigned to building a rich shrine and chapel dedicated to Edward the Confessor; a project to which Licoricia was also required to donate 2,500 marks from her own inheritance (Bartlett 2009: 57–8).

Licoricia then returned to Winchester and took up residence in an extensive property in Jewry Street, which also housed the community synagogue within its grounds (ibid.: 69); she continued to be involved with senior magnates, the court and the king, who personally intervened on her behalf in several disputes (ibid.: 63–7). Henry III (1216–72) was a regular visitor to Winchester both to meet his former tutor, Bishop de Roches, and to make improvements to the Castle (Ottaway 2017: 290–2; 312); these would have enabled Licoricia's contacts with him and the other members of the court. Licoricia is recorded as having business interests in Bedford, Hampshire, Norfolk, Oxford, Surrey, Warwick and Wiltshire (Brown and McCartney 2004: 18). She and her family survived the younger Simon de Montfort's three-day rampage through Winchester in 1264 (ibid.: 89), but such upheavals seem to have affected Licoricia's business, as she rarely appears in the records during the 1260s–70s (ibid.: 109). Her son, Benedict, however, appears to have been both very successful in business and able to work closely with the Gentile powerbrokers in Winchester, as in 1268 he was elected a guildsman – uniquely for England and possibly anywhere in medieval western Europe (ibid.: 97). His success continued into Edward I's reign when, in 1274, Benedict became Keeper of the Queen's Gold, but at some time in 1278–9, he was hanged for the crime of coin-clipping (ibid.: 130). There is little evidence that he and Licoricia had worked together and when, in 1277, Licoricia and her Christian maid were stabbed to death, it was her other sons who tried to bring her murderers to justice (ibid.: 109–10). In 1290, Edward I expelled all Jews (except doctors) from England (Mortimer 2023: 98–9) so Winchester lost its Jewish citizens, but their presence was recorded in the name of street where they predominately lived, becoming known as Jewry Street (Keene 1985: 1479; Griffiths 2021: 231).

Documentary sources give an idea of the extent of Licoricia's house and land, but these have not been explored archaeologically. The most investigated part of medieval Winchester is the Brooks area, where there is

FIGURE 6.1 *View N-W across Lower Brook Street excavation in 1966 with the remains of St Mary's church prominent at centre* © WEC.

also documentary evidence to complement the results of archaeological investigations (Keene 1985: 703, 746, 792–3) and waterlogged conditions to provide environmental evidence (Green 2022: 255–75). The Winchester Excavations Committee's investigations revealed a number of structures that appear to have combined living spaces and workshops, firstly tanning and then, in the twelfth and thirteenth centuries, fulling, dyeing and other cloth preparation (Biddle 1968b: 267). At the same time, other properties in the area had their earlier timber structures replaced in stone and light industry (including non-ferrous metalworking) continued on the same plots (Ottoway 2017: 343). Later excavations in the Brooks area revealed the impressive holding of the rich wool merchant, John de Tytying (90) (Scobie, Zant and Whinney 1991). From the archaeological and documentary evidence (Keene 1985: 712–13), between 1299 and 1312 John developed the plot into a major urban property reflecting his wealth and status. Entering through a gatehouse, the visitor would see at least two halls (one apparently stone built with an undercroft), ancillary buildings (including a chalk-lined latrine and a kitchen), gardens and a possible dovecote (Ottaway 2017: 325). Elsewhere, excavations in Staple Gardens provided evidence of fourteen tenements which had early medieval origins but underwent two further phases of development in the periods 1050–1225 and 1225–1550 (Teague and Hardy 2011). In the early thirteenth century, the Archdeacon of Winchester owned one very large plot with two stone buildings, a chapel and a hall with undercroft (Cunliffe 1964). Although it appears that many of these properties were unoccupied by the early fourteenth century, one with a deep undercroft was still standing and the original steps were later modified to a ramp possibly to make it easier to get goods in and out (Teague and Hardy 2011). A pit from a nearby property contained bones of squirrel, fox, stoat and polecat as well as those of cats, suggesting that it had been occupied by a furrier (Strid 2011). A recent study has combined evidence from historic sources, archaeological material and aDNA analysis to demonstrate the presence of *M. leprae* strains belonging to the same genotype from both these squirrel bones and human remains from the extramural St Mary Magdalen leper hospital, possibly through transmission from squirrel fur lining of garments (Urban et al. 2024).

Outside the walled area, the western suburb expanded beyond its early medieval predecessor probably in response to the need for labour and services at the Castle; certainly, there appears to have been a contraction in the suburb when it declined in the fourteenth century (Ottaway and Qualmann 2018). Timber structures, churches and evidence of industrial activity dating to the eleventh and twelfth centuries were found and the discovery of the bones of a gyrfalcon (Coy 2011: 43) attests to the royal hawk mews known from documentary sources in Henry II's reign (1154–89) (Biddle and Keene 1976a: 238; Keene 1985: 937–8). Once Hyde Abbey had been established in the early twelfth century (105), it appears that an enclosed northern suburb grew up there with at least two churches (Ottaway 2017: 333–4). Numerous pits dating from the thirteenth and fourteenth centuries, and a number of dwellings were found there; later robbing and buildings destroyed much of their detail, but some seem to have been abandoned by the fourteenth century (ibid.: 334–6). Two further churches survive that were founded in the twelfth century to serve the eastern suburb below St Giles Hill and the limited excavations carried out confirmed settlement activity in the area (ibid.: 336). The southern suburb is known primarily from documentary sources that record a number of parish churches as well as the *Sustren Spiral*, Carmelite, and Augustinian Friaries (Biddle and Keene 1976: 267). In 1301 a College was established there, dedicated to St Elizabeth of Hungary, and which was recorded at the Dissolution as having a church and belfry, cemetery, bakehouse, barns, brewhouse, dovecotes, granaries, houses and kitchen gardens (ibid.: 338). Limited WARG excavations at the church produced tiles and building materials as well as a range of decorative stonework whose preservation the excavators attributed to the building having been in existence for only a limited time (Old, Backhouse and WARG 2022: 49–52). In 1231 Bishop des Roches initiated the creation of *The Soke*, a separate ecclesiastical jurisdiction in the southern and eastern suburbs (Biddle and Keene 1976a: 255; Keene 1985: 72); this was later extended to include land outside West and North Gates (ibid.). The documentary sources record too that in the early twelfth century, powerful ecclesiastical figures and also secular magnates spent time in Winchester, most likely when the court was present at the royal palace and the castle (Barlow et al. 1976: 389–91).

As with the earlier periods (79), environmental and recovery circumstances affect the evidence that can be found for the diet of the medieval population of Winchester (Green 2022: 251–3; 339). That finds of charred grains come predominantly from the suburban sites suggest that it was there that grain was being processed, with cereals being used in the town as milled flour, so unlikely to leave archaeological traces (ibid.: 236). Winchester has extensive records of mills along the Itchen from early medieval times onwards; some served individual monastic communities and others the town as a whole (Keene 2022: 68). Twelfth-century documentary sources record some six bakers in Winchester and women selling loaves at various places around the town (ibid.: 69). Analysis of the Bishop of Winchester's Pipe Rolls revealed the pattern of cultivation from his fields in the town's hinterland, where about equal areas of wheat and barley were sown, as well as some oats probably exploiting the richer soils of the valley bottoms; elsewhere oats predominated on less fertile soils (Keene 2022: 62). Keene also argues that these fields' proximity to the town may have also influenced what was grown; wheat would have been in demand for bread and barley for brewing (ibid.: 63). The Bishop's own Wolvesey estate included a large garden between the Palace buildings and the town wall: documentary evidence indicates that fruit and vegetables were grown there on a considerable scale, under the direction of a gardener (ibid.: 64). In addition to garlic, onions, leeks and other vegetables, a large area was used for fruit trees and a vineyard. A good deal of land on the south side of the city was devoted to viticulture; in the thirteenth and fourteenth centuries, a church on land belonging to St Mary's Abbey was called 'All Saints in the Vines' (ibid.). As in previous periods (90), the Brook Street excavations provided evidence of continuing exploitation of orchard crops and hedgerow berries, which are also found at the monastic and castle sites from the eleventh century (Green 2022: 327), as are strawberries, raspberries and blackberries (ibid.: 329). The garderobes excavated at high-status sites (Wolvesey Palace and the Castle) produced grape pips and fig seeds which may reflect preservation in such contexts, but they – and two peach stones – imply that their inhabitants had a more luxurious diet (ibid.: 329–30); there is still little evidence generally of legumes, although documentary sources record that peas and beans were produced in the Wolvesey garden (Keene 2022: 64). The brassica species recovered probably come from rape that was cultivated as a source of oil possibly for both lighting and cooking (Green 2022: 332). The animal bone analyses indicate that beef, pork and lamb continued to be consumed as well as eel, fish and geese (Strid 2011; Brown 2011; Nicolson 2011).

In considering life in the medieval town, it is important to recognize the significance of religion for medieval people for whom 'Christianity permeated every part of daily life' (Cybulski 2019: 100). As Rosman outlines:

> Wherever people looked they saw religious symbols. At street crossings ... and on bridges, carved crosses and statues proclaimed that God was guarding those who lived there and travellers who journeyed through ... Interspersed among the major festivals were vast numbers of saints' days. These constituted the most commonly recognized calendar in a largely unlettered age.
>
> ROSMAN 1996: 1

Everyone was expected to attend church regularly, including three services every Sunday and on feast days, although most received communion only once a year, at Easter (Gilchrist 2012: 169–70). The year was organized around the great festivals of the Church which also affected diet, with meat being forbidden in Advent and Lent (when eggs were also forbidden) (Mortimer 2009: 169). In the medieval period, parish churches looked very different from the primarily post-Reformation decor that we see:

> Roofs and walls were often brightly painted ... Above and around the great central arch there was often a doom painting. Beneath it was a

'rood screen' a wood or stone partition, carved or painted with images of saints, and surmounted by a great crucifix ... It is important to realize that these images were not mere illustrations of the biblical message. They were themselves primary means of communication.

ROSMAN 1996: 9–10

An intimate and reciprocal relationship developed between parishioners and their patron saints, with prayers offered and candles lit before images of the saints; in return, the saints served as personal intercessors for those expressing their devotion (Gilchrist 2012: 173). Furthermore, these representations of the saints were also touched, kissed, dressed and carried in procession on feast days (ibid.: 174). The Church also played a key role in managing the transition from life to death, and in shortening the time souls spent confined in purgatory until their sins had been purged by means of demonic torture (Gilchrist 2012: 169). By the late twelfth century, the idea had been established that an individual's time in purgatory could be shortened by acts performed in life, including the endowment of churches and by pilgrimage (Duffy 2006: 314–18). As later sections about Winchester Cathedral will explore, those with resources could establish chantries where priests performed masses to alleviate the donor's sufferings in purgatory (Duffy 2006: 308–9) (104).

Documentary evidence suggests that in the late twelfth century, Winchester had at least fifty-seven parish churches within the walls and in the suburbs (Keene 1985: 106), although that number later shrank to twelve (Ottaway 2017: 315); some have been excavated and show modifications made to accommodate growing populations (ibid.: 315–16). In addition to the churches and great monastic houses, from the thirteenth century there were friaries of four major orders – Franciscan, Dominican, Augustinian and Carmelite (ibid.: 317–18). Their mission differed from the established monastic orders in focusing on preaching, initially often on the street and later in their own establishments; friars were better educated than most parish priests, with some lecturing at universities and running their own educational establishments (Duffy 2006: 299–301). Their presence on occasion led to conflicts with the parochial clergy who saw them as rivals for congregations and their donations (ibid.: 301). Despite having to establish their communities on the margins of the town, the friaries' records at the Dissolution indicate substantial establishments, confirmed by the limited excavations that have been carried out on their sites (Wessex Archaeology 2011; Bower 2014; Teague 1999; Southern Archaeological Services 2007). In the twelfth century, Winchester's estimated wealth was about equal to Norwich and more than at York and Lincoln (Thomas, Biddle and Morris 2017: 41); between the eleventh and thirteenth century, Winchester appears to have been thriving.

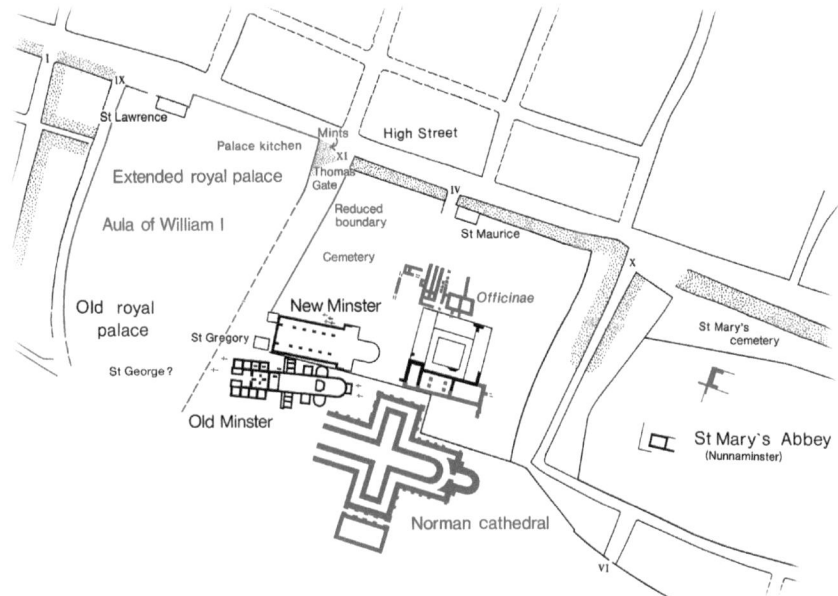

FIGURE 6.2 *The royal quarter of Winchester in 1093 on the eve of the demolition of Old Minster: the Norman royal palace has been extended over the western part of the New Minster precinct. The eastern part of the Norman cathedral was dedicated on 8 April 1093. Old Minster was demolished during the following year* © WEC.

Royal Winchester

The royal palace

Although William I chose to be crowned in Westminster Abbey, he appears to have felt the need to stress an element of continuity with Winchester and instigated a regular ritual of 'crown-wearing' in the Old Minster (Biddle 1986; Bates 2020: 521). He also ordered the enlargement of the precinct of the early medieval royal palace at Winchester, more than doubling its size to 2 hectares (Biddle and Keene 2017: 38). It was extended northwards over part of the New Minster cemetery, and possibly also required the demolition of some monastic buildings (Barlow et al. 1976: 292–4). Houses and workshops on the south side of High Street were also demolished and a street blocked to make room for a kitchen extension to the palace (Thomas, Biddle and Morris 2017: 38). No archaeological evidence or detailed description of the palace have yet been found, although Gerald of Wales (1146–1223) recorded a palace and hall – 'royal buildings second in neither quality nor quantity to the palace in London' (ibid.). However, Henry I (1100–35) preferred to stay at the castle and by 1141 the palace had passed into the hands of the Bishop of Winchester. It is recorded as being burnt down in the aftermath of the fighting between the forces of Stephen and Matilda (Hanley 2021: 163), after which time it appears to have been used as a quarry for Wolvesey Palace (Barlow et al. 1976: 296–7).

The castle

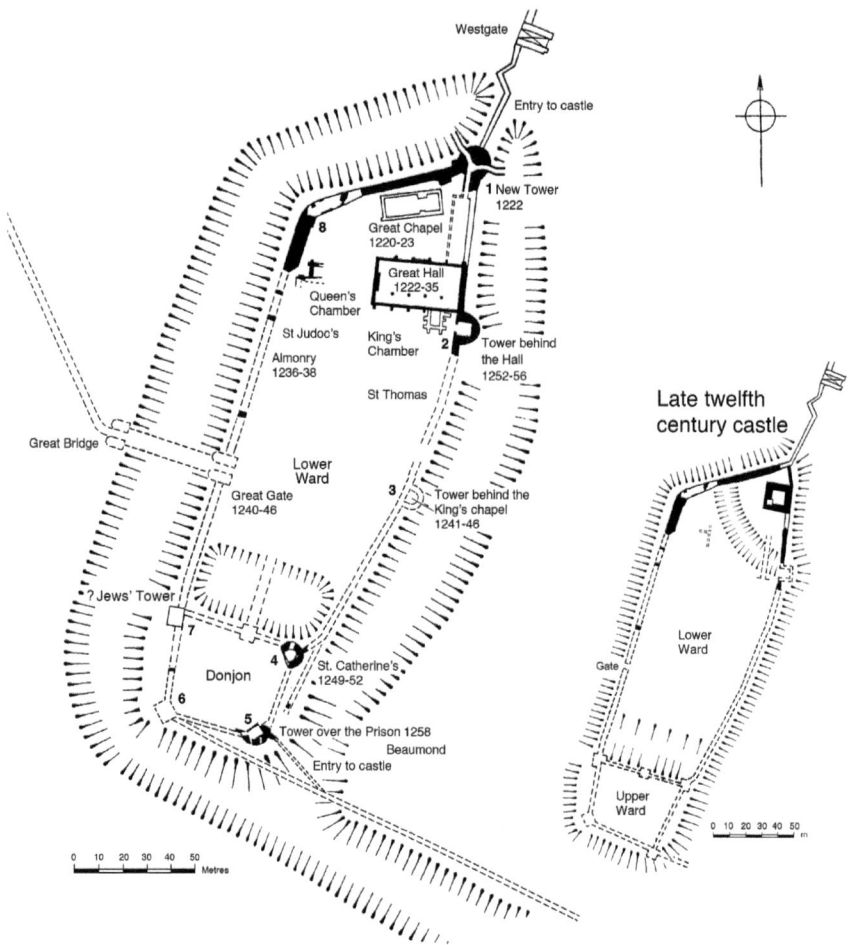

FIGURE 6.3 *Winchester Castle: outline plans of the principal elements in the late twelfth and thirteenth centuries* © WEC.

Castles were much more than simply military bases: as seigneurial residences, they were potent symbols of authority and status, centres of honorial lordship and royal administration.

STRICKLAND 2022: 235

The castle built at William I's command in Winchester by William FitzOsbern in 1066–7 well illustrates this statement; it is sited on the highest point of the walled area, taking advantage of the existing defences of the town, and with a new 5-metre-high bank and ditch built, enclosing an area of 2.4 hectares. Its construction required the demolition of several streets' worth of existing houses, so overall was a potent and very visible manifestation of the new regime (Thomas, Biddle and Morris 2017: 38). A combination of archaeological and documentary sources reveal how the Castle developed (Ottaway 2017: 287–94; Clayre and Biddle forthcoming). Usually, an earthwork motte would complete the initial castle design, but a chapel preceded it at Winchester (Thomas, Biddle and Morris 2017: 38). There is no evidence to indicate whether this was because the town appears to have accepted Norman rule easily or because William wanted an impressively sited ecclesiastical venue for his hosting of the Papal legate at Easter 1072 (ibid.: 6). In Henry I's reign, the royal treasury was relocated to the castle; in the early twelfth century, the previous buildings were levelled and a square

FIGURE 6.4 *Excavation at Winchester Castle in 1967, with the foundation of the twelfth-century Great Tower (centre)* © WEC.

FIGURE 6.5 *Winchester Castle: looking S-W at Great Hall (left) and the visitors' centre. Photo: P. Kemball © WEC.*

stone keep erected (Ottaway 2017: 288). Although in 1194 Richard I (1189–99) chose Winchester Cathedral for an apparent revival of the lapsed crown-wearing ceremony (and possible reassertion of his monarchy after his imprisonment) (Ashbridge 2019: 83), there appears to have been no further royal investment in the castle until Henry III (1216–72) both repaired the destruction from the Barons' War and added a number of massive towers to the castle (Ottaway 2017: 290–2).

In 1222–5, Henry had built the 'Great Hall' that survives to this day (Biddle, Clayre and Morris 2000: 68), as well as a number of chapels and enhancements to the royal apartments, including new gardens (Clayre and Biddle 2022: 74). Edward I maintained the castle defences but after a major fire in 1302 that destroyed the royal apartments, the Castle ceased to be maintained as a royal residence (Biddle, Clayre and Morris 2000: 69).

The Round Table

In 1976, the Round Table that hangs in the Castle's Great Hall was lowered for study and conservation; in 2000, a major historical, scientific and art historical study of its construction and subsequent history was published (Biddle 2000a). Analysis of the various Arthurian Romances indicate that by the thirteenth century, Winchester had become associated with a number of the stories including the holding of a great tournament (Biddle 2000b: 356). Biddle argues that it was the holding of a tournament in Winchester in 1290 by Edward I to celebrate the marriages of his children that is the most likely date for the Table's construction (ibid.: 374), which also fits with the dendrochronological date (ibid.: 390). It appears that in its original form the table was not painted nor had a permanent covering (Biddle 2000c: 403) but based on the evidence of the surviving later Tudor painting and other decoration within the Hall, Biddle argues that the most likely decoration was a leather cover with a central sunburst around which were divisions for the various knights, possibly with their names (ibid.: 417).

Ecclesiastical Winchester

The Cathedral Priory

At the time of the Conquest, Winchester's two greatest Anglo-Saxon Minsters stood side by side, opposite the early medieval palace complex (95); the Norman expansion of this site that impinged on the New Minster precinct signalled that change was afoot (95). Appointed Bishop in 1070, the Norman Walkelin oversaw in 1079 the layout of a cathedral immediately to the south of Old Minster. It was designed in the new (Romanesque) style; oak and beech trunks were driven into the peaty waterlogged ground to provide a stable platform for the east end of the building (Ottaway 2017: 295–6). The first part of the new church was dedicated in 1093 and St Swithun's

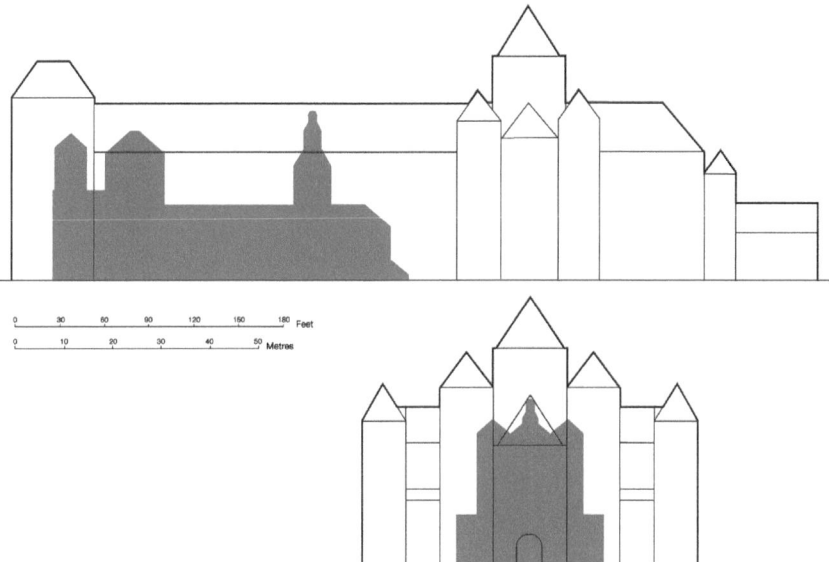

FIGURE 6.6 *The size of Old Minster as completed in 992–4 (solid) compared with the outline of the Norman cathedral as built 1079–c. 1120: in length, looking N (above); in width, looking E (right).* © WEC.

FIGURE 6.7 *New Minster (left), the site of demolished Old Minster, and the nave of the new cathedral under construction, looking east c. 1120. In the memorial court (foreground), before a fragment of Old Minster, a rectangular monument lies over the site of St Swithun's grave, with stone coffins around it. Artist's impression by Simon Hayfield © WEC.*

reliquary was transferred there that same year on the anniversary of his 971 translation.

The archaeological evidence for the subsequent demolition of Old Minster to enable the completion of the nave, and the subsequent twelfth-century destruction of New Minster will be discussed in WS 4.i (Kjølbye-Biddle and Biddle forthcoming) and this section draws on that analysis. The robber trench of Old Minster's West Work was used as a charnel pit for burials disturbed by the building works; later a plaster surface was laid over it to form what the excavators describe as a 'memorial court', surrounding a stone monument on the alignment of Old Minster and on the exact site of St Swithun's original tomb. Burials were cut into the surface of the court and a number of stone coffins were preserved in situ from their early medieval positions; the bones of Cnut and his family were transferred into the new Cathedral. During the episcopate of Henri de Blois (*c.* 1096–1171) in the late

FIGURE 6.8 *Winchester Cathedral, Norman tower and north transept, and Perpendicular nave. Photo: P. Kemball © WEC.*

twelfth century, he arranged for them to be moved again (Crook 2021: 102–6), as part of his remodelling of the shrine of St Swithun in which a 'feretory platform' was created to more prominently display the reliquary; beneath the platform was a short tunnel, the 'Holy Hole', allowing pilgrims greater access to the saint's bones (Crook 2001: 15); Crook has suggested that this unusual arrangements may have been inspired by the ring crypts in Rome (2021: 100).

Built of Quarr stone from the Isle of Wight, Bath Stone and stone recycled from Old Minster, the new Cathedral was cruciform in shape, and *c.* 162 metres long, making it the longest cathedral in Europe at this time (Ottaway 2017: 208). Crook has argued that at the west end, there were twin towers flanking a central structure which he suggests consisted of a 'tribune' platform above the western portal from where the king would have greeted people on ceremonial occasions (Crook 2010). By the early thirteenth century, the instability of the east end in particular necessitated repairs to the foundations; a retrochoir was created which provided greater space for accessing St Swithun's tomb and also included the installation of a Lady Chapel flanked by rectangular chapels (Ottaway 2017: 299). More remodelling of the east end was undertaken in the early fourteenth century further enhancing the area of St Swithun's tomb and the royal burials (Crook 2001: 27). The western towers were demolished in *c.* 1350 and the west front and nave remodelled in the Perpendicular style. Although the building campaign was initiated by Bishop Edlington, it was his successor William of Wykeham (1320/24–1404) and his master mason William of Wynford (1360–1405) who were responsible for the majority of the work (Crook and Kusaba 1993; Hare 2012). At the behest of Cardinal Beaufort (*c*. 1375–1447), St Swithun's early medieval reliquary was melted down, to be replaced by a new reliquary and shrine consecrated in 1476 (Lapidge 2003: 35). In the late fifteenth and early sixteenth centuries, further work was undertaken to remodel the Lady Chapel and the chancel; several elaborate chantry chapels for the bishops were also installed in the nave and retrochoir (Crook 2001: 39; Ottaway 2017: 364).

The church was only part of the great monastic priory complex. Defined by a precinct wall to its south, there would have been a cloister, chapter house, prior's hall, buildings to feed and house the monks and lay brothers, and to tend the sick and accommodate visitors, as well as gardens, barns, brewhouses, orchards and workshops (including a *scriptorium*) (Cybulski 2021: 104–5). Although some individual buildings survive, such as the fourteenth-century timber-framed guest house now known as the 'Pilgrims' Hall' (Crook 2001: 44–6), much else is only known from fragments incorporated into later structures (Ottaway 2017: 300–3).

New Minster

There are records of a major fire destroying New Minster's domestic buildings in 1065 (Biddle and Keene 1976a: 316), which excavations suggest were rebuilt with some additions (Biddle and Quirk 1964: 165–72; Kjølbye-Biddle and Biddle forthcoming) and (as was explored earlier) the expansion of the royal place in 1069–70 was at the expense of New Minster (95). Generally, the site was increasingly cramped, and Henry I appears to have ensured that the necessary land transfers and arrangements were put in place to facilitate the moving of the relics of the Alfredian royal family (Yorke 2021b: 27). Building works at Hyde Abbey started around 1110 and their transfer there was made the next year. Osteological investigations of bones from Hyde Abbey confirmed the presence of at least part of one of the Alfredian royal house (Albert and Tucker 2015: 209–28). The timing and circumstances of the demolition of New Minster were not documented; excavations revealed extensive robbing (Kjølbye-Biddle and Biddle forthcoming) and the site was then incorporated into the Cathedral cemetery, which continued in use until the nineteenth century (Ottaway 2017: 300).

Hyde Abbey

Once the remains of the Alfredian royal family were re-interred in front of the altar of the new church, further construction continued; it appears in its first phase that the east end of the abbey church was apsidal with an

FIGURE 6.9 *Hyde Abbey's fifteenth-century southern gatehouse, seen from inside the abbey precinct. Photo: P. Kemball © WEC.*

ambulatory that Klingelhöfer (2003) has identified as part of a distinctive Anglo-Norman style paralleled at Cluny Abbey in France, and also at Bermondsey Abbey and Lewes Priory in England. Documentary sources record that in 1141 the new Hyde Abbey church was burnt down during the fighting between the faction supporting Stephen and that supporting Matilda, and a particular loss was the great gold cross given to New Minster by Cnut (Hare 2021: 28); (105). No evidence of fire was detected in excavations although remodelling of the east end appears to confirm the documentary evidence of the creation there of a Lady Chapel, probably in the early thirteenth century (Ottaway 2021: 303). Because of the later reuse of the site and the limited areas available for excavation, the full plan of the monastery buildings is difficult to reconstruct but it seems there were three areas of the monastic precinct. It was entered through a main gateway on Hyde Street. The Inner Court accommodated the abbey church and cloisters, ancillary buildings, and fishponds (Ottaway 2017: 312–15; the Forecourt contained the pre-existing (and still extant) Church of St Bartholomew and its cemetery, which appears to have served as the parish church for much of the northern suburb (Keene 1985: 953); to its south was the Outer Court with a number of structures including the Almoner's Hall and the Abbey Mill (Ottaway 2017: 312). Since 2016 Hyde900's community excavations have uncovered further features of the Abbey buildings, including a stretch of an intact vaulted twelfth-century culvert, a number of large architectural fragments, painted window glass from the twelfth-century cloisters, and traces of what has been interpreted as a *lavabo*, for handwashing (Hilts 2024). As inheritor of the majority of New Minster's endowments, Hyde Abbey was the second wealthiest abbey in Hampshire (after the Cathedral Priory), with forty monks at its most populous in the twelfth century (Hare 2021: 29); fourteenth-century records indicate that the majority of the monks came from Hampshire and the surrounding counties where the Abbey held land (ibid.: 30).

St Mary's Abbey (Nunnaminster)

The nunnery (68) was rededicated as the Abbey of St Mary and St Eadburga in 1108 (Biddle and Keene 1976a: 322; Yorke forthcoming) and excavations revealed that the Abbey Church was rebuilt, with a nave 21 metres in width, twice as wide as the previous structure (Qualmann 1986: 206; Morris and Qualmann forthcoming). The fine masonry of the church is comparable with that of the Cathedral transepts, which suggests a twelfth-century date for the work. In the thirteenth century, a font was added and there was some remodelling and reflooring; a number of high-status burials were discovered in the nave and north aisle of the church from this period; six had coffins made of a single piece of stone including one of polished Purbeck marble. Watching briefs recorded walls that may belong to the Abbey's other buildings which at the time of the Dissolution were described as including a hospital and a Chapel of the Holy Trinity dedicated by a wealthy merchant, Roger de Inkpen. Coldicott has reviewed the later medieval document in an analysis of the visitations to St Mary's made by various Bishops of Winchester with concerns about some of the nuns spending too much time outside the Abbey, including with the monks of the Cathedral Priory. The nunnery seems to have remained popular, though, as concerns were also expressed about there being too many nuns (Coldicott forthcoming).

Wolvesey Palace

As was outlined in the previous chapter Bishop Aethelwold established the first monastic precinct and building at Wolvesey (72); the later Bishop's Palace was extensively excavated by WEC and will be published fully in Winchester Studies 6ii. The most recent account of the evidence is provided in Biddle's article (2021a), produced as part of a major review of Henri de Blois' life and contribution (Kynan-Wilson 2021). Although a building that dates from the preConquest period has been discovered (Biddle 2021a: 126), the majority of what was found on the site dates from the twelfth century onwards, but Ottaway (2017: 311) has argued that some of its preconquest buildings were still standing at least initially, affecting the layout of the subsequent medieval buildings. Although its commissioner is not recorded, the excavators argue that radiocarbon dating and analogies

FIGURE 6.10 *Wolvesey Palace, looking west with the remains of the East Hall right, the West Hall and keep to the left, and the extant chapel beyond* © *P. J. Ottaway.*

with the building style visible at the Cathedral suggest that Bishop Giffard (1107–29) commissioned in *c.* 1110 the substantial stone West Hall (measuring 50 by 24.5 metres) (Biddle 2021a: 127–30). It is likely that this building included the Bishop's private apartments, which continued to be used for housing royal and other distinguished visitors throughout the Palace's life especially after the Castle's decline (100). Biddle argues that a parterre was created giving views of the Cathedral and was the garden associated in the documentary sources with the visit of Edward I and Queen Margaret in 1306 (ibid.: 130).

Bishop Henri de Blois (1096–1171) was the brother of King Stephen and played an important part in the struggle between Stephen and Matilda (Hanley 2021: 162–3) (96). Henri played a key role in the ecclesiastical and political life of England and the mainland Angevin Empire (Kynan-Wilson and Munns 2021). What Henri de Blois had constructed at Wolvesey in 1138 was described as 'a house like a palace with a very strong tower' (Biddle 2021a): 131–2) and before commissioning any new buildings, it appears that the Bishop first had added an external flight of stairs and a Caen stone porch to the north side of the existing West Hall to create an impressive first floor entrance (ibid.: 134–5). Probably in 1137–9 the East Hall was then built at a slight angle to the West Hall but separate from it, on the opposite side of what became the Palace's central courtyard. Overall, the East Hall was smaller than the West, but its principal room was much larger and the full height of the building, although at either end the hall was two storey; it is likely to have been used for the two papal legatine assemblies Henri is known to have held in Winchester, as well as for other official occasions (ibid.: 136). Possibly because of the worsening political situation between 1139 and 1141 defensive walls were erected around the residential buildings and apparently protected the Palace from capture in 1141 (ibid.: 138). Probably between 1141 and 1153 further defensive works followed, with the erection of a massive 'keep-like' structure that was built against the east wall of the East Hall, and immediately to the south, a much smaller but similar tower, Wymond's Tower, was built around the latrine tower previously added to the south-east corner of the East Hall (ibid.: 138–9). A gatehouse and further northern defences were then added, and the main assembly hall of the East Hall was moved to a first floor location, possibly between 1153 and 1171 (ibid.: 139) as the final phase of Henri's building project (ibid.: 139–43). This move was reversed in the thirteenth century, possibly by Bishop Peter des Roches (ibid.: 144). In the late fourteenth century, during William of Wykeham's bishopric, the moat was widened and deepened with a new bridge constructed over it at Woodman's Gate; the Bishop's apartments in the West Hall were also being remodelled (ibid.: 139–43). In the fifteenth century, the still-surviving chapel was rebuilt and at the same time a screen was added to separate the cross passage from the body of the hall. This arrangement persisted until the Hall was demolished in the 1680s (ibid.). Evidence of the quality of the windows has been provided both by the window glass found in the Hall itself and also from a large unstratified deposit of coloured glass with figures, canopies, inscriptions and foliage trails found at Woodman's Gate (Keene 1990; Kerr 1990).

The Hospital of St Cross

Possibly inspired by the example of Archbishop Lanfranc's hospital in Canterbury, in c. 1132–5 Henri de Blois established an alms-house (hospital) dedicated to the Holy Cross. It is on land acquired from the Cathedral Priory, south of the town, and set back from the line of what had been the Roman road to Southampton (Crook 2011: 2–4). Henri is recorded as stressing that the purpose of the hospital was 'for the good of his soul, and those of his predecessors and the kings of England' (ibid.: 2). In addition, it was to accommodate and support thirteen 'poor men who are so feeble and lacking in strength that they can scarcely if at all look after themselves without the help of others'; as well as the residents, 100 other poor men were to be clothed and given a daily meal at St Cross (ibid.: 3). The remains of a twelfth-century hall (probably the original brothers' communal lodging) was excavated in 2009 by WARG (Old, Backhouse and WARG 2022: 52–6) and part of the church also dates to this period (Crook 2011: 5). Possibly during his exile, Henri handed over control of St Cross to the Knights Hospitaller and for the next 200 years there were numerous and protracted disputes between their Order and the Bishops of Winchester, who in a partial resolution of the issue eventually regained the right to appoint the Master in 1212, although full control was not returned until the mid-fourteenth century (ibid.: 25–6). Documentary and archaeological evidence suggest that the accommodation for the brothers, their chaplains and other staff was in the eastern half of the precinct, furthest away from the road, with

FIGURE 6.11 *The alms-houses (left) and church at St Cross, seen from the water meadows, site of the abbey's fishponds. Photo: P. Kemball © WEC.*

gardens, the cemetery and the church occupying the western section (ibid.: 30). Probably in the late fourteenth century the surviving buildings known as 'The Brethren's Hall' and 'Beaufort's Tower' were added (ibid.: 31–4). William of Wykeham conducted an enquiry into St Cross which again resulted in protracted legal arguments (ibid.: 34–7); documents prepared as part of the dispute provide a picture of life at the community at this time. In addition to the thirteen brethren there were four chaplains, a cook, three bakers, three brewers and other servants as well as a choir of twenty clerks and singing boys (ibid.: 37). The choristers were recruited from the local poor and given a basic education as well as daily food and beer rations; the brothers received three meals a day (ibid.).

Henry (later Cardinal) Beaufort was another royal (in this case half-) brother of a king – Henry IV – and was both Chancellor of England and Bishop of Winchester; he began to acquire land for an additional institution at St Cross which was founded formally in 1446 and completed in 1449 (ibid.: 47–8). This 'Almshouse of Noble Poverty' was to accommodate three sisters and thirty-five brethren who, unlike those of the original foundation, were intended to be either men of aristocratic birth who had fallen on hard times or members of Beaufort's own household (ibid.: 47); it appears that the sisters received the same stipend as the brothers, had their own hall, and duties that included 'washing the brothers' clothes' (ibid.: 48). It was intended that the two foundations would run in parallel, use the same church and have the same Master, although the buildings erected were on a much grander scale, with a great quadrangle and still surviving 'staircases' of individual apartments for the brothers, strongly resembling the layout of Oxbridge colleges (ibid.: 49–54). The Hall was remodelled with the addition of an integral kitchen and two other rooms (ibid.: 54–60); Beaufort also commissioned the enhancement of the gatehouse, including his own heraldry in the decoration and had rebuilt the 'Hundred Men's Hall' that still survives (ibid.: 60–1). For some reason, after Cardinal Beaufort's death a 'New Almshouse of Noble Poverty' was created, which received its charter in 1455 having been given an additional annual grant of £300 direct from Cardinal Beaufort's nephew, Henry VI (ibid.: 63). With the accession of Edward IV in 1461, many of Beaufort's manors were re-possessed and neither the king nor his successor appears to have had any interest in funding the enterprise, so in 1486 Bishop Waynflete issued a third charter stating that there would be a chaplain, and two brethren charged with saying prayers for Cardinal Beaufort in perpetuity (ibid.: 65). Given these reduced circumstances, the only major architectural addition of the late fifteenth century was the construction of a first-floor galley between the church and the Master's lodgings (ibid.: 70–1). In the early sixteenth century, Bishop Foxe refurbished the east end of the church to create a small, enclosed choir with choir stalls in the new (Renaissance) style (ibid.: 73–5). Early sixteenth-century documentary sources suggest that the fortunes of St Cross had improved with its annual income being £500, leaving a profit of £90 over expenses (ibid.: 77). Although there were only eleven brethren, there were servants and fifteen chaplains, as well as clerks who sang the services together with boy choristers who were in the care of a school master (ibid.). The food provided for the Hundred appears to have been of good quality, including white and red herrings, mushrooms and sticklebacks, as well as spices and figs from London and 'divers kinds of wine' bought at Southampton (ibid.).

St Mary Magdalen Leper Hospital

On the eastern approaches at Morn Hill, located outside the walled town, the *Leprosarium* has its first documentary record in the Winton Domesday of 1148 (Biddle and Keen 1976a: 328), although the extensive archaeological excavations have demonstrated that the first phase of the site consisted of timber structures, a stone chapel and an organized cemetery dating to 1070–90. A remodelling of the site took place in the mid-twelfth century when a new chapel and masonry infirmary were built, and a new cemetery came into use (Roffey 2020: 545). A combination of osteological (Roffey and Tucker 2012) and documentary research (Roffey 2012) have led the excavators to challenge the established view of individuals with leprosy as shunned outcasts (Roffey 2020: 541–3). Roffey has shown that before the fourteenth century there is some documentary evidence that leprosy was believed to be a mark of divine favour, and its occurrence a religious calling as well as a 'passport to paradise' comparable with Christ's suffering (ibid.: 545). He argues that *leprosaria* therefore combined a type of religious community with a mechanism for segregation; their burial styles are comparable with those found in religious communities in Winchester and elsewhere (ibid.: 546–9). Eighty-five percent of the men, women and children buried in the St Mary Magdalen cemeteries showed signs of leprosy, recently shown to be the same genotype as in leprous squirrel bones from central Winchester (Urban et al. 2024) (see above 93). Roffey endorses Keene's view of Winchester, with its many religious houses and shrines both within the town, at its limits and on the hilltops (including the chapel on St Catherine's Hill), as expressing:

> Winchester's role as a point of departure for places of pilgrimage overseas and itself a destination for pilgrims.
>
> KEENE 2015: 443

> St Mary Magdalen was not only physically connected, but also visually and spatially interconnected to other landscape features and religious institutions, contributing to a complex network of sacralisation in the medieval urban hinterland.
>
> KEENE 2021: 551

Certainly, the institution continued to thrive with further additions to the hospital buildings in the thirteenth century, and it survived the Dissolution of the Monasteries, continuing to receive endowments (Ottaway 2017: 373). In the late sixteenth century, the hospital was partly demolished to make way for a row of brick-built alms-houses, although the chapel remained intact, and the Master's house was modified at this time (ibid.).

St Giles Fair

Held annually on St Giles Hill, the fair was probably already well established by 1096 when William II granted it jointly to the Bishop and the Cathedral Priory; soon after the Bishop took overall control, paying the Priory a fixed annual sum. It grew from an initial three days to a great international fair lasting for an eventual sixteen in 1155 (Thomas, Biddle and Morris 2017: 42). The site lay within the Bishop's estate of Winnall and was referred to in 1287 as *nova villa*, laid out around St Giles' Church with a grid of streets named after the trades practised there, including Spice Street and Cutler Row, or the origin of the traders, including French Street and Spanish Row (Keene 1985: 1092). The peak of the Fair's prosperity was between the late twelfth and the late thirteenth century; there was a sustained decline probably caused by the general economic conditions and the course of the Hundred Years' War, especially the raids by the French fleets along the southern English coasts in the late fourteenth century (ibid. 356). By 1393 the Bishop had ceased to collect tolls (Ottaway 2017: 337), although the fair continued and was confirmed in the town's sixteenth-century charter (Atkinson 1963: 49–55).

The Winchester Bible

Few documents survive from the medieval Cathedral Priory (15), so it is fortunate that the Winchester Bible produced in the late 1180s was preserved (Donovan 2021: 151). It is the largest of the large-scale twelfth-century English Bibles, with 468 folios measuring 583 x 396 mm, and was designed to be illuminated with ninety-three large historiated initials, of which forty-two survive (ibid.: 149). Donovan emphasizes that for the clerics of the time, the text was of prime importance, and she identifies a single scribe undertaking its production (ibid.: 153; 158–9). In addition, there are full-page illustrations ('miniatures') produced by six masters, whose identification was first made by Oakeshott (1945) and confirmed by Donovan (2021: 156–71), although she proposes a different process for how their work was brought together (ibid.: 171–4). There is a general acceptance that there was no 'Master' overseeing the complete design of the Bible; Donovan argues for the bringing together of a team of makers that drew on the established skills and resources of the Winchester *scriptorium*, as well as six masters coming from a range of different artistic traditions and locations (ibid.: 172:). Although Norton (2018) has challenged the idea of Henri de Blois as the patron of the Winchester Bible, Donovan argues both that there is strong evidence of his commissioning bibles and other works while he was Abbott of Glastonbury and also that he had the international contacts (and resources) to bring together the eclectic team of experts whose work is seen in the Winchester Bible (Donovan 2021: 173–4). Donovan also supports her attribution to Henri by arguing that it was his death in 1171 that caused the final illuminations not to have been added, even though the text was by that stage complete (ibid.: 174–5). Furthermore, the Bishop had the resources to fund the huge amounts of vellum required for the work, as well as the gold and lapis lazuli (mined in Afghanistan) used in the illuminations, possibly sourced from St Giles' Fair or through Henri's European contacts (West 2008).

St Mary's College (now Winchester College)

It is important to remember just how rich the Bishopric of Winchester was; even after founding both New College, Oxford, and Winchester College – as well as his building projects at the Cathedral (103) and Wolvesey Palace

(108) – William of Wykeham made bequests of more than £6 million in modern money (Partner 1982: 22). He was Bishop of Winchester from 1366 to 1404; in 1382, Richard II granted him a two-hectare site just south of the walled area to accommodate seventy scholars and a 'support staff' that James (2009: 106) calculates was a community of 123. The young men being educated included both Scholars (to be admitted on merit), who would then progress to Wykeham's foundation at New College, Oxford, to train as priests (Lytle 1982: 69), and Commoners, the 'sons of noble and powerful persons who are special friends to . . . the College' (ibid.: 172). The extensive site granted by the king included seven tenements on the south side of what became College Street and a meadow to their south (Keene 1982: 55–60). Building work began in 1387 under the direction of William of Wynford, who had also been responsible for the construction of Wykeham's other foundation of New College, Oxford (Harvey 1982: 82–3; 86). It appears that the buildings around the main Winchester quadrangle, including the chapel and school room, were completed by 1394, with the Outer Court that opened on to College Street being finished by the time of Wykeham's death in 1404 (Keene 1982: 70).

Late Medieval Winchester

For a number of reasons, Winchester in the medieval period was not as central to the kingdom as it had been in earlier centuries. Nevertheless, as the foregoing sections have shown, great architectural projects and artistic endeavours (97, 99, 101, 107, 110) were undertaken in a town with a thriving economy, that was still the location for some significant royal occasions (97, 98, 105). Documentary sources attest to Winchester being a major centre of the textile industry in the twelfth and thirteenth centuries (Keene 1990) and the archaeological record reveals evidence for fulling and other processes associated with the finishing of cloth (ibid.: 201–2; 208–10). In 1326 the 'Staple', to control the export of wool under royal supervision, was established with Winchester being one of the ten Staple Towns (Keene 1985: 472–5). As early as 1312, however, there is a record of an 'insurrection' in Winchester:

> Against the mayor's and king's prohibitions, the rebels held meetings, refused to be brought to justice, 'deprived certain citizens of the city of their liberty', and perhaps most seriously, as suggested by its position in the document, 'of their own authority . . . admitted strangers to that liberty' and imposed tallages on 'some of the citizens . . . not only to the prejudice of the mayor and king's minister, but also in derogation and contempt of the king's mandates . . . to the impoverishment of the city of Winchester'.
>
> COHN and AITON 2012: 146

Unfortunately, the records do not indicate what the rebels' complaints or demands were, but clearly something of significance occurred (ibid.).

It has been the analysis of documentary evidence that has emphasized a late medieval decline in Winchester's fortunes, especially as a result of the Black Death (Keene 1985: 366–8). DNA analysis suggests that Kyrgyzstan is likely to have been the source of the variety of *Yersinia pestis* that caused the Black Death but the exact routes by which it reached western Eurasia are unknown (Spyrou et al. 2022: 723). Frankopan (2023: 400–1) has argued that the devastating effect of this pestilence may be partly attributed to adverse weather conditions, severe cattle disease and subsequent protein loss, and crop failure in previous decades that cumulatively had weakened the population before they were confronted by this highly infectious pandemic. Certainly, documentary sources show the impact of the Black Death on the ecclesiastical communities of the Winchester diocese, with 44 per cent of monks and 49 per cent of other clergy being recorded as dying; this was more than in any other diocese in England (Morris, Thomas, and Clayre 2017: 50). Benedictow outlines that issues with the documentary evidence for plague deaths makes it difficult to calculate the total population loss from pandemic episodes, but he estimates that overall, it may have been 65 per cent of the rural population (Benedictow 2021: 862–3). Keene's analysis of the Tarrage Roll suggests that the 1300 population of 11,625 had fallen to 7,710 in 1417, and as documented in the 1524 Subsidy Roll, to between 3,245 and 4,316 (Keene 1985: 366–8). For the first time, some houses from this period survive above ground (Ottaway 2017: 358; 362–3; 377) showing that there were people in the town with the resources to erect new buildings in the High Street as well as in the northern and eastern suburbs, although Ottaway argues that there is evidence of abandonment and demolition in other areas (ibid.: 385).

The population losses resulting from the Black Death had profound social and economic effects in England with the surviving workers demanding higher wages, and rural populations (in particular) demanding more freedoms as well as higher wages (Jones 2009: 20–1). At the same time, the king required resources for the war against France and imposed for the first time in 1377 a flat-rate poll tax; two further poll taxes were levied, and a fourth one was ordered in 1381 with royal commissioners being sent out to ensure that the (much greater) sums were collected (ibid.: 48–50). Starting in Essex, representatives of local communities began to challenge the commissioners (ibid.: 53–4) and in both Essex and Kent these challenges led to armed insurrections which have become known as 'The Peasants' Revolt'; although one of Wat Tyler's eventual demands was the abolition of serfdom (ibid.: 128), documentary evidence shows that many leading the insurrection were already community leaders (ibid.: 58). Royal officials, and places where documents were held (on the basis of which taxes could be levied), were the rebels' main targets (ibid.: 72; 82; 104; 207).

What happened in Winchester has certain elements in common with these insurrections but there are differences suggesting that local tensions may have been as important as the national issues (Hincke 2010). Possibly participants in the London events, and inspired by reports of insurrection in Guildford (ibid.: 114), William Wygge and his companions led a three-day insurrection in Winchester during which they were joined by a number of other local citizens, occupied the Guildhall, murdered someone (who may have been the town clerk), and burnt the records stored in the Staple which could have included other royal records in addition to those relating to the wool trade (ibid.: 114–16). Wygge had held a number of municipal offices and the indictments against others leading the rebellion indicate that they were guildsmen predominantly active in cloth finishing; some other insurgents were brewers, a smith and a hosier, as well as two men identified as servants (Keene 1985: 396; Hincke 2010: 123). Retribution followed swiftly however, with the investigation in Winchester being the first commission outside London to try insurgents; it resulted in the execution of seven of them (ibid.: 118) but not Wygge (ibid.: 113), who had secured a pardon for himself and continued as successful guildsman in Winchester subsequently, as did several others who had been involved (ibid.: 124). Interestingly there is no record of monastic houses in Winchester being attacked, although they were elsewhere (ibid.). Hincke identifies another, earlier, Winchester insurrection (in addition to that of 1312) (111) when eleven months previously up to 300 citizens were reported as attacking the Prior of Southwark, who was in Winchester as part of a royal initiative to raise troops for the war (ibid.: 123); a number of those involved in this insurrection were also involved in the 1381 event.

In 1418, the authorities made a parliamentary petition claiming that as one-third of the town was desolate they were unable to make the required tax payments (Carpenter Turner 1980: 78). During the fifteenth century, Winchester's cloth industry appears to have suffered from competition, especially from the West Country, and a further petition was made in 1452 stating that ten streets were almost depopulated, with 1,000 empty houses and seventeen parish churches without incumbents (Keene 1985: 903).

7

Reduced Horizons

Tudor times

Prince Arthur

Despite the decline in the town's fortunes and its dilapidation (Chapter 6), after the accession of Henry VII (1485–1509), royal attention turned again to Winchester in 1486 when the new king brought his pregnant wife, Elizabeth (Breverton 2019: 76), there. Their son was born at the Cathedral Priory, given the title of Prince of Wales, and named 'Arthur' (ibid.: 77). Contemporary chroniclers were explicit in recounting that his name and place of birth were deliberate choices, as Breverton reports Francis Bacon's account:

> The Queen was delivered of her first born son, whom the King, in honour of the British race, of which himself was, named Arthur, according to the name of the ancient King of the Britons, in whose acts there is truth enough to make him famous.
>
> ibid.: 78

Arthur was christened in Winchester Cathedral; numerous Welsh poems celebrated his birth as symbolically representing the final union of York and Lancaster (ibid.: 81–2). He then spent the next two years at the Bishop of Winchester's palace at Farnham (ibid.: 81) before moving to Ludlow where, shortly after marrying Katherine of Aragon, he died in 1502 (Weir 2009: 48).

The Round Table

In 1506 Philip of Burgundy, son of the Emperor Maximilian, was shipwrecked off the south coast of England, making land at Weymouth (Biddle 2000c: 422); Henry VII arranged an escort, and despatched his heir Prince Henry to join the royal party, who were entertained by Bishop Foxe at Wolvesey

FIGURE 7.1 *King Arthur's Round Table today. The legs of the table were knocked out and the table hung on the east wall of the hall, perhaps in 1348. The present design is from 1516, repainted in 1789. Photo: P. Kemball © WEC.*

(ibid.: 423). Philip was married to Joanna, half-sister (ibid.: 422) of Katherine of Aragon (widow of Prince Arthur) (Weir 2009: 24). In the account of Philip's visit prepared by Henry VII afterwards, much was made of Arthurian traditions, and he alludes to Philip having visited the Round Table in Winchester (Biddle 2003dc: 424). In 1513, Henry VIII spent time in mainland Europe with Emperor Maximilian who, Biddle has discovered, felt a special connection with King Arthur, commissioning a least one statue of the king for his own tomb, identifying with him at tournaments and apparently appropriating him as a Hapsburg (ibid.: 663–72). It is in this context that it appears that in 1516 Henry had the Round Table repaired and repainted; there is no record of any direct connection with Maximilian, but it may have been part of Henry's imperial aspirations (ibid.: 444; 672). Whitman has argued:

> The Round Table relic is situated in a context that extends far beyond a hall in Winchester. It exhibits more than an overlap between the faces of Arthur and Henry, or the fellowships of the Round Table and the Garter, or the kingdoms of ancient and modern Britain ... It is still a number of years before King Henry VIII will assert himself to be the supreme authority in both secular and sacred spheres in England. Yet even before the official formulation of that far-reaching act, one of Henry's closest associates in the early 1530s defends the king's refusal to submit to papal jurisdiction partly by appealing to the precedent of Arthur's conquest of Rome.
>
> WHITMAN 2008: 52

In addition to meeting Maximilian, Henry was in regular touch with Philip's son, Charles, who in 1519 was elected as Holy Roman Emperor (ibid.: 448–63). In 1522, Charles and a large entourage were welcomed to England (ibid.: 425–8) and entertained with a series of pageants in London, one of which emphasized the shared heritage of Charles, Henry and Katherine (married in 1509) through John of Gaunt (ibid.: 428). Henry and Charles then enjoyed hunting in the Hampshire countryside, after which they arrived at Winchester. From the Winchester College records, it appears that the royal party dined there and probably stayed at the nearby Bishop's Palace. Spanish documents record a visit to the Round Table before the king and the emperor moved on for a week's stay at the Bishop's residence at Bishop's Waltham (ibid.: 429). Subsequently though, 'The King's Great Matter' of Henry's divorce from Charles' aunt Katherine (beginning in 1529) put them firmly at odds (Weir 2009: 353, Wabuda 2018: 394)

The Reformation and the Dissolution of the Monasteries

> Sixteenth and seventeenth century people knew that they were living through a period of religious upheaval, but they did not know it was 'the English Reformation' any more than the soldiers at the battle of Agincourt knew they were fighting in 'The Hundred Years' War'.
>
> RYRIE 2020: 9

By the early sixteenth century, Bishop Foxe had already carried out a number of 'visitations' (inspections) of the religious houses within the diocese of Winchester (Hare 1999: 5–8). In 1507 it was found that women had access to Hyde Abbey, whose monks apparently frequented taverns (ibid.: 5–8). Foxe was committed to promoting the values of monasticism and produced a new English translation of the Rule of St Benedict especially aimed at his diocese's convents (Collet 2007). Two years after the establishment in 1534 of the Church of England with the king as its Supreme Head (Wabuda 2018:

391), Parliament agreed that all religious houses with an annual income of less than £200 would be 'dissolved' and their assets transferred to that Supreme Head (Ryrie 2020: 30). Apparently because of an administrative error that under-reported its income, St Mary's Abbey was initially scheduled for closure in this first wave, but at the price of a massive fine and the loss of two of its richest manors (as well as a favourable report of both spiritual health of the community and the state of its buildings), the Abbey survived briefly (Hare 1999: 3, 9).

In 1538, the Commissioner, Thomas Wriothesley, oversaw the destruction of St Swithun's Shrine in the Cathedral, reporting to Thomas Cromwell that the local town officials were strongly in support of this, although Wriothesley took pains to carry this act out at 3 a.m. (ibid.: 10). In 1539, all of Winchester's religious houses surrendered, with their members being offered pensions and monks able to seek employment as parish priests (Hare 1999: 11–12). Winchester Cathedral Priory became transformed into a chapter of canons, presided over by the previous prior as Dean (ibid.: 16). The position for nuns was, however, less favourable; not only did they receive smaller pensions but there were no alternative careers open to them (ibid.: 12). It appears that the nuns of St Mary's continued to live in an informal community for some time, probably in part of the nunnery buildings (ibid.: 12; 15–16). As late as Edward VI's reign (1547–53) they were reported as wearing their habits in public and condemning the reformed liturgy; they were finally suppressed in 1551 (MacCulloch 2000: 112–13). Excavations at the site of St Mary's Abbey produced evidence of the careful opening of tombs (presumably for the reburial of their occupants), as well as of stripping lead off the chapel roof, and the melting-down of precious metals (Ottaway 2017: 364).

By 1540, England's shrines, pilgrimage sites and relics had been systematically plundered and destroyed, with all religious houses in England having their assets stripped to enrich the Crown (Wabuda 2018: 395). It is difficult to assess what the impact of these changes was for the wider Winchester community; religious houses had had a duty to provide for poor local people and certainly St Mary's is recorded as supporting 'many poor households' (Hare 1999: 11). The cessation of pilgrimages must have affected suppliers of refreshment to travellers. Wabada (2018: 395) argues that the abolition of saints' holidays and the imbedded veneration of saints had a significant impact, leading to the Pilgrimage of Grace in the North. Ryrie (2020: 33) argues further that it was the more explicitly Protestant reforms of Edward VI's reign (1547–53) that would have had the most impact on people's lives, with major liturgical changes and modifications to the parish churches including the removal of rood screens and stone altars. Mary's reign (1553–8) brought about a temporary halt to the reforms (ibid.: 37) but Elizabeth's queenship (1558–1603) ensured the steady march of Protestantism (ibid.: 37–8), although – as will be discussed – some wished to maintain a more traditional approach to Christianity (ibid.: 38–40) (122–3). There were of course people who benefited from the land acquisitions, including Thomas Wriothesley himself, who acquired 22 per cent of the monastic land in Hampshire; he and his successors as Earls of Southampton became prominent in both regional and national affairs (Hare 1999: 13). On a more mundane level, subsequently many of Winchester's buildings incorporated stone from Hyde Abbey and St Mary's Abbey and some monastic buildings became the core of private dwellings (ibid.: 15–16).

The marriage of Mary I and Philip II

Apart from a visit by Edward VI to Winchester College in 1552 (McGrath 1982: 243), the next significant royal event in Winchester was the marriage ceremony of Mary I (1553–8) and Philip II of Spain, held at the Cathedral in 1554 (Samson 2005). The negotiations for her marriage contract as England's first Queen Regnant had been long and complex, and were eventually set out in an Act of Parliament presented by the Bishop of Winchester, Stephen Gardiner, also Chancellor of England, and stated that Philip:

> would vouchsaff so to humble himself, as in this maryadge to take apon him rather as a subject then otherwise; and that the quene shoulde rule all thinges as she doth nowe
>
> ibid.: 763

The Spanish ambassador reported the dissemination of a family tree that emphasized Philip's English ancestry dating back to Henry III (ibid.: 765). The contemporary account of the wedding ceremony in Winchester describes strenuous efforts being made to accomplish the complex balancing act that recognized the formal legal position of a woman being subject to her husband (ibid.: 772) and the need to stress that Philip was not going to become the King of England automatically as a result of his marriage (Hyde 2022: 74). The Cathedral was very much 'staged' for the occasion, as the English Heralds' account documents:

> First the said church was richlie hanged with Arras and cloath of gold, and there was a stage made along the bodie of the Churche ... The Stage and Mounte covered with Redd saie and underneath the Rode Loft was there ii traverses made, one for the queues Matie. on the right hand another for the Prince on the left side ... The quier was aloft hung with rich cloath of gold, and on eche side the high Aulter was there a rich Travers one for the queen on the right side another for the Prince on the left side
>
> SAMSON 2005: 761–2

Mary's location on the right side was the 'king's position' and she also stressed her status by processing from Wolvesey Palace (followed by her officials but no one to 'give her away') into the right-hand side of the Cathedral after Philip had been installed in a 'Closett' on the left (ibid.: 761). Furthermore, although both Mary and Philip were dressed in white cloth of gold, he was clothed in dress in the English court style given to him by the queen, and he also wore the Order of the Garter (ibid.: 764). Possibly because there was no church precedent, however, the vows exchanged harked back to Mary's subordinate position as a woman with her swearing 'from henceforth to be compliant and obedient to you as much in mind as in body'. The ballad composed in honour of the wedding by John Heywood again stresses the complexity of the situation (Hyde 2022). The song opens by announcing that the new king, Philip (represented by the symbol of the Habsburg monarchy, the eagle), had travelled to England to be with Mary, who is represented both as England's lion and a lamb. The ballad then finishes with a prayer that everyone should demonstrate their allegiance to the 'lamblyke lyon, and lamblike burde' and to their Catholic faith (Hyde 2022: 78). Mary and Philip's reign was characterized by continuing efforts to square the circle of their joint rulership, further complicated by the lack of an heir (Samson 2005: 782–4).

Town life

In 1587 Elizabeth I granted the charter that confirmed the town's constitution, rights and obligations (Atkinson 1963: 49–55), at the behest of her powerful courtier Sir Francis Walsingham, who in 1582 had been invited by Winchester's civic leaders to become their first High Steward (ibid.: 49). The Mayor and his officers were responsible for ensuring the health of the community through rules about the perennial problems of industrial pollution of the water supplies as well as restricting access to Winchester from areas affected by plague (ibid.: 204). They also organized citizens to keep overnight law and order – The Watch – as well as mustering men in case of invasion (ibid.: 221–8). In addition to the rules about trade and markets (ibid.: 182–203), they also had responsibility for enforcing religious regulations, being required to carry out searches of houses thought to be harbouring religious rebels (ibid.: 105–6). Throughout the sixteenth century, various Bishops of Winchester complained about the numbers of citizens who were both recusants (paying a fine for not attending church) and generally not adhering to the required religious observances (ibid.: 234; 240–1); in 1599 a notable example was the escape of a priest who had been detained (ibid.: 241–2). It could be that this atmosphere encouraged Queen Elizabeth's alchemist, Dr John Dee, to plan to establish at St Cross a research institute for those who might elsewhere be considered atheists or necromancers; unfortunately for Dee, Elizabeth did not appoint him to the Mastership (Woolley 2002: 312). After an investigation of religious practice there, new rules were introduced at Winchester College in 1572 (McGrath

1983: 253–4) and three Wykehamists were executed after returning from Europe as priests (ibid.: 256–7); some were imprisoned, and yet others recorded as supporting the training of priests at Douai and other European seminaries (ibid.: 258–60). In 1606 another Wykehamist, the Jesuit Henry Garnet, was executed for his part in the Gunpowder Plot (Childs 2014: 349–51). Morris, Thomas and Clayre (2017: 53) outline how, in the late sixteenth and early seventeenth centuries, Winchester suffered economic harm from the decline of the cloth trade, poor harvests and plague outbreaks, with increasing numbers of people needing civic support as well as that funded by contributions from wealthy individual benefactors. Rosen (1981: 152; 161) describes how, in the early seventeenth century, Winchester was beginning its transition to become primarily a regional centre, with a population that included lawyers supporting the Bishop's courts and the Assizes, the Cathedral clergy, College masters, physicians and booksellers. Local gentry and the wider nobility were also attracted to the town, including to the racecourse on Worthy Down that was established in 1591 (Morris, Thomas and Clayre 2017: 54).

Stuart highs and lows, Georgian gentility

After the trial in of Sir Walter Raleigh in 1603, held in the Great Hall because of plague in London (ibid.), Winchester was next involved in national affairs through the Civil War, from 1642. There were specific organized attacks, but the poor state of the town's defences meant that it was regularly raided by passing troops who demanded money, food and lodgings, as well as holding to ransom local dignitaries and gentry (Rosen 1981: 165). The most dramatic attack was in 1642, when troops under the command of Sir William Waller entered the town in pursuit of a Royalist Commander, Lord Grandison (ibid.: 55). Waller's troops not only pillaged shops and homes, but also vandalized the Cathedral, scattering the bones of the early medieval kings and bishops as well as destroying its stained glass (Crook 1993: 98). In 1643, further stress was put on the local population by the garrisoning of 5,000 Royalist troops at the Castle, with further attacks by Parliamentary forces necessitating defensive measures by the Royalists (Rosen 1981: 105). Winchester eventually fell to Parliament in 1645 after a determined bombardment of the Castle led by Oliver Cromwell; troops garrisoning the town in 1647 plundered the Cathedral Chapter House and burnt its records (ibid.: 165). In 1649, the Castle was finally slighted (ibid.: 169) and the site sold to the town (Clayre and Thomas 2017: 56). It appears that much of the walled town had fallen into disrepair with many houses badly damaged and the parish churches being closed (ibid.: 55), although Rosen (1981: 166) has identified that many discharged soldiers with a range of peacetime skills settled in Winchester, thus beginning its recovery.

In 1682, the civic leaders attempted to change Winchester's fortunes by extolling the virtues of the town, and especially its horse-racing, by publishing in the London Gazette an 'advertisement' inviting the king to attend the Autumn race meeting (Thurley 2009: 41). Charles II (1630–85), the queen and much of the court accepted the invitation. It was during this visit that the king conceived the idea of commissioning a dwelling not just to

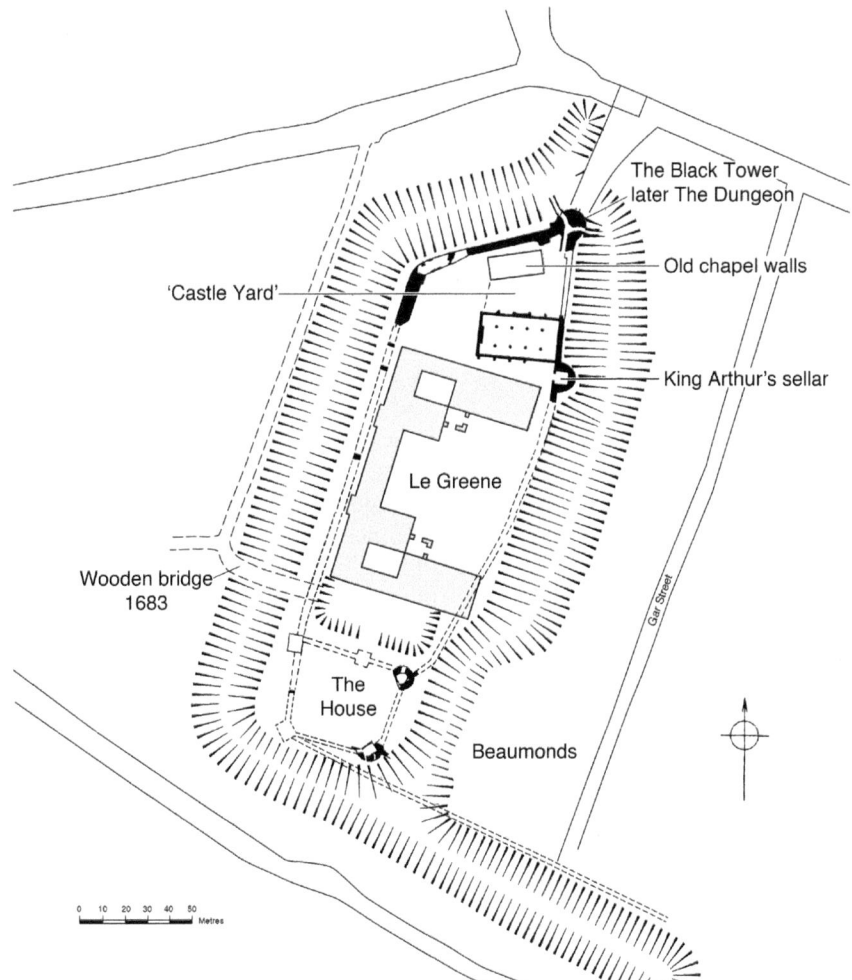

FIGURE 7.2 *Winchester Castle in the late seventeenth century with, in grey, the plan of the palace, or King's House, as built in 1683–5, showing the constraints/ limitations that the site imposed on Wren's plan. Walls are shown solid where excavated, otherwise by dashed lines, but in 1682, many walls especially on the W and S, were still standing.* © WEC.

accommodate him during the races, but something more on the scale of Versailles (Ottaway 2017: 391); the Corporation offered to sell him the site of the now ruined castle for five shillings (Clayre and Thomas 2017: 57). Within three months Sir Christopher Wren had drawn up plans for a grand palace, to include not only private royal apartments but also public rooms to enable the business of state to be conducted there (Thurley 2009: 229). In addition, the design incorporated the creation of an avenue flanked by terraces of housing for the court, to lead from the palace to the west front of the Cathedral, as well as a great park to the west and south of the palace enclosing an area of 142 hectares (Clayre and Thomas 2017: 57). What became known as the King's House was begun in March 1683 and Charles made two visits to inspect progress before he died in 1685; James II did not formally halt work for two more years (Thurley 2009: 228).

Although the full plans were not realized, it appears that that the project stimulated the construction of private residences, both individual houses (e.g.in Kingsgate and Southgate Streets) and terraces (particularly the north side of St Peter's Street) (Morris and Hover 1994: 102–8), as well as public buildings. The new baroque-style Bishop's Palace at Wolvesey was completed in 1715, the new Guildhall in 1713, and a new hospital in Parchment Street opened in 1758–9 (Clayre and Thomas 2017: 57). The Corporation also arranged weekly assemblies with tea and coffee, card games and country dances which were attended by young ladies from the countryside as well as from the town (Rosen 1981: 180). Inns provided more accommodation for visitors than anywhere else in Hampshire (ibid.: 181). In 1724, Daniel Defoe wrote that Winchester was a 'place of no trade, no manufacture, no navigation'. On the other hand, he added: 'here is a great deal of good company the abundance of gentry being in the neighbourhood, it adds to the sociableness of the place. The clergy here are generally speaking very rich and numerous' (Defoe 1724: 215).

A further boost to the Winchester social scene was provided by army officers during the French campaigns of the 1690s and subsequently (Thomas and Clayre 2017: 58). The presence of the Hessian contingent among forces involved in the Seven Years' War was noted earlier (29) and from the mid-eighteenth century, part-time militias were raised, with regular camps being established at Winchester and its hinterland (ibid.: 60). From this time the King's House was used to house prisoners of war, first French, followed by those from the American War of Independence in 1775 (Lewis 1965: 15). In 1796, the site was leased to the Barrack Department that rapidly built it up to become a major centre for the British Army, with many military buildings being constructed (Lewis 1965; Thomas and Clayre 2017: 60).

Jane Austen's novels give an idea of what provincial life was like at the time. with representatives of 'the regiments' providing both glamour and danger to the genteel rural communities (Worsley 2017: 72). In 1809, Jane herself moved to a cottage on her brother's estate at nearby Chawton, in settled circumstances that enabled her to write more novels including *Pride and Prejudice* (ibid.: 250). Once her final illness progressed beyond the skills of the local doctors, Jane came to Winchester to take advantage of specialist medical care provided by its hospital doctors (ibid.: 311) and was nursed in rented rooms in College Street (ibid.: 312). In July 1817, Jane penned a last poem expressing the hope that the rain would keep away on St Swithun's Day for the sake of the Winchester races (ibid.: 316); she died on 18 July (ibid.: 318). Her body was carried in procession to the Cathedral on 24 July and a memorial stone installed that makes no mention of her novels but praised 'the benevolence of her heart, the sweetness of her temper and the extraordinary endowments of her mind' (ibid.: 319). After her death Jane's family published both *Northanger Abbey* and *Persuasion*, accompanied by 'A biographical note' on her life, and her fame grew. Recently controversy has arisen about the design of a commemorative statue proposed to be erected at Winchester Cathedral (Atkinson 2024). Jane's reference to St Swithun's Day relates to the legend which states that if it rains on 'his day' – 15 July – it will rain for a further forty days, apparently a mark of the saint's displeasure at his bones being moved indoors from his previous outdoor grave. This story cannot, however, be traced back earlier than the sixteenth century and is at odds with medieval sources, but apparently accords with established weather patterns (https://www.weatheronline.co.uk/reports/wxfacts/St-Swithuns-Day.htm).

The Victorian city

Population and buildings

Although Winchester City Foundry in Lower Brook Street made axles for the Great Western Railway (Ottaway 2017: 420), Winchester was never part of the Industrial Revolution that so changed much of Britain. In many ways, life in the city in the nineteenth century was very much the same as previously. The population still grew, however, from 6,069 in 1801 to 19,670 in 1891 (James 2009: 142), filling the walled area and expanding gradually into the suburbs. Nineteenth-century census data and trade directories emphasize retail and service sectors as the predominant areas of employment. In 1859 Baker's Directory lists thirty-one bakers, twenty-seven grocers, twenty-seven general shopkeepers and twenty butchers as well as forty booksellers, ten banks and fifty-seven insurance offices, although the largest single category of businesses was those providing hospitality, including hotels, inns and beer houses (James 2009: 153).

Winchester's importance as a judicial centre is attested in 1859 by the record of twenty-two attorneys (James 2009: 143–4) who would doubtless have been supplemented by those pleading cases at the Assize Courts, which in 1874 were relocated from the Great Hall to a new building built to its east (Ottaway 2017: 415). The existing gaol in Jewry Street was expanded, but was then replaced in 1848–50 by a new Winchester Prison next to the headquarters of the Hampshire Constabulary on Romsey Road; a new hospital joined them there in 1863–8 (ibid.: 417). The workhouse had been built at Oram's Arbour in 1834/5 to accommodate 300 people, although its population rarely exceeded 160 (James 2009: 151). It is likely that locating these major building projects was partially linked to the availability of land but also to the continuing problems of disease within the old walled area, with regular outbreaks of cholera especially in the Brooks area (James 2009: 142). Eventually, thirty years after the initial damning report by the city's sanitary inspector in 1844 and a long-standing dispute between the civic leaders and ratepayers (Carpenter Turner 1980: 168–9), drains were improved and in 1875 a new sewage pumping station was built (Clayre and Thomas 2107b: 62–3). Throughout the nineteenth century, a wide range of military buildings (The Lower Barracks) were erected over an extensive area running up from Southgate Street to the land cleared for the Palace complex, especially after 1858 when it became the home base and training depot of both the King's Royal Rifle Corps and the Rifle Brigade (ibid.: 62). After a fire destroyed the King's House in 1894, new barracks replaced it that emulated the brick construction of the 'Wren' style, and in 1901 to the east of the Lower Barracks, further buildings were erected for the Hampshire Regiment whose headquarters were located in Serle's House in Southgate Street (ibid.: 64).

Slavery

On the website of University College London's Centre for the Study of the Legacies of British Slavery, there are fourteen individuals with addresses in or around Winchester who applied for or received compensation for freeing their enslaved people upon abolition in 1833 (https://www.ucl.ac.uk/lbs/). Although the lowest number recorded was twenty-two enslaved people, others sought compensation for more than 200, making them eligible for some £3,500; and one local individual who held 546 in slavery claimed some £13,529 (ibid.) which would (using the Bank of England historic calculator) be worth in the region of £1.2 million today. In the 1871 Census, whilst 67 per cent of the population was born locally, 250 people were recorded as born abroad, including 120 in India or the 'East Indies' and twenty in the West Indies (ibid.: 143–4). Amongst these may have been the first people of colour recorded as living in Winchester, although there could have been unrecorded enslaved people and servants from the eighteenth century onwards or even earlier (Gerzina 2022: 4–6; 21–30). There is likely to have been some abolitionist activity in Winchester through the Society of Friends (The Quakers), who established a burial ground outside the City in 1750 (Ottaway 2017: 407), but no record of protest survives.

Reform at St Cross

In the nineteenth century, the terms of the finances of the Hospital of St Cross came under scrutiny (Crook 2011b: 95). The 'Custumury' set out that, when any of the leases on properties belonging to the Hospital came up for renewal, a fee was payable to the Master, the majority of which went to him directly rather than to the Hospital (ibid.: 96). In the 1840s, *The Hampshire Independent* newspaper highlighted that of the £13,000 to be paid for a lease renewal, £10,706 would go to the Master and in 1849 the issue was raised in Parliament, which voted for an enquiry to be established. After a hearing in the Court of Chancery, the Attorney General ruled in 1853 that the Custumury was flawed, the Master was guilty of a gross breach of trust, the Hospital was a lay foundation and that a new scheme of government needed to be established. The Master was also required to repay any sums he had accrued since the start of the enquiry, but he did not resign for a further two years (ibid.: 87). By 1857, a new 'Scheme' had been devised under which the Hospital would be overseen by a board of fourteen trustees including (ex officio) the Master of St Cross, the Dean of Winchester and the Warden of Winchester College. The lease renewal fee was abolished, and the finances were to be closely monitored, with the thirteen brethren being fed and housed, given a gown each year, and paid a weekly stipend of five shillings; the 'hundred men poor' were to receive one shilling a week (ibid.: 98). In 1881, the funding situation had improved sufficiently to allow the reinstatement of Cardinal Beaufort's 'Almshouse of Noble Poverty' with its nine brothers (ibid.: 101). Crook has argued that Hiram's Hospital in Anthony Trollope's *The Warden* is not based on St Cross as that is a secular foundation, and the issues arose because of financial arrangements not because of an internal revolt; however, he acknowledges that some elements of the novel are borrowed from the St Cross case (ibid.: 95).

John Keats and other visitors

Another author who drew attention to the abuses at St Cross is John Keats, who mentions in a letter to his brother, George, that the Hospital was:

> a very interesting old place ... and for the appropriation of its rich rents to a relation of the Bishop of Winchester ... a charity greatly abused.
>
> KEATS 2011: 233–4

In 1819, John Keats spent two months in Winchester and formed a favourable impression of the town, describing it in a letter as:

> the pleasantest Town I ever was in ... There is a fine Cathedral ... From the Hill at the eastern extremity, you see a prospect of Streets, and old Buildings mixed up with Trees.
>
> ibid.: 233–4

> How beautiful the season is now – How fine the air ... This struck me so much in my Sunday's walk that I composed upon it.
>
> ibid.: 320

His poem *To Autumn,* inspired by this walk, was the last in the series of odes that Keats wrote and remains one of his most popular compositions (Turley, Archer, and Thomas 2012: 797). These authors argue that the route that Keats followed from his lodgings in College Street to the water meadows is one that Charles Ball had set out in his 1818 publication – *Descriptive Walks*. They suggest that he might have bought this from the nearby shop in College Street run by James Robbins (ibid.: 798), arguing that:

> the printer-publisher represented an ideological arm of what we might ... call the 'new men' of Winchester, a coterie of bourgeois citizens including bankers-turned-farmers and millers-turned-mayors who were assiduously refashioning the decayed market city as a centre of finance, culture and tourism.
>
> ibid.: 800

The coming of the railways in the nineteenth century certainly facilitated travel to Winchester (James 2009: 145), which not only benefitted from day visitors to the city itself but also by being included as a destination in longer tours to Wilton and Stonehenge; more restaurants and hotels opened to meet this demand (Carpenter Turner 1980: 182–3). Histories, paintings and views of the city were produced in increasing numbers (James 2009: 156) and in 1868 William Savage published the first guide to Winchester illustrated with photographs. He also ran a series of souvenir shops, selling a range of Winchester-themed transfer-printed pottery as well as miniature copies of the Cathedral font and of the famous 'Winchester bushel' (Carpenter Turner 1980: 183).

Troubles at Winchester College

The military took part in the city's life and in 1815 put out a fire at Winchester College (Bell 1982: 367). However, in 1818, the colonel of the 'local regiment' was told by the boys barricading in the Warden and other staff 'that if his soldiers came near enough, they would have their heads broken by stones from the tower' (ibid.: 871). Nevertheless, after the headmaster had negotiated a truce under which the boys would go home, one of the ringleaders of rebellion (later Lord Hatherley) recorded that 'they met the military in the churchyard, who were ordered to charge them, when ... the boys ignominiously fled, happily having no weapons but bludgeons at hand, and the military being fully armed' (ibid.). This was not the first rebellion at the College; they arose for a number of reasons both parochial (ibid.: 370) and more general: in the 1793 rebellion, the Red Cap of Liberty as the symbol of the French Revolution flew over the school (Turner 2015: 57); in 1808, a revolt broke out when the headmaster tried to make a saint's day a holiday without consulting the prefects (ibid.: 58); and in 1828, another was instigated by six younger boys who objected to acting effectively as servants ('fags') to older boys (ibid.: 57). Turner quotes a contemporary summary of the power wielded by these senior boys 'there were only three absolute rulers in the World: the Great Mogul, the captain of a man of war and the Prefect of Hall at Winchester' (ibid.: 58). Winchester was not alone however both in the revolts and the power relations which characterized the major public schools of the time (ibid.: 56–9), until Thomas Arnold's reconfiguration of the prefect system as a force for good at Rugby brought change to the system (ibid.: 93–7). Arnold had himself experienced the 'old regime' when he had been attacked on his first night at Winchester for kneeling at his bed to pray (ibid.: 93).

8

The Legacy of Past Glories and New Beginnings

Twentieth-century developments

King Alfred's millennium celebrations

Alfred's story was adapted and retold in history, fiction and art to meet the imperial view of history, until – in the reign of Queen Victoria – 'Alfredomania' peaked when he was 'hailed as the founder of the Royal Navy, and even of the British Empire, as the father of English prose, and as the archetype of all heroic qualities' (Keynes 1999: 333). As explored earlier (20) locally in Winchester this led to Mellor's scrabbled campaign at Hyde Abbey to recover the bones of the Alfredian royal family (ibid.: 345–6). In 1897, Frederick Harrison first suggested that a colossal statue of King Alfred should be erected in Winchester to coincide with his millennium of his death (wrongly assumed to be 1901) but it was the newly elected young mayor of the city, Alfred Bowker, who provided the impetus for the delivery of the project (ibid.: 1–2). In 1899, a National Committee had been convened with Bowker as Secretary and the subscription list opened; the main work was, however, carried out by a small Executive Committee, with again Bowker as Secretary and the Lord Mayor of London as chairman. In addition to the statue, the £30,000 funding target was to build a 'Museum of Early English History' in Winchester (ibid.: 7) (see below 136). However, by the summer of 1901, £1,500 was still needed just to pay for the statue; fortunately, the US Ambassador had been a member of the National Committee and promoted the cause in his home country, such that donations reached the required £6,000 by the end of August 1901 (ibid.: 9).

A local committee had also been formed to organize and fund-raise both for the celebrations and for the museum, which was first proposed to be located at Wolvesey Palace, but in the face of opposition from the Bishop of Winchester, the alternative site of Hyde Abbey was suggested. Although there were insufficient funds to build the museum, the owner of Hyde Abbey agreed to sell the site and adjoining land to the Corporation for a park, which became the North Walls Recreation Ground (ibid.). After the (probably quite predictable) problems encountered in erecting the 5.4-tonne, 4.1-metre-

FIGURE 8.1 *Alfred in bronze as the heroic warrior king, by Hamo Thornycroft, erected 1901, dominates the east end of The Broadway* © *Lance Bellers / Dreamstime. com.*

high bronze statue onto the two granite block slabs, it was put in place in September 1901 (ibid.: 10–12). A large contingent of American visitors joined in the three-day celebrations: they began in London with a visit to the British Museum to view various artefacts associated with Alfred, before moving on to Winchester for tours of Alfredian sites, church services, mayoral receptions and historical tableaux, culminating on 20 September in a large procession to the Broadway and the unveiling of the statue (ibid.: 14–15). Four hundred dignitaries then lunched at Guildhall, and in the afternoon 2,000 children were entertained to tea and presented with commemorative medals; there were also general celebrations for local people on St Giles Hill and in Abbey Gardens (ibid.: 16). After Bowker and his sister were presented to President Roosevelt, the main commemoration of the day of Alfred's death was held in New York on 28 October (ibid.: 16–17). As Yorke has emphasized, Alfred's millennium crystallized the emphasis on the racial superiority of the English-speaking peoples and the British Empire that had been developing throughout the nineteenth century (ibid.: 20), a paradigm which has come under increasing scrutiny and criticism in recent scholarship (e.g. Karkow 2020: 195–239). She has argued that:

> many, perhaps most of us, want the medieval to have meaning in and for the present, and it is useful to speak out about its (mis)interpretations and (mis)appropriations, and its weaponizing by far right and white supremacist groups and racist individuals and institutions.
>
> ibid.: 237

The Great War in Winchester

In June 2014, outside the Castle's Great Hall a stone sculpture was unveiled, of a bench on which a soldier's pack rests (Neal 2014). This was the fulfilment of a promise made in 1919 by the Mayor of Winchester to erect a monument to the two million First World War troops who passed through the various transit camps around Winchester on their way to the Western Front (Eddleston 2015: 30–2). The first and most investigated camp is at Morn Hill, which was initially set up as a tented camp in the winter of 1914, but it was so cold that the site had to be abandoned, and the troops billeted in Winchester itself (ibid.: 30). Subsequently at Morn Hill – which would eventually accommodate 50,000 men at a time – wooden huts were built along with stables, garages, a cookhouse and a cinema. British and colonial troops were based there until 1917, when they were replaced by American soldiers, and a large military hospital was added (Eddleston 2015: 30). Recent excavations have explored the camp stockade as well as unearthing a range of everyday items (Napier 2021). Although Olusoga's study (2014) demonstrates that black troops serving as part of all armies were treated less favourably than their white counterparts, it appears that the ordinary people of Winchester were equally welcoming to all troops:

> They brought all these men over from India in bitter weather clad just in shorts. People used to go out with jugs of cocoa or bring them in, poor things ... towards the end of the war, it would be one mass of black troops coming along ... we used to have them in and give them a meal. Everyone did.
>
> BUSSEY 2002: 61

FIGURE 8.2 A Promise Honoured, *by Simon Smith. Photo: P. Kemball* © WEC.

Winchester witnessed an event in 1919 which illustrates that racist attitudes from home countries could surface:

> An American soldier had made a derogatory remark about a black South African soldier who was walking out with a local white woman in the High Street. The South African drew out a knife and made to stab the American but fortunately he was disarmed by the police. No charges were laid but he was warned as to his future conduct.
>
> EDDLESTON 2015: 100

Shortly afterwards, the South African returned to the High Street with his comrades looking for any American soldiers and it was only with difficulty that the police calmed down the ensuing fight. That night, American soldiers descended on the South African troops' quarters and a further pitched battle ensued, which was quelled thirty minutes later by the intervention of armed members of the Rifle Brigade (ibid.: 102).

An account of the wartime city was given by Winchester College's headmaster as quoted in Seldon and Walsh's account:

> Day and night we have lived in the presence of military sights and sounds ... College Street has been crowded with men in khaki ... Old Wykehamists en route to the front have spent their last few hours among old friends in the School.
>
> 2018: 138

Seldon and Walsh also record the feelings of the mother of a young Wykehamist killed in July 1915:

> We spent his last Saturday in England in Winchester with the charm and beauty of the place at their highest. The last service before going to the front in the Chapel of so many loved associations could not fail to be very moving.
>
> ibid.: 240

The government decision that those who had died in the First World War would not be repatriated caused considerable anguish amongst bereaved relatives and made the creation of commemorative memorials in the United Kingdom all the more important (ibid.: 304–6). The headmaster of Winchester College, Montagu Randall, was one of the first public school headmasters to propose a collective war memorial to their dead (ibid.: 308–9). By 1917, he had consulted widely including with old Wykehamists still serving in France, on the form that the memorial should take (ibid.: 309) and commissioned Herbert Baker, who had been involved in the design of the European collective war memorials (ibid.: 308) and created for Winchester College a four-sided War Cloister that recorded the names of the Wykehamists who had died in the conflict – the largest private war memorial ever erected (ibid.). Baker's autobiography (quoted by Mowl) outlines his inspiration and experience of the project:

> Working at Winchester amid all that is best in England was a glorious experience for me; its venerable buildings, its romance and traditions; King Arthur, the Round Table and Camelot; King Alfred; the cathedral, Wykeham and the first public school, its youthful manhood, inspired by the learning of the past with ideals and adventures for the future.
>
> MOWL 2024: 32

FIGURE 8.3 *Winchester College Cloister designed by Herbert Baker © Basphoto / Dreamstime.com.*

Unlike the radical designs of the continental war memorials (Seldon and Walsh: 308) and of Lutyens' London Cenotaph (ibid.: 304), the conscious medievalism of the design carried echoes of conflicts very different from the mud of the trenches or the deserts of Mesopotamia and its message is confirmed by Randall writing in 1924 when it was dedicated:

> Mr Baker's genius has not only erected a worthy monument to the 500 but has translated into stone an idea which I have come to associate with Winchester: that Public Schools carry on as a direct inheritance, in peace and war, the traditions of Christian Chivalry.
>
> ibid.: 318

The Battle of Twyford Down

In 1970, the Government published a plan to extend the M3 motorway in order to improve its connection to the major freight port of Southampton; despite there being a possible westerly rural route around Winchester, the proposal was to build the new motorway to the east, by the existing A33 bypass, impinging on the water meadows between St Catherine's Hill and the city. The M3 Joint Action Group was formed in 1976 and by both building community support and involving powerful local stakeholders like

FIGURE 8.4 *Twyford Down protests (1991–3)* © Jonathan Mitchell / Dreamstime.com.

Winchester College, they persuaded the public enquiry that this route was too damaging (Bryant 1996: 9). In 1983, a new scheme proposed that the M3 should run through a cutting east of St Catherine's Hill through Twyford Down (ibid.: 11). Barbara Bryant's exposition of how she, her husband Dudley and landscape architect Merrick Denton-Thompson realized the scale of the destruction being proposed, and how they brought it to the attention of the 1985 public enquiry, is one of the first examples of how determined individuals can challenge the accepted wisdom of institutions, including government (ibid.: 17–48). Martin Biddle was another key supporter of the campaign identifying that Twyford Down 'preserved an archive of information on social, economic and historical aspects concerning human settlements in the Itchen Valley for half a millennium' (ibid.: 40). In the late 1980s and early 1990s, the Twyford Down Association's efforts expanded from a local to a national campaign, involving a High Court challenge to the planning inspector's agreement to the route, a tactical voting campaign in the 1992 General Election, proposals for a toll-funded tunnel and the involvement of the then Director of Friends of the Earth, Jonathan Porrit, as well as one of the first tussles on environmental issues between the European Union and the UK government (ibid.: 123–78). However, despite all the campaigning, the M3 route was confirmed. Another chapter in the saga began when a group calling themselves 'Earth First' and then 'The Dongas Tribe' occupied the site and took direct action physically to block the construction work, ushering in environmentalism, something new in the UK political scene (Benyon 2020). As Porritt outlined:

> That's where the new style anti-roads protest was born. The experience there has fed through to one campaign after another.
>
> 1996: 301

Locally, another long-running environmental campaign ended in 2011 when the building of 2,000 homes was permitted north of the City, despite the 'Save Barton Farm' campaigners arguing that 'Winchester is a national treasure, they [government] need to take a national strategic view to protect all our historic cities' (Napier 2013).

Twenty-first century

Heritage reborn

In the twenty-first century, Alfred again won a place in popular culture through Bernard Cornwell's six-book series about the Northumbrian, Uhtred. who fought alongside (and with!) Alfred and his family; the first is *The Last Kingdom* (Cornwell 2004). This became the title of a television series for BBC and Netflix; although shot in Hungary, it included sets portraying an early medieval Winchester that the production designer for Series 1 and 2 envisaged as needing to show its Roman antecedents (Martyn John pers. com.). Alfred also appears in three series of *The Vikings* (inspired by the sagas of Ragnar Lodbrok) for The History Channel: Alfred is portrayed as ruling in both Wessex and Mercia as well as interacting and fighting with the various Viking protagonists of the series. Aronstein has argued:

> Adaptation takes place within a context of producers, consumers, and medium. No story gets adapted, especially to expensive mediums such as film and television, unless there is something in it for the producers paying for that adaptation; as such, a tale must have the potential both to deliver a pre-existing audience and to attract a new one.
>
> ARONSTEIN 2023: 260

Alfred has also reached a worldwide audience as one of the key characters in Ubisoft's *Assassin's Creed Valhalla* computer game, where in addition to being the King of Wessex he was also secretly the fictional Grand Maegester of the polytheist Order of the Ancients. In the game and in line with Alfred's attested strong Christianity – the character turns against the Order and seeks to undermine it; he follows the historical narrative of defeating the Vikings and championing learning (https://www.ubisoft.com/en-gb/game/assassins-creed/valhalla).

In 2012 Winchester Studies 8 *The Mint* was published, followed by WS 9.1 *The People of Early Winchester* (2017), WS 10 *The Environment and Agriculture of Early Winchester* (2022), and WS 3.i *Venta Belgarum: Prehistoric, Roman and Post-Roman Winchester* (2023). In 2014 WEC, Winchester College and the University organized an interdisciplinary conference, '*Winchester Archaeology and Memory*', that attracted over 200 international delegates. 2017 saw the publication of Patrick Ottaway's *Winchester – Swithun's City of Happiness and Good Fortune: An Urban Archaeological Assessment*, summarizing past archaeological investigations and identifying future areas for investigation. In addition, and in collaboration with the Historic Towns Trust, Biddle and Keene published *Winchester: British Historical Town Atlas for Winchester* (WS 11), which explores the history of Winchester with early and modern maps, historic aerial photographs and colour illustrations, as well as a detailed gazetteer.

In 2014 Hampshire County Council and Winchester City Council established a new charitable body – Hampshire Cultural Trust (HCT). Alongside its responsibilities for the county museums' services, it manages the buildings, collections and assets of Winchester's museums service via a lease agreement (Masker 2013). One early project was *Winchester, The Royal City*, a partnership between HCT, Hyde900, The English Project, the University of Winchester, Winchester Cathedral, WEC, Hampshire County Council and Winchester City Council; it aimed to 'celebrate and promote the ancient city as a centre of key significance to the development of England and English culture'[1]. In addition to a number of conferences and public events, there were explorations of establishing a new museum of Englishness, thereby reviving the ideas proposed more than a century ago to celebrate Alfred's millennium, discussed above (129). However, HCT's 2019–20 annual report stated:

> The Winchester, The Royal City project was redefined to articulate a clearer vision and to align with Winchester City Council's Central Winchester Regeneration plans.

In 2023, it was announced that HCT is exploring with Hampshire County Council plans to

> enhance the heritage offer in the city by creating a joined-up 'Winchester Castle' visitor experience, re-connecting The Great Hall to both the ruined keep and the city's only surviving medieval gateway, the Westgate, through new interpretation.

ATKINSON 2023

In 2022, a new 'immersive experience' – *878 AD* – opened in Winchester as a partnership between HCT and Ubisoft and in collaboration with Sugar Creative, one of the UK's leading immersive tech innovation studios. The project consists of an augmented reality physical attraction, and an app that enables visitors to explore an imaginary version of ninth-century Winchester based primarily on the *Assassin's Creed Valhalla* game rather than on the historical and archaeological evidence (https://878ad.co.uk/).

In 2019 the Central Winchester Regeneration Area was named as 'Saxongate': as the then leader of Winchester Council explained: 'The new name for the area draws from history, tradition and heritage and we can't wait to make it part of Winchester's exciting future.' The name was not adopted by the successor Liberal Democrat administration (Belgarum 2023). In the wake of that Belgarum article, a letter to the *Hampshire Chronicle* suggested that the area should be named after the medieval woman Juliana de la Floude discussed above (88). In 2023, the first trenches were dug to explore the archaeology of the Central Winchester Regeneration Area in advance of the redevelopment (Bouchard 2023).

In 2014 a five-year £22-million project began at Winchester Cathedral to conserve the building's fabric and to create a new mezzanine level and lift to access a newly developed three-level exhibition space. In addition, the project transformed the visitor experience of the seventeenth-century Bishop Morley library through increased physical access and development of interactive tools to allow virtual access to the books. Conservation diaries were also created as a tool via which future generations would be able to understand processes and methodologies of past repairs and renovation work[2].

In 2017, a charity was established to fund a statue of Licoricia (89) as a way of promoting an understanding of her life and the role of the Jewish community in Winchester and more widely. In early 2022, the unveiling of the statue of Licoricia and one of her sons in Jewry Street was attended by the Chief Rabbi as well as Christian, Muslim, Sikh, Buddhist and civic community leaders. The (then) Prince of Wales was prevented by Covid from attending the unveiling until later, when he linked her to the work of modern Jewish charities. The Licoricia of Winchester charity is continuing its work by creating Key Stage 3 materials focusing on the contribution of the city's Jewish community and its royal connections and promoting religious tolerance and community diversity as well challenging prejudice[3] https//licoricia.org.

In addition to guided tours of the City, Visit Winchester now offers a series of self-guided walks including *Accessible Winchester* and a *Medieval Jewish Trail*. In 2024, Winchester College organized a fund-raising campaign and series of events to commemorate the centenary of the dedication of the War Cloister (Mowl 2024). These included raising £1 million to support a physical restoration programme, lectures, visits, a podcast series, battlefield tour and exhibition at the College Museum[4]

FIGURE 8.5 *Licoricia and her son, by Ian Rank-Broadley. Photo: P. Kemball © WEC.*

The best/happiest place to live in England?

The current (2013–36) Winchester Local Plan states that:

> Winchester's heritage and environment are of international importance with a wealth of historic sites and buildings and a townscape of the highest quality . . . Winchester needs to meet its housing and community requirements and to diversify its economy through the promotion of the

FIGURE 8.6 *Winchester from St Giles Hill, looking west. The Itchen runs in the foreground, right to left under City Bridge, the clock tower of Guildhall is at the centre, the cathedral to its left, with the courts and long blocks of county administration either side of Westgate beyond. © Getty Images.*

knowledge, tourism, creative and education sectors, whilst respecting the highly valued features and setting of the Town ... A critical issue is how to deliver the amount and type of development required to respond to these needs without compromising the qualities and character of the Town recognised and valued by so many.[5]

The most recent summary of the profile of the residents of twenty-first-century Winchester comes from the 2021 Census, which recorded an overall 10 per cent growth in population since 2011:

1 93% of the population is white with Asian ethnicity being the next largest at 2%.
2 14% work in human health and social work activities, 11.4% in wholesale and retail trades, 11.3% in education, 9% in professional, scientific and technical activities, 8.8% in public administration and defence, 7% in construction, 6.7% in information and communications, 5.2% in manufacturing, 5% in administrative and support services, 4.5% in accommodation and food services,

3.7% in financial and insurance activities, and 3.3% in transport and storage.
3. 36.2% live in detached houses, 25% in semi-detached properties, 20.1% in terraced houses and 13.1% in purpose-built flats or tenements.[6]

In 2016, *The Sunday Times* identified Winchester as the 'Best place to live in England' with the summary:

> Now that it has a branch of middle England's favourite supermarket, this cathedral city is practically perfect ... "Winch" is all things to all its residents: a historic, cultured, foodie hub with fine period architecture and a decent selection of independent stores.

However, the following year Winchester had lost its crown, and the paper published this comment:

> What's changed in the 12 months since we crowned this wonderful little city as the Best Place to Live 2016? There's Smug, a new satirical magazine that aims to "keep Winchester from disappearing up its own bottom (http://smugwinchester.com)", but the biggest difference is that it's even harder to get a seat on the fast, morning trains to Waterloo.

However, by 2021 Winchester was back in the South-east regional list:

> Historic and hospitable, the former capital of England is one of our favourite places to raise a family thanks to its 12 outstanding schools and excellent train connections.

In 2023, a Rightmove survey identified Winchester as the second happiest place to live in England based on its annual 'Happy at Home Index' that asks residents how they feel about their area. In March 2024, *The Daily Telegraph* included Winchester amongst its 'most desirable towns in England' list and the next month *The Times and Sunday Times* listed it in the South-east region's 'Best Places to Live' with the comment:

> You have to go back a long way to find a time when life wasn't good in Winchester. Possibly as far back as 1141, when there was a siege, a bloody battle and a great fire ... The city was once a Roman stronghold and is the former capital of Wessex. Its atmospheric cathedral, more than 900 years old, is used today as a venue for Pilates classes, silent discos and an annual pancake race. The only dent in the stellar reputation of this city, regularly named one of the happiest places to live, is the planned closure of the A&E department.

FIGURE 8.7 *Looking through Westgate down High St, c. 1900 – the same view as the cover. Photographer unknown. Courtesy of Winchester City Museums/HCT.*

Afterword

Shippey has argued that:

> England has a kind of mythical geography, a network of associations and oppositions, now dwindled largely to humour and tourism, but once a vital part of the country's being: a geography which accords special roles to Oxford and Cambridge, to Stratford and Glastonbury, to Wigan and Jarrow ... In this geography Winchester has a place full of significance.
>
> SHIPPEY 1992: 18

More recently, Catherine Clarke recorded her reflections about the city while preparing an episode on Norman Winchester for *Britain's Most Historic Towns*:

> Winchester's history is one of re-use, re-appropriation, and transformation; the cityscape always folding its material into new configurations and meanings ... As the site of powerful crosscurrents of time and desire, the city becomes, rather, a space of folded temporalities and shifting, elusive glimpses, in which disparate historical moments are willed into proximity. 'Heritage', of course, relies on the mobilization of affect and desire, transforming 'history' into a version of the past contingent on subjective individual perspective and identification ... The historic urban environment today is an expanding space, enlarging to encompass versions of the past desired, sought, and recuperated by diverse communities, as well as the various realms – material, conceptual, and digital (virtual or hybrid) – which increasingly constitute it ... These emerging possibilities offer exciting new ways of working for those engaged in heritage management or conservation, as well as for those in the academy exploring intersections between place and history. More than ever, tools and technologies exist which allow scholars of the historic city to make interventions in the urban environment today, in ways which go far beyond factual interpretation or physical conservation to include playful re-imaginings, creative, subjective, and experimental responses, and virtual transformation.
>
> CLARKE 2019: 97; 100–1

Throughout this book we have attempted the sort of approach that Clarke is advocating by setting out the available evidence and interrogating the contexts that produced it, as well as attempting to present the diversity of Winchester's past communities. As we have seen, Winchester and its various icons thread their way through the national as well as local consciousness; while science has brought much to our understanding of the city's past, creative imaginations have also brought emotive responses to its buildings and landscapes which have connected with modern game-designers as much as with romantic Victorians and Tudor monarchs. There is much to be known about: from over 90 per cent of the walled city still to be excavated, DNA and isotype analyses will help us discover much more clearly from where Winchester's people came and with whom they interacted, and many documentary sources remain to be analysed. What makes Winchester special may nevertheless still elude us, but all the evidence suggests that it will continue to be so.

CHRONOLOGY

When	What
BCE	
c. 800,000–10,000	First human presence in Winchester area indicated by finds of stone tools.
c. 10,000–4000	First woodland clearances indicated by pollen cores.
Neolithic and Bronze Ages	Agricultural settlements established on downlands and in valleys; probable replacement of Neolithic communities by people associated with Beaker pottery.
Iron Age	Large enclosures created on St Catherine's Hill and Oram's Arbour in Middle Iron Age but no evidence of late Iron Age occupation.
CE	
1st century	*Venta Belgarum* established as a Roman town with a defensive circuit, *forum*, street grid, domestic buildings and workshops, water supply, extramural cremation cemeteries and evidence of connections with rest of Roman Empire.
2nd century	Defensive circuit expanded, many houses enlarged and rebuilt in stone with wall plaster and mosaics.
3rd century	Stone gatehouse added at south gate as well as masonry defensive walls, houses continue to be extended with more hypocausts and mosaics; extramural inhumation cemeteries established, evidence of workshops and trade.
4th century	External bastions added to defences, increasing evidence of decline within urban area; presence of people with Pannonian origins at Lankhills cemetery.
5th century	*Venta Belgarum* ceased as an urban centre although some evidence of continuing activity, rural settlements continued possibly with some Germanic settlers.

CHRONOLOGY

When	What
6th–7th century	Increasing number of cemeteries with Germanic artefacts, rural settlements continued, documentary sources record rise of Wessex Anglo-Saxon kingdom, erection of first stone church at site later known as Old Minster.
8th century	Documentary accounts of re-establishment of urban settlement in Winchester supported by evidence of high-status burials; Viking raid on Winchester recorded.
9th century	Swithun became Bishop of Winchester in 852 until his death in 863; new street grid and intramural road formed inside refurbished defences; Winchester flourished as political and cultural centre during reign of King Alfred, who was buried in Old Minster in 899.
10th century	Alongside Old Minster Alfred's son, Edward built New Minster into which Alfred's bones were transferred; another monastic site established at Nunnminster, with patronage of King Edgar; Bishop Aethelwold instigated monastic reform; translation of St Swithun to Old Minster; town develops with more houses and workshops; artistic ideas of 'Winchester School' inspired a range of artefacts across England.
Early 11th century	After chaotic reign of Aethelred, new Scandinavian ruler Cnut, favoured Winchester, donating magnificent gold cross to New Minster, depicted in manuscript – *Liber Vitae;* stone freeze added to New Minster with Anglo-Scandinavian iconography.
1066 onwards	Castle built in 1067; new cathedral built in the style known now as Romanesque begun, necessitating demolition of Old Minster; international trading flourished at St Giles Fair; leper hospital established at St Mary Magdalen; importance of Winchester declined with increasing focus on London.
12th century	In 1110, 'Winton Domesday' survey recorded 300 properties in the town belonging to the Crown; castle buildings significantly remodelled with new stone keep; bones of Alfredian royal house transferred to Hyde Abbey; substantial stone buildings erected at Bishop's Palace at Wolvesey; Bishop Henri du Blois established alms-house of St Cross and was probable commissioner of the Winchester Bible; Winchester flourished with some fifty-seven parish churches, and timber and stone dwelling houses, many with workshops for various trades.

When	What
13th century	Under Henry III, castle greatly enhanced including building extant Great Hall, where Edward I's replica of Round Table installed in 1290; more town houses rebuilt in stone often with workshops; suburbs expanded.
14th century	After major fire in 1302 destroyed royal apartments, castle ceased to be a royal residence, in 1347 outbreak of Black Death led to town's decline, over 40 per cent of Winchester's monks and priests recorded as dying; in many areas of the town houses were abandoned; opposition to new taxes led to insurrection in 1381 as part of Peasants' Revolt; building of Bishop William of Wykeham's St Mary's College (now Winchester College) began in 1382.
15th century	In 1418, town authorities petitioned Henry VI for reduction in taxes arguing one-third of town desolate and in 1452, petition asserted ten streets almost depopulated with 1,000 empty houses. In 1486, as part of establishing the Tudor dynasty, Henry VII arranged for his son, named for King Arthur, to be born at Winchester (identified by Thomas Malory as Camelot).
16th century	In 1522, Henry VIII displayed the newly refurbished Round Table to Emperor Charles V; in 1538, following establishment of Church of England, Thomas Wriothesley oversaw destruction of St Swithun's tomb; by 1540 all monastic houses were closed except the Cathedral Priory, where in 1554, lavish wedding ceremony of Mary I to Philip II of Spain took place.
17th century	During Civil War, town suffered multiple attacks from forces of both king and Parliament; Castle slighted and much of the town in ruins; in 1682, Charles II commissioned Sir Christopher Wren to design palace complex comparable with Versailles; King's House begun in 1683 but after Charles' death, no other part of design completed.
18th century	Construction of both houses and public buildings; weekly civic assemblies attended by army officers, increasingly after palace site leased to army; Milner's popular *History, Civil and Ecclesiastical and Survey of the Antiquities of Winchester* had eleven editions 1789–1839.

When	What
19th century	Winchester's population rose from 6069 (1801) to 19,670 (1891); Censuses record retailers and hospitality workers predominated, alongside lawyers, clergy and school masters with first people of colour recorded in 1871; interest in the city's past grew with Roman finds recorded; city increasingly popular with tourists including John Keats, who composed *To Autumn* in 1819; Brooks area redeveloped for workers but poor conditions led to successive cholera epidemics until drains improved and new pumping station built.
20th century	In 1901, King Alfred commemorated by local and national celebrations and with erection of large statue; in 1914 first transit camp established on Morn Hill and in all two million troops passed through en route to Western Front. In 1961, Martin Biddle directed excavation in Cathedral car park and conceived of interdisciplinary study of city's past followed in 1962 by creation of Winchester Excavations Committee sponsored programme of excavations involving *c*. 3,000 diggers over eleven seasons. Campaigns opposed government plans for M3 extension and although ultimately unsuccessful, 'The Battle of Twyford Down' in 1991 now identified as the start of modern environmentalism.
21st century	Continuing publication of Winchester Studies and Winchester Museums' Service series; scientific analyses confirmed late Roman Germanic presence at Lankhills; bones from Alfredian royal house at Hyde Abbey, and Queen Emma's remains in Cathedral's mortuary chests; 2004–20, Bernard Cornwell's 'Saxon Series' of books (and later *Last Kingdom* TV series) brought Alfred and Winchester back into popular imagination and this has continued through Ubisoft's *Assassin's Creed Valhalla* computer game. Since 2016, Winchester regularly voted best or happiest place to live in England.

DRAMATIS PERSONAE

Alfred the Great
Ruler of Wessex from 871, and from 888, King of the Anglo-Saxons – icon of Winchester and England.

Alfred Bowker
Mayor of Winchester 1898–1901; animator of King Alfred's millennial celebrations in Winchester in 1901.

Aethelwold
Bishop of Winchester 963–84; monastic reformer.

Benedict
Son of Licoricia and only medieval Jew to be elected as a guildsman in England, and possibly the whole of Europe.

Charles II
King of England, Scotland and Ireland 1680–5; in 1682 commissioned Sir Christopher Wren to build 'an English Versailles' at Winchester.

Cnut
King of England 1016–35, Scandinavian; donor of great golden cross to New Minster, where he was buried.

Eadburg
Daughter of Edward the Elder, born 921; patron saint of Nunnaminster (later St Mary's Abbey).

Ealswith
Mercian, wife of King Alfred; named as the *aedificatrix* (founder) of Nunnaminster.

Edward the Elder
Son of Alfred and Ealswith and King of the Anglo-Saxons 899–924; commissioner of New Minster.

Edward I
King of England 1237–77; in 1275 commissioner of the Round Table still in Winchester Castle.

Emma/Ælfgifu
Born 990, Queen Consort of England, wife of both Aethelred and Cnut, mother of Harthacnut and Edward the Confessor; her bones were probably identified in one of the Winchester Cathedral Mortuary Chests.

Guy of Warwick
Fictional medieval Romance character associated with defeat of the giant, Colebrand, at Winchester.

Herbert Baker
Architect: in 1918 designed neo-medieval War Cloister, the biggest private memorial in Europe, to commemorate the dead of Winchester College.

Henri de Blois
Bishop of Winchester 1129–71, brother of King Stephen; commissioned expansion of Wolvesey Palace, founder of St Cross alms-house and probably commissioner of Winchester Bible.

Henry VII
King of England 1485–1509; enhanced the Tudor dynasty's heritage credentials by arranging for his son, Arthur to be born at Winchester in 1486.

Henry VIII
King of England 1509–47; 1516 had the Round Table repainted, and displayed in 1522 to the Emperor Charles V.

Henry Beaufort
Cardinal, Bishop of Winchester 1404–47; added the Almshouse of Noble Poverty to St Cross foundation, commissioned a chantry chapel in Winchester Cathedral, melted down and replaced the early medieval shrine of St Swithun.

Juliana de la Floude
Laundress: in 1299 won case against neighbour John de Tyting for interrupting her water supply, with King Edward I's ruling 'water has always been common', later adopted by United Nation as a Sustainable Development Goal.

Jane Austen
Author: died 1817 at Winchester, buried in the Cathedral.

John Keats
Poet; wrote *To Autumn* during a stay at Winchester in 1819.

Licoricia
Jewish entrepreneur; lived at Winchester in mid-thirteenth century, commemorated 2022 by a statue in the city.

Mary I
First Queen Regnant of England; married, 1552, Philip II of Spain, in Winchester Cathedral.

Swithun
Bishop of Winchester 852–63, later sanctified; his bones were translated in 971, into Old Minster, and in 1093, to the Norman cathedral, a major pilgrimage site until the sixteenth-century Reformation.

Walkelin
First Norman Bishop of Winchester 1070–98; in 1079 commissioned the present Cathedral, necessitating the demolition of Old Minster.

William of Wykeham
Bishop of Winchester 1367–1404; founded Winchester College in 1382, commissioned additions to Wolvesey Palace and Winchester Cathedral.

William of Wynford
Fourteenth-century master mason who built Winchester College and remodelled Winchester Cathedral in the style now identified as the Perpendicular for his patron, William of Wykeham.

William Wygge
Winchester guildsman who led an insurrection in Winchester as part of the 1381 Peasants' Revolt.

Scholars of Winchester's past

Martin Biddle
Professor of Medieval Archaeology, University of Oxford 1997–2002, Director, Winchester Excavations, instigator of the interdisciplinary approach to the study of Winchester's past and of modern urban archaeology, General Editor, Winchester Studies.

Frank Cottrill
Appointed first paid Curator of Winchester in 1947, reorganized its collections and oversaw first systematic modern excavations in Winchester.

Derek Keene
Professor of Comparative Metropolitan History, University of London 2002–6, Deputy Director, Winchester Research Unit, then founding Director, Centre for Metropolitan History, University of London, 1987–2002, main author on documentary history of Winchester.

John Milner
Author, *History, Civil and Ecclesiastical, and Survey of the Antiquities of Winchester*, published 1789–90, so popular there were eleven editions by 1839.

Patrick Ottaway
Archaeologist at many excavations in Winchester and elsewhere, editor of Winchester Museums Service publications, principal author of Winchester's *Urban Archaeology Assessment*, and editor of Winchester Studies volumes on Environment, Brook Street, and Wolvesey Palace.

Sydney Ward-Evans
Sydney Ward Evans identified himself as 'Honorary Archaeologist' of Winchester in 1926, observing and recording at hundreds of building sites and funding displays of his findings.

Barbara Yorke
Professor of Early Medieval History, University of Winchester, 2001–14, author of a range of publications on early medieval Winchester and on the 1901 King Alfred millennium.

NOTES

1 The Uniqueness of Winchester

1 https://winchester.anglican.org/colonial-countryside-walk-explains-links-with-slave-trade/.

8 The Legacy of Past Glories and New Beginnings

1 https://www.hampshireculture.org.uk/winchester-and-norman-conquest.
2 https://historicengland.org.uk/advice/caring-for-heritage/places-of-worship/cathedrals/winchester/).
3 https//licoricia.org.
4 https://wincollsoc.org/pages/war-cloister-centenary.
5 https://www.winchester.gov.uk/planning-policy/winchester-district-local-plan-2011-2036-adopted/local-plan-part-1-joint-core-strategy-adopted-march-2013-local-plan-review-2006/local-plan-part-1-joint-core-strategy-adopted-2013.
6 https://www.nomisweb.co.uk/sources/census_2021/report?compare=E07000094.

FURTHER READING

Ottaway, P (2017), *Winchester: St Swithun's 'City of Happiness and Good Fortune': An Archaeological Assessment.* Oxford and Philadelphia: Oxbow Books.

Winchester Studies

https://www.archaeopress.com/Archaeopress/Search/Winchester.

BIBLIOGRAPHY

Abrama, R. (2022), *Licoricia of Winchester: Power and Prejudice in Medieval England*. Winchester: The Licoricia of Winchester Appeal.
Allason-Jones, L., and B. McKay (1985), *Coventina's Well: A Shrine on Hadrian's Wall*. Chesters: Trustees of the Clayton Collection.
Allason-Jones, L. (2023), 'Jet pin', in F. M. Morris and M. Biddle, *Venta Belgarum: Prehistoric, Roman and Early Medieval Winchester. Winchester Studies 3.i*, 279–81. Oxford: Archaeopress.
Albert, E., and K. Tucker (2015), *In Search of Alfred the Great*. Stroud: Amberley Publishing.
Anderson, E. R. (1991), 'Malory's Camelot, Winchester and the "Chirche of Seynte Stevins"', *Neuphilologische Mitteilungen*, 92 (2): 211–13.
Armit, I., and D. Reich (2021), 'The Return of the Beaker Folk? Rethinking Migration and Population Change in British Prehistory', *Antiquity*, 95 (384): 1464–77.
Aronstein S. (2023), 'Romance in Twentieth- and Twenty-First-Century Popular Culture', in R. L. Krueger (ed.), *The New Cambridge Companion to Medieval Romance. Cambridge Companions to Literature,* 257–71. Cambridge: Cambridge University Press.
Ashbridge, T. (2019), *Richard I, The Crusader King. Penguin Monarchs*. London: Allen Lane.
Atkinson, C. (2023), 'Hampshire Cultural Trust to Potentially Take Over Great Hall', *Hampshire Chronicle*, 4 December. Available online: https://www.hampshirechronicle.co.uk/news/23967230.hampshire-cultural-trust-potentially-take-great-hall/.
Atkinson, C. (2024), 'Winchester Cathedral Responds to Backlash to Jane Austen Statue', *Hampshire Chronicle,* 8 March. Available online: https://www.hampshirechronicle.co.uk/news/24170317.winchester-cathedral-responds-backlash-jane-austen-statue/.
Atkinson, T. (1963), *Elizabethan Winchester*. London: Faber and Faber.
Backhouse, J. D., D. H. Turner and L. Webster (1984), *The Golden Age of Anglo-Saxon Art, 966–1066*. London: British Museum.
Banham, D., and R. Faith (2014), *Anglo-Saxon Farms and Farming*. Oxford. Oxford University Press.
Barker, P. (1993), *Techniques of archaeological excavation*. London: Batsford.
Barker, S., and C. Haydon, eds (1992) *Winchester: History and Literature: The proceedings of a Conference in celebration of the 150th Anniversary of the founding of King Alfred's College held on 16th March 1991*. York: Coward Printers.

Barlow, F., M. Biddle, O. Feilitzen and D. J. Keene, eds (1976), *Winchester in the Early Middle Ages: An Edition and Discussion of the Winton Domesday. Winchester Studies 1.* Oxford: Oxford University Press.

Barrow, J. (2008), 'The Chronology of the Benedictine Reform', in D. Scragg (ed.), *Edgar, King of the English 959–975: New Interpretations,* 211–23. Woodbridge: Boydell & Brewer.

Bartlett, S. (2009), *Licoricia of Winchester: Marriage, Motherhood and Murder in the Anglo-Jewish Community,* ed. P. Skinner. Edgware and Portland: Vallentine Mitchell.

Bates, D. (2020), 'William the Conqueror and Wessex', in A. Langlands and R. Lavelle (eds), *The Land of the English Kin: Studies in Wessex and Anglo-Saxon England in Honour of Professor Barbara Yorke,* 517–37. Leiden: Brill.

Beard, M. (2016), *SPQR: A History of Ancient Rome.* London: Profile Books.

Belgarum (2023), 'Nearing the end for the Saxongate development hoarding', *Hampshire Chronicle,* 26 October. Available online: https://www.hampshirechronicle.co.uk/news/indepth/silverhill/23872977.nearing-end-saxongate-development-hoarding/.

Bell, A. (1982), 'Warden Huntingford and the old conservatism', in R. Custance (ed.), *Winchester College: Sixth-centenary Essays,* 351–74. Oxford: Oxford University Press.

Benedictow, O. J. (2021), *The Complete History of the Black Death,* 791–868. Woodbridge: Boydell & Brewer.

Bengry, J. (2021), 'Can and should we queer the past?', in H. Carr and S. Lipscomb (eds), *What Is History Now? How the Past and the Present Speak to Each Other,* 49–65. London: Weidenfeld & Nicolson.

Benyon, H. (2020), *Twyford Rising: Land and Resistance.* Winchester: Sarsen Press.

Biddle, M. (1964), 'Excavations at Winchester 1962–3. Second interim report', *Antiquaries Journal,* 44: 188–219.

Biddle, M. (1965), 'Excavations at Winchester 1964. Third interim report', *Antiquaries Journal,* 45: 295–329.

Biddle, M. (1967), 'Excavations at Winchester 1966; Fifth interim report', *Antiquaries Journal,* 47: 251–79.

Biddle, M. (1968), 'Excavations at Winchester 1967. Sixth interim report', *Antiquaries Journal,* 48: 250–84.

Biddle, M. (1974), 'The Archaeology of Winchester', *Scientific American,* 230 (v): 32–4.

Biddle, M. (1975), 'Excavations at Winchester 1971; tenth and final interim report', *Antiquaries Journal,* 55: 96–126 and 295–337.

Biddle, M. (1983), 'The Study of Winchester: Archaeology and History in a British Town, 1961–83'. Albert Reckitt Archaeology Trust Lecture, *Proceedings of the British Academy,* 69: 93–135.

Biddle, M. (1986), 'Seasonal Festivals and Residence: Winchester, Westminster and Gloucester in the Tenth to Twelfth Centuries', *Anglo-Norman Studies 8, Proceedings of Battle Conference 1985,* 51–72. Woodbridge: Boydell & Brewer.

Biddle, M. (1990), *Object and Economy in Early Medieval Winchester. Winchester Studies 7.ii.* Oxford: Oxford University Press.

Biddle, M., ed. (2000a), *King Arthur's Round Table: An Archaeological Investigation.* Woodbridge: Boydell & Brewer.

Biddle, M. (2000b), 'The making of the Round Table', in M. Biddle (ed.), *King Arthur's Round Table: An Archaeological Investigation*, 377–92. Woodbridge: Boydell & Brewer.

Biddle, M. (2000c), 'The hanging of the Round Table', in M. Biddle (ed.), *King Arthur's Round Table: An Archaeological Investigation*, 393–424. Woodbridge: Boydell & Brewer.

Biddle, M. (2000d), 'The painting of the Round Table', in M. Biddle (ed.), *King Arthur's Round Table: An Archaeological Investigation*, 454–73. Woodbridge: Boydell & Brewer.

Biddle, M., ed. (2012), *The Winchester Mint and Coins and Related finds from the Excavations 1961–1971. Winchester Studies 8*. Oxford: Oxford University Press.

Biddle, M. (2017), 'Planned Town and Early Capital: Mid Ninth Century to 1066', in M. Biddle and D. Keene (eds), *Winchester, The Atlas of British Historic Towns vi. Winchester Studies 11*, 26–37. Oxford: Oxbow Books.

Biddle, M. (2020), 'Winchester: A city of two planned towns', in A. Langlands and R. Lavelle (eds), *The Land of the English Kin: Studies in Wessex and Anglo-Saxon England in Honour of Professor Barbara Yorke*, 26–49. Leiden: Brill.

Biddle, M. (2021a), 'Henri of Blois' Domus Quasi palatium in Winchester', in W. Kynan-Wilson (ed.), *Henry of Blois: New Interpretations*, 119–44. Woodbridge: Boydell & Brewer.

Biddle, M. (2021b), 'Capital Considerations: Winchester and the Birth of Urban Archaeology', in R. Lavalle, S. Roffey, and K. Weikert (eds), *Early medieval Winchester: Communities, Authority in an Urban Space*, 19–39. Oxford and Philadelphia: Oxbow Books.

Biddle, M., and R. Quirk (1964), 'Excavations near Winchester Cathedral 1961 (Excavations at Winchester, 1st Interim Report), *Archaeological Journal*, 119: 150–94.

Biddle, M., and D. J. Keene (1976a), 'Winchester in the eleventh and twelfth centuries', in F. Barlow, M. Biddle, O. Feilitzen and D. J. Keene (eds), *Winchester in the Early Middle Ages: An Edition and Discussion of the Winton Domesday. Winchester Studies 1*, 241–448. Oxford: Oxford University Press.

Biddle, M., and D. J. Keene (1976b), 'The early place names of Winchester', in F. Barlow, M. Biddle, O. Feilitzen and D. J. Keene (eds), *Winchester in the Early Middle Ages: An Edition and Discussion of the Winton Domesday. Winchester Studies 1*, 231–9. Oxford: Oxford University Press.

Biddle, M., and B. Kjølbye-Biddle (1995), 'The Excavated Sculptures from Winchester', in D. Tweddle, M. Biddle and B. Kjølbye-Biddle, *Corpus of Anglo-Saxon Sculpture, Volume 4, South East England*, https://ascorpus.ac.uk/vol4_chap8.php. London: British Academy.

Biddle, M., and D. J. Keene, eds (2017), *Winchester: British Historic Towns Atlas – 6. Winchester Studies 11*. Oxford and Philadelphia: Oxbow Books.

Biddle, M., and B. Kjølbye-Biddle (2007), 'Winchester: from *Venta* to *Wintancæstir*', in L. Gilmour (ed.), *Pagans and Christians – from Antiquity to the Middle Ages. Papers in Honour of Martin Henig, Presented on the Occasion of his 65th Birthday, BAR International Series 1610*, 189–214. Oxford: British Archaeological Reports

Biddle, M., B. Clayre and M. Morris (2000), 'The setting of the Round Table: Winchester Castle and Great Hall', in M. Biddle (ed.), *King Arthur's Round Table: An Archaeological Investigation*, 59–101. Woodbridge: Boydell & Brewer

Biddle, M., J. Renfrew and P. Ottaway, eds (2022), *Environment and Agriculture of Early Winchester. Winchester Studies 10*. Oxford: Archaeopress.

Biddulph, E. (2011a), 'The Roman Occupation (Phase II)', in B. M. Ford and S. Teague, *Winchester – A City in the Making: Archaeological Investigations between 2002 and 2007 on the sites of Northgate House, Staple Gardens and the Former Winchester Library, Jewry Street. Oxford Archaeology Monograph 12*, 48–72. Oxford: Oxford Archaeology.

Biddulph, E. (2011b), 'The Roman Town', in B. M. Ford and S. Teague, *Winchester – A City in the Making: Archaeological Investigations between 2002 and 2007 on the sites of Northgate House, Staple Gardens and the Former Winchester Library, Jewry Street. Oxford Archaeology Monograph 12*, 179–87. Oxford: Oxford Archaeology.

Blagg, T. F. C., and M. Biddle (2023), 'Ornamental Stone', in F. M. Morris and M. Biddle, *Venta Belgarum: Prehistoric, Roman and Early Medieval Winchester. Winchester Studies 3.i*, 777–89. Oxford: Archaeopress

Booth, P., A. Simmonds, A. Boyle, S. Clough, H. E. M. Cool and D. Poore (2010), *The Late Roman Cemetery at Lankhills: Excavations 2000–2005*. Oxford. Oxford Archaeology, Information Press.

Bouchard, A. (2023), 'Archaeologists share Victorian and medieval finds from Winchester site', *Hampshire Chronicle*, 29 June. Available online: https://www.hampshirechronicle.co.uk/news/23688164.archaeologists-share-victorian-medieval-finds-winchester-site/.

Borman, T. (2014), *Thomas Cromwell: The Untold Story of Henry VIII's Most Faithful Servant*. London: Hodder.

Bowker, A. (1902), *The King Alfred Millenary: a Record of the Proceedings of the National Commemoration*. London and New York: Macmillan and Co.

Boyd, D., and G. Dear (1998), *The Stained-glass Windows of William Morris and his Circle in Hampshire and the Isle of Wight. Hampshire Papers 13*. Winchester: Hampshire County Council.

Bradley R. (2019), *The Prehistory of Britain and Ireland. Cambridge World Archaeology*. Cambridge: Cambridge University Press.

Breverton, T. (2019), *Henry VII: The Maligned Tudor King*. Stroud: Amberley Publishing.

Brown, R. B., and S. McCartney (2004), 'David of Oxford and Licoricia of Winchester: Glimpses into a Jewish family in Thirteenth-century England', *Jewish Historical Studies*, 39: 1–34.

Brownrigg, L. L. (1978), 'Manuscripts Containing English Decoration 871–1066, Catalogued and Illustrated: A Review', *Anglo-Saxon England*, 7: 239–66.

Brooks, N. P. (1982), 'The Oldest Document in the College Archives? The Micheldever Forgery', in R. Custance (ed.), *Winchester College: Sixth-centenary Essays*, 189–288. Oxford: Oxford University Press.

Brookes, S. (2020), 'On the Territorial Organisation of Early Medieval Hampshire', in A. Langlands and R. Lavelle (eds), *The Land of the English Kin: Studies in Wessex and Anglo-Saxon England in Honour of Professor Barbara Yorke*, 276–93. Leiden: Brill.

Bruce Mitford, R. L. S. (2005), *Corpus of Late Celtic Hanging Bowls*. Oxford: Oxford University Press.

Bryant, B. (1996), *Twyford Down: Roads, Campaigning and Environmental Law*. London: E and F Spon.

Bussey, S. (2002), *Voices of Winchester*. Cheltenham: The History Press.
Campbell, M. (1987), 'The Hyde Abbey Crozier', in J. Alexander and P. Binski, *Age of Chivalry: Art in Plantagenet England 1200–1400,* 306. London: Royal Academy of Arts
Campbell, A., and S. Keynes, eds (1998), *Encomium Emmae Reginae*. Cambridge: Cambridge University Press.
Carpenter Turner, B. (1980), *Winchester*. Southampton: Paul Cave Publications Ltd.
Carr, E. H. ([1961] 2018), *What Is History? The George Macaulay Trevelyan Lectures Delivered in the University of Cambridge January–March 1961 (Penguin Modern Classics)*. London: Penguin Books.
Carr. H., and S. Lipscomb, eds (2021), *What Is History Now? How the Past and the Present Speak to Each Other*. London: Weidenfeld & Nicolson.
Carreras, C. (2023), 'Amphorae', in F. M. Morris and M. Biddle, *Venta Belgarum: Prehistoric, Roman and Early Medieval Winchester. Winchester Studies 3.i,* 719–30. Oxford: Archaeopress.
Carver, M. (1987), *Underneath English Towns: Interpreting Urban Archaeology*. London: Batsford.
Champness, C., S. Teague and B. M. Ford (2012), 'Holocene environmental change and Roman floodplain management at Pilgrim's School, Cathedral Close, Winchester', *Proceedings of the Hampshire Field Club and Archaeology Society, Hampshire Studies,* 6 (I): 25–68.
Chandler J., ed. (1993), *John Leland's Itinerary: Travels in Tudor England*. Stroud: Alan Sutton.
Chedzey, J. (2003), 'Manuscript Production in Medieval Winchester', *Reading Medieval Studies,* XXIX: 1–18.
Childe, V. G. (1923), *What Happened in History*. London: Penguin Books.
Childs, J. (2014), *God's Traitors: Terror and Faith in Elizabethan England*. London: The Bodley Head.
Clarke. D.L (1972), 'Models and paradigms in archaeology', in D. L. Clarke (ed.), *Models in Archaeology,* 1–60. London: Methuen and Co.
Clarke, G (1979), *The Roman Cemetery at Lankhills. Winchester Studies 3.ii*. Oxford: Oxford University Press.
Clarke, G, (2023), 'Lankhills reconsidered', in F. M. Morris and M. Biddle, *Venta Belgarum: Prehistoric, Roman and Early Medieval Winchester. Winchester Studies 3.i,* 1213–44. Oxford: Archaeopress.
Clayre, B., and M. Biddle (2022), 'Gardens in medieval and later Winchester: the Castle, Wolvesey Palace and Eastgate House', in M. Biddle, J. Renfrew and P. Ottaway (eds), *Environment and Agriculture of Early Winchester. Winchester Studies 10,* 72–85. Oxford: Archaeopress.
Clayre, B., and M. Biddle (forthcoming), *Winchester Castle: Fortress, Palace, Garrison and Country Seat. Winchester Studies 5*. Oxford: Archaeopress.
Clayre, B., and E. Thomas (2017a), 'Contested city and social centre 1642–1800', in M. Biddle and D. J. Keene (eds), *Winchester, The Atlas of British Historic Towns vi. Winchester Studies 11,* 55–61. Oxford: Oxbow Books.
Clayre, B., and E. Thomas (2017b), 'Postscript: Winchester since 1800', in M. Biddle and D. J. Keene (eds), *Winchester, The Atlas of British Historic Towns vi. Winchester Studies 11,* 61–7. Oxford: Oxbow Books.
Cohn, S. K., and D. Aiton (2012), *Popular Protest in Late Medieval English Towns*. Cambridge: Cambridge University Press.

Coldicott, D. K. (forthcoming), 'St Mary's Abbey in the Later Middle Ages', in B. Kjølbye-Biddle and M. Biddle, *The Anglo-Saxon Minsters of Winchester. Winchester Studies 4.i.* Oxford: Archaeopress.

Collett B. (2007), 'Holy Expectations: The Female Monastic Vocation in the Diocese of Winchester on the Eve of the Reformation', in J. G. Clark (ed.), *The Culture of Medieval English Monasticism. Studies in the History of Medieval Religion,* 147–66. Woodbridge: Boydell & Brewer.

Collis, J. (1978), *Winchester Excavations 1949–1960. 2: Excavations in the Suburbs and Western Parts of the Town.* Winchester: Winchester City Museum.

Collis, J. (1981), 'A theoretical study of hillforts', in G. Guilbert (ed.), *Hillfort Studies: Essays for A.H.A Hogg,* 66–76. Leicester. Leicester University Press

Collis, J (2011), 'The Urban Revolution: Martin Biddle's Excavations in Winchester, 1961–1971', in J. Schoefield (ed.), *Great Excavations: Shaping the Archaeological Profession,* 74–86. Oxford: Oxbow Books.

Cooper, A., and T. Yarrow (2012), 'The Age of Innocence: Personal Histories of the 1960s "Digging Circuit" in Britain', *International Journal of Historical Archaeology,* 16 (2): 300–18.

Cornwell, B. (2004), *The Last Kingdom.* London: Harper Collins.

Cotton, M. A., and P. W. Gathercole (1958), *Excavations at Clausentum, Southampton, 1951–1954. Ministry of Works Archaeological Reports, 2.* London: Her Majesty's Stationery Office.

Coumert, M. (2019), 'Gildas', in J. Jahner, E, Steiner and E. M. Tyler (eds), *Medieval Historical Writing: Britain and Ireland, 500–1500,* 19–34. Cambridge: Cambridge University Press.

Cowell, B. (2009), *The Heritage Obsession: The Battle for England's Past.* Stroud: The History Press.

Coy, J. (2009), 'Late Saxon and Medieval Animal Bone from the Western Suburbs', in D. Serjeantson and H. Rees (eds), *Food, Craft and Status in Medieval Winchester: The Plant and Animal Remains from the Suburbs and City Defences,* 27–54. Winchester: Winchester Museums Service.

Crabtree, P, J. (2018), *Early Medieval Britain: The Rebirth of Towns in the Post-Roman West.* Case Studies in Early Societies. Cambridge: Cambridge University Press.

Cramp, R. J. (2001), 'Window glass from the British Isles 7th–10th centuries', in F. Dell'Acqua and R. Lucca Silva, *Il colore nel Medioevo arte, simbolo, tecnica la vetrata in Occidente dal IV all'XI secolo atti delle giornate di studi.* Lucca, 23–5, Istituto storico lucchese. Collana di studi sul colore 3: 67–85.

Crook, J., ed. (1993), *Winchester Cathedral: 900 Years.* Holmfirth: Philmore and Co.

Crook, J. (2001), *Winchester Cathedral.* Andover: Pitkin Unichrome.

Crook, J. (2003), 'Early Historians of Winchester Cathedral', *Proceedings of the Hampshire Field Club and Archaeology Society,* 23: 226–41.

Crook, J. (2011), *The Hospital of St Cross and Almshouse of Noble Poverty.* Exeter: Short Run Press.

Crook J. (2021), 'The Architectural Heritage of Bishop Henry of Blois at Winchester Cathedral', in W. Kynan-Wilson (ed.), *Henry of Blois: New Interpretations,* 93–118. Woodbridge: Boydell & Brewer.

Crook, J. (2022), 'Medieval Royal and Episcopal Burials in Winchester Cathedral', *Antiquaries Journal,* 102: 134–62.

Crook, J., and Y. Kusaba (1993), 'The Perpendicular Remodelling of the Nave: Problems and Interpretation, in J. Crook (ed.), *Winchester Cathedral: 900 Years*, 215–30. Holmfirth: Philmore and Co.

Crowfoot, E. (1990), 'Textiles', in M. Biddle, *Object and Economy in Early Medieval Winchester. Winchester Studies 7.ii*, 467–88. Oxford: Oxford University Press.

Cunliffe, B. W. (1964), *Winchester Excavations 1949–1960, 1*. Winchester: Winchester City Museum.

Custance, R., ed. (1982a), *Winchester College: Sixth-centenary Essays*. Oxford: Oxford University Press.

Custance, R. (1982b), 'Warden Nicholas and the Mutiny at Winchester College', in R. Custance (ed.), *Winchester College: Sixth-centenary Essays,* 313–50. Oxford: Oxford University Press.

Cybulski, D. (2021), *Life in Medieval Europe: Fact and Fiction*. Barnsley: Pen and Sword History.

Dannell, G. B. (2023), 'The Samian Ware: a Summary', in F. M. Morris and M. Biddle, *Venta Belgarum: Prehistoric, Roman and Early Medieval Winchester. Winchester Studies 3.i*, 681–5. Oxford: Archaeopress.

Davis, O. (2015), 'From Football Stadium to Iron Age Hillfort: Creating a Taxonomy of Wessex Hillfort Communities', *Archaeological Dialogues*, 1: 45–64.

de la Bédoyère, G. (2013), *Roman Britain: A New History*. London: Thames and Hudson.

Defoe, D. (1724), *A Tour Throughout the Whole Island of Britain, Divided into Journeys and Circuits*, Volume 1. London.

Delamarre, X. (2010–12), '*Notes d'onomastique vieille-celtique*', *Keltische Forschungen*, 5: 99–137.

Dempsey, K. (2019), 'Gender and Medieval Archaeology: Storming the Castle', *Antiquity*, 93 (369): 772–88.

Deshman, R. (1995), *The Benedictional of Æthelwold*. Princeton: Princeton University Press

Donovan C. (2021), 'Bishop Henry's Bible', in W. Kynan-Wilson (ed.), *Henry of Blois: New Interpretations,* 145–84. Woodbridge: Boydell & Brewer

Duffy E. (2006), 'Religious belief', in R. Horrox and W. M. Ormrod (eds), *A Social History of England, 1200–1500*, 293–339. Cambridge: Cambridge University Press.

Dunning, G. C. (1964), 'The Badorf Amphora', in M. Biddle and R. Quirk, 'Excavations near Winchester Cathedral 1961 (Excavations in Winchester 1st Interim Report)', *Archaeological Journal*, 119: 183.

Eddleston, J. J. (2015), *Winchester in the Great War*. Barnsley: Pen and Sword Military.

Esmonde Cleary, S. (2003), 'Civil Defences in the West under the High Empire', in P. Wilson (ed.), *The Archaeology of Roman Towns*, 73–85. Oxford: Oxford University Press.

Fafinski, M. (2021), *Roman Infrastructure in Early Medieval Britain: The Adaptations of the Past in Text and Stone*. Amsterdam: Amsterdam University Press.

Fasham, P. J. (1985), *The Neolithic Settlement at Winnall Down, Winchester*. Hampshire Field Club and Archaeology Society Monograph 2. Winchester.

Fasham, P. J., D.E Farwell and R. J. B. Whinney (1989), *The Archaeological Site at Easton Lane, Winchester. Hampshire Field Club and Archaeological Society Monograph 7*, Winchester.

Fasham, P. J., and R. J. B. Whinney (1991), *Archaeology and the M3. Hampshire Field Club and Archaeology Society Monograph 7*, Winchester.

Frankopan, P. (2023), *The Earth Transformed: An Untold History*. London: Bloomsbury Publishing.

Gardner, A. (2013), 'Thinking about Roman Imperialism: Postcolonialism, Globalisation and Beyond?', *Britannia*, 44: 1–25.

Gerzina, G. (2022), *Black England: A Forgotten Georgian History*. London: John Murray.

Gilchrist, R. (2012), *Medieval Life: Archaeology and the Life Course*. Woodbridge: Boydell & Brewer.

Gnecco, C., and A. S. Dias (2015), 'On Contract Archaeology', *International Journal of Historical Archaeology*, 19 (4): 687–98.

Graafstal, E. P. (2023), 'Roman "Grand Strategy" in Action? Claudius and the Annexation of Britain and Thrace', *Britannia*, 54: 23–50.

Green, F. J. (2022), 'Plant Remains and Agriculture in Early Norman and Later Medieval Winchester', in M. Biddle, J. Renfrew and P. Ottaway (eds), *Environment and Agriculture of Early Winchester. Winchester Studies 10*, 251–341. Oxford: Archaeopress.

Greenwood, C. E., L. J. E. Cramp and T. Hodos (2023), 'What's in the pots? Identifying Possible Extensification in Roman Britain Through Analysis of Organic Residues in Pottery', *Britannia*, 54: 137–65.

Gretsch, M. (2006), *Aelfric and the Cult of Saints in Late Anglo-Saxon England. Cambridge Studies in Anglo-Saxon England, 34*. Cambridge: Cambridge University Press.

Gretzinger, J., D. Sayer and P. Justeau et al. (2022), 'The Anglo-Saxon Migration and the Formation of the Early English Gene Pool', *Nature*, 610: 112–19.

Griffiths, T. (2021), 'The Jewish Community in Twelfth Century Winchester: an Interdisciplinary View', in R. Lavelle, S. Roffey and K. Weikert (eds), *Early Medieval Winchester: Communities, Authority in an Urban Space*, 225–39. Oxford and Philadelphia: Oxbow Books.

Grimmer, M. (2007), 'Britons in Early Wessex: The Evidence of the Law Code of Ine', in N. Higham (ed.), *Britons in Anglo-Saxon England*, 102–14. Woodbridge: Boydell & Brewer.

Guest, P., H. Ma, L. Mion, A. Lamb and R. Madgwick (2023), 'Feeding the Roman Army in Britain', *Antiquity*, 97 (395): e29, Project Gallery, 1–5.

Hanley, C. (2021), *Matilda: Empress, Queen, Warrior*. New Haven and London: Yale University Press.

Harding, D. W. (2020), *Rewriting History: Changing Perceptions of the Archaeological Past*. Oxford: Oxford University Press.

Hare, J. (1999), *The Dissolution of the Monasteries in Hampshire. Hampshire Papers 16*. Winchester: Hampshire County Council.

Hare J. (2012), 'The Architectural Patronage of Two Late Medieval Bishops: Edington, Wykeham and the rebuilding of Winchester Cathedral Nave', *The Antiquaries Journal*, 92: 273–305.

Hare, J. (2021), 'Hyde Abbey, after circa 1110', in K. Qualmann, G. Scobie and J. Zant, *Excavations at Hyde Abbey, Winchester 1972–1999, collated and edited* by Patrick Ottaway, 27–32. Winchester: Winchester Museums Service/Hampshire Cultural Trust Publications Series.

Harvey, J. (1982), 'The Buildings of Winchester College', in R. Custance (ed.), *Winchester College: Sixth-centenary Essays*, 77–128. Oxford: Oxford University Press.

Haselgrove, C. C., and R. Pope (2007), *The Earlier Iron Age in Britain and the Near Continent*. Barnsley: Oxbow Books.

Haselgrove, S (1979), 'Romano-Saxon Attitudes', in P. J. Casey (ed.), *The End of Roman Britain*, 15–27. British Archaeological Reports: Oxford.

Haslam J. (2016), 'The Burghal Hidage and the West Saxon Burhs: a Reappraisal', *Anglo-Saxon England*, 45: 141–82.

Haverfield, F. (1912), *The Romanization of Roman Britain*. Oxford: Clarendon Press.

Hawkes, C. F. C, J. N. L. Myres and C. G. Stevens (1930), *Saint Catherine's Hill, Winchester. Proceedings of the Hampshire Field Club and Archaeology Society*. Winchester: The Wykeham Press.

Hawkes, S. C. (1990), 'The Anglo-Saxon necklace from Lower Brook Street', in M. Biddle, *Object and Economy in Early Medieval Winchester. Winchester Studies 7.ii*, 621–6. Oxford: Oxford University Press.

Hayward, K. (2023), 'Building Stone: Petrography and Provenance', in F. M. Morris and M. Biddle, *Venta Belgarum: Prehistoric, Roman and Early Medieval Winchester. Winchester Studies 3.i*, 754–6. Oxford: Archaeopress.

Henig, M. (2023), 'Wooden statuette', in F. M. Morris and M. Biddle, *Venta Belgarum: Prehistoric, Roman and Early Medieval Winchester. Winchester Studies 3.i*, 857–9. Oxford: Archaeopress.

Higgs, E., and M. Biddle (1960), 'The animal bones', in J. Alexander, 'Report on the Investigation of a Round Barrow on Arreton Down, Isle of Wight', *Proceedings of the Prehistoric Society*, 26: 301–2.

Higham N., ed. (2007a), *Britons in Anglo-Saxon England*. Woodbridge: Boydell & Brewer.

Higham N. (2007b), 'Britons in Anglo-Saxon England: An Introduction', in N. Higham (ed.), *Britons in Anglo-Saxon England*, 1–15. Woodbridge: Boydell & Brewer.

Hill, J. D., A. J. Spence, S. L. Niece and S. Worrell (2004), 'The Winchester Hoard: A Find of Unique Iron Age Gold Jewellery from Southern England', *Antiquaries Journal*, 84: 1–22.

Hill, J. D. (2012), 'How did Middle and Late Iron Age Societies in Britain Work (if they did)?', in T. Moore and X. Armada (eds), *Atlantic Europe in the First Millennium B.C.: Crossing the Divide*, 242–6. Oxford: Oxford, Academic.

Hilts, C. (2015), 'Winchester Uncovered: Revisiting One of England's Greatest Excavations', *Current Archaeology*, 300: 35–41.

Hilts, C. (2024), 'Monastic Memories; Continuing the Search for Hyde Abbey,' *Current Archaeology*, 406: 14–15.

Hincke, H. (2010), 'The Rising of 1381 in Winchester', *The English Historical Review*, 125 (512): 112–31.

Hinton, D. (1990), 'Relief-decorated Strap-Ends', in M. Biddle (ed.), *Object and Economy in Medieval Winchester. Winchester Studies 7.ii*, 494–500. Oxford: Clarendon Press.

Hinton, D. (2008), *The Alfred Jewel and other Anglo-Saxon Decorated Metalwork, Ashmolean Museum*. Dorchester: Henry Ling.

Hinton, D., S. Keene and K. Qualmann (1981), 'The Winchester Reliquary', *Medieval Archaeology*, 25: 45–77.

Hodges, R (2025), 'Hamwic Deconstructed: Imported Pottery and Issues of Middle Saxon Urban Discontinuity', in M. Maltby and D. Hodges (eds), *Producers, Traders and Consumers in Urban Societies in Southern Britain and Europe*, 1–12. Oxford: Archaeopress.

Hofstetter W. (1988), 'Winchester and the Standardization of Old English Vocabulary', *Anglo-Saxon England*, 17: 139–61.

Holland, T. (2016), *Athelstan: The Making of England*. London: Allen Lane.

Hooke D. (2011), *Trees in Anglo-Saxon England: Literature, Lore and Landscape. (Anglo-Saxon Studies)*. Woodbridge: Boydell & Brewer.

Hudson, A. (2022), *Bishop Æthelwold, his Followers, and Saints' Cults in Early Medieval England: Power, Belief, and Religious Reform*. Woodbridge: Boydell & Brewer.

Hughes, I. (2013), *Imperial Brothers: Valentinian, Valens and the Disaster at Adrianople*. Barnsley: Pen and Sword Military.

Hyde, J. (2022), 'Popular Propaganda: John Heywood's Wedding Ballad and Mary I's Spanish Match', *Transactions of the Royal Historical Society*, 32: 73–91.

Irvine, S. (2002), *The Anglo-Saxon Chronicle: A Collaborative Edition MS E*. Woodbridge: Boydell & Brewer.

Isenberg, E., and J. Renfrew (2022), 'Pollen Analysis from the Archaeological Deposits in Winchester', in M. Biddle, J. Renfrew and P. Ottaway (eds), *Environment and Agriculture of Early Winchester. Winchester Studies 10*, 139–59. Oxford: Archaeopress.

Jackson, K. (1970), 'Romano-British Names in the Antonine Itinerary', in A. L. F. Rivet, 'British Section of the Antonine Itinerary', *Britannia*, 1: 34–82.

James, T. (2009), *Winchester: From Prehistory to the Present*. Stroud: The History Press.

Jarman, C. (2021), *The River Kings: The Vikings from Scandinavia to the Silk Roads*. London: William Collins.

Jarman, C. (2023), *The Bone Chests: Unlocking the History of the Anglo-Saxons*. London: William Collins.

Johnston, D. E., and J. Dicks (2014), *Sparsholt Roman Villa Hampshire: Excavations. Hampshire Field Club Monograph 11*. Winchester.

Jones, D. (2009), *Summer of Blood: The Peasants' Revolt of 1381*. London: Harper Press.

Joyce, S. J. (2022), *The Legacy of Gildas: Constructions of Authority in the Early Medieval West. Studies in Celtic History*. Woodbridge: Boydell & Brewer.

Karasawa, K. (2022), 'Historical Origins of a Mythical History: The Formation of the Myth Supporting Anglo-Saxonism Reconsidered', in K. L. Jolly and B. E. Brooks (eds), *Global Perspectives on Early Medieval England. Anglo-Saxon Studies*, 171–89. Woodbridge: Boydell & Brewer.

Karkov, C. E. (2004), *The Ruler Portraits of Anglo-Saxon England. Anglo-Saxon Studies*. Woodbridge: Boydell & Brewer.

Karkov, C. E. (2008), 'The Frontispiece to the New Minster Charter and the King's Two Bodies', in D. Scragg (ed.), *Edgar, King of the English 959–975: New Interpretations*, 224–41. Woodbridge: Boydell & Brewer.

Karkov, C. E. (2020), *Imagining Anglo-Saxon England: Utopia, Heterotopia, Dystopia*. Woodbridge: Boydell & Brewer.

Keats, J. ([1816] 2011), *Letters of John Keats to His Family and Friends*, ed. S. Colvin. Cambridge: Cambridge University Press

Keene, D. J. (1982), 'Town into Gown: The Site of the College and Other College Lands in Winchester Before The Reformation', in R. Custance (ed.), *Winchester College: Sixth-centenary Essays*, 37–76. Oxford: Oxford University Press.

Keene, D. J. (1985), *A Survey of Medieval Winchester. Winchester Studies 2*. Oxford: Oxford University Press.

Keene, D. J. (1990), 'The Textile Industry', in M. Biddle, *Object and Economy in Early Medieval Winchester. Winchester Studies 7.ii*, 200–14. Oxford: Oxford University Press.

Keene, D. J. (2015), 'Early Medieval Winchester: Symbolic Landscapes', in A. Simms and H B. Clarke (eds.), *Lords and Towns in Medieval Europe: The European Historic Towns Atlas Project*, 419–45. London: Routledge.

Keene, D. J. (2022), 'Agriculture and the Use of Plants in Medieval Winchester: The Documentary Evidence', in M. Biddle, J. Renfrew and P. Ottaway (eds), *Environment and Agriculture of Early Winchester. Winchester Studies 10*, 57–81. Oxford: Archaeopress.

Kendrick. T. D. (1950), *British Antiquity*. London: Methuen.

Kennedy, P. (2023), *Pathogenesis: How Germs Made History*. London: Torva.

Kernot, C. F. (1927), *British Public Schools' War Memorials*. London: Roberts and Newton Limited.

Kerr, J. (1990), 'Later medieval window glass from Wolvesey Palace', in M. Biddle, *Object and Economy in Early Medieval Winchester. Winchester Studies 7.ii*, 397–423. Oxford: Oxford University Press.

Kershaw, J. (2008), 'The Distribution of the "Winchester" Style in Late Saxon England: Metalwork Finds from the Danelaw', *Anglo-Saxon Studies in Archaeology and History*, 15: 254–69.

Keynes S. (1986), 'A Tale of Two Kings: Alfred the Great and Æthelred the Unready', *Transactions of the Royal Historical Society*, 36: 195–217.

Keynes, S. (1999), 'The cult of King Alfred the Great', *Anglo-Saxon England*, 28: 225–356.

Keynes, S. (2008), 'Edgar, *rex admirabilis*', in D. Scragg (ed.), *Edgar, King of the English 959–975: New Interpretations*, 3–59. Woodbridge: Boydell & Brewer.

Keynes, S., and M. Lapidge (1983), *Alfred the Great: Asser's Life of King Alfred and Other Contemporary Sources*. London: Penguin Random House.

King, A. (2020), 'Venta Belgarum: What Is in the Name for Roman Winchester?', in A. Langlands and R. Lavelle (eds), *The Land of the English Kin: Studies in Wessex and Anglo-Saxon England in Honour of Professor Barbara Yorke*, 13–25. Leiden: Brill.

Kjølbye-Biddle, B., and M. Biddle (forthcoming), *The Anglo-Saxon Minsters of Winchester. Winchester Studies 4.i*. Oxford: Archaeopress.

Klingelhöfer, E. (2003), 'Cluniac Architectural Influences at Hyde Abbey Church, Winchester', *Medieval Archaeology*, 47: 190–5.

Konshuh, C. (2020), Constructing Early Anglo-Saxon Identity in the Anglo-Saxon Chronicles, in A. Langlands and R. Lavelle (eds), *The Land of the English Kin: Studies in Wessex and Anglo-Saxon England in Honour of Professor Barbara Yorke*, 154–81. Leiden: Brill.

Kornexl, L. (2013), '*Regularis Concordia*', in M. Lapidge, J. Blair, S. Keynes and D. Scragg (eds), *The Wiley Blackwell Encyclopaedia of Anglo-Saxon England* (2nd edn), 399–400. Oxford: Wiley Blackwell.

Kynan-Wilson, W., ed. (2021), *Henry of Blois: New Interpretations*. Woodbridge: Boydell & Brewer.

Kynan-Wilson, W., and J. Munns (2021), 'Introduction: Approaches to Henry of Blois', in W. Kynan-Wilson (ed.), *Henry of Blois: New Interpretations*, 1–25. Woodbridge: Boydell & Brewer.

Langlands, A., and R. Lavelle, eds (2020), *The Land of the English Kin: Studies in Wessex and Anglo-Saxon England in Honour of Professor Barbara Yorke*. Leiden: Brill.

Lapidge, M. (2003), *The Cult of St Swithun. Winchester Studies 4.ii*. Oxford: Oxford University Press.

Lavelle, R. (2020), 'Places I'll Remember? Reflections on Alfred, Asser and the Power of Memory in the West Saxon Landscape', in A. Langlands and R. Lavelle (eds), *The Land of the English Kin: Studies in Wessex and Anglo-Saxon England in Honour of Professor Barbara Yorke*, 312–35. Leiden: Brill.

Lavelle, R., S. Roffey and K. Weikert, eds (2021), *Early Medieval Winchester: Communities, Authority in an Urban Space*. Oxford and Philadelphia: Oxbow Books.

Lawson, A. J. (2023), 'Miscellaneous shale objects', in F. M. Morris and M. Biddle, *Venta Belgarum: Prehistoric, Roman and Early Medieval Winchester. Winchester Studies 3.i*, 1165. Oxford: Archaeopress.

Lawton, D. (2001), 'The Surveying Subject and the "Whole World" of Belief: Three Case Studies', in W. Scase, R. Copeland and D. Lawton (eds), *New Medieval Literatures*, 9–32. Oxford: Oxford Academic.

Laycock, S. (2008), *Britannia The Failed State: Tribal conflicts and the end of Roman Britain*. Stroud: Tempus.

Leland, J. ([1535–45] 1907), *The Itinerary of John Leland*, ed. Lucy Toulmin Smith. London: Bell.

Lewis, W. (1965), *A History of the Peninsula Barracks*. Winchester: Culverlands. Available online: https://web.archive.org/web/20131008030852/http://krrcassociation.com/archives/history_peninsula_barracks.pdf

Lloyd, R. (1962), *The Troubling of the City*. London: Allen and Unwin.

Lodwick, L. (2017), 'Arable Farming, Plant Foods, and Resources', in M. Allen, L. Lodwick, T. Brindle, M. Fulford and A. T. Smith (eds), *The Rural Economy of Roman Britain*, 11–84. London: Society for the Promotion of Roman Studies.

Lodwick, L. (2023), 'Cultivating Villa Economies: Archaeobotanical and Isotopic Evidence for Iron Age to Roman Agricultural Practices on the Chalk Downlands of Southern Britain', *European Journal of Archaeology*, 26 (4): 445–66.

Lorden, J. A. (2016), 'Landscapes of Devotion: the Settings of St Swithun's early *uitae*', *Anglo-Saxon England*, 45: 285–309.

Lyon, S. (2012), 'Minting in Winchester: an Introduction and Statistical Analysis', in M. Biddle (ed.), *The Winchester Mint and Coins and Related Finds from the excavations 1961–1971. Winchester Studies 8*, 3–55. Oxford: Oxford University Press.

Lytle, G. F. (1982), '"Wykehamist culture" in Pre-Reformation England', in R. Custance (ed.), *Winchester College: Sixth-centenary Essays*, 120–66. Oxford: Oxford University Press.

MacCulloch, D. (2000), *Tudor Church Militant: Edward VI and the Protestant Reformation*. London: Allen Lane

MacPhail, R. J., H. Galinié and F. Verhaeghe (2015), 'A Future for Dark Earth', *Antiquity*, 77 (296): 349–58.

Maltby, M. (2010), *Feeding a Roman Town: Environmental Evidence from Excavations in Winchester 1972–1985*. Winchester Museums Service: Winchester

Margraff Turley, R., J. Archer and H. Thomas (2012), 'Keats "To Autumn" and the New Men of Winchester', *The Review of English Studies*, 63 (262): 797–817.

Masker, R. (2013), 'Council approve new trust to run Hampshire and Winchester museums', *Hampshire Chronicle*, 27 September. Available online: https://www.hampshirechronicle.co.uk/news/10703326.council-approve-new-trust-to-run-hampshire-and-winchester-museums/.

Mason, E. (1991), '"The Site of King-Making and Consecration": Westminster Abbey and the Crown in the Eleventh and Twelfth Centuries', *Studies in Church History Subsidia*, 9: 57–76.

Mattingley, D. (2008), *An Imperial Possession: Britain in the Roman Empire, 54 BC–AD 409. Penguin History of Britain*. London: Penguin.

McCulloch, P., and R. Osgood (2018), 'The Hessians of Barton Farm: Uncovering When a German Army Saved Britain, *Current Archaeology*, 345: 20–5.

McGrath, P. (1982), 'Winchester College and the Old Religion in the Sixteenth Century', in R. Custance (ed.), *Winchester College: Sixth-centenary Essays*, 229–80. Oxford: Oxford University Press.

Mees K. (2019), *Burial, Landscape and Identity in Early Medieval Wessex*. Woodbridge: Boydell & Brewer

Mills, C., I. Armit, K. J. Edwards, P. Grinter and Y. Mulder (2004), 'Neolithic Land-Use and Environmental Degradation: a Study from the Western Isles of Scotland', *Antiquity*, 78 (302): 888–95.

Milner, J. (1789), *History, Civil and Ecclesiastical, and Survey of the Antiquities of Winchester*. Winchester: Robbins.

Molleson, T., R. Powers, R. Price and P. Sheppard (2017), 'Anglo-Saxon and medieval populations from the Old and New Minster and Cathedral Cemeteries', in C. Stuckert (ed.), *The People of Early Winchester. Winchester Studies 9.i*, 261–390. Oxford: Oxford University Press.

Monk, M. (2022), 'The Plant Economy and Vegetation of Anglo-Saxon Winchester', in M. Biddle, J. Renfrew and P. Ottaway (eds), *Environment and Agriculture of Early Winchester. Winchester Studies 10*, 185–250. Oxford: Archaeopress.

Morony, M. (2019), 'The Early Islamic Mining Boom', *Journal of the Economic and Social History of the Orient*, 62 (1): 166–221.

Morris, F. M., E. Thomas and B. Clayre (2017), 'Provincial City in Decline: 1300–1642', in M. Biddle and D. J. Keene (eds), *Winchester: British Historic Towns Atlas – 6. Winchester Studies 11*, 38–54. Oxford and Philadelphia: Oxbow Books.

Morris, F. M., and M. Biddle (2023), *Venta Belgarum: Prehistoric, Roman and Early Medieval Winchester. Winchester Studies 3.i*. Oxford: Archaeopress.

Morris, M. (2021), *The Anglo-Saxons: A History of the Beginnings of England*. London: Hutchinson.

Morris, M. N., and K. E. Qualmann (forthcoming), 'Nunnaminster/St Mary's Abbey: Archaeological Evidence', in B. Kjølbye-Biddle and M. Biddle, *The*

Anglo-Saxon Minsters of Winchester. Winchester Studies 4.i. Oxford: Archaeopress.

Morris, R. K., and K. Hoverd (1994), *The Buildings of Winchester*. Stroud: Alan Sutton.

Mortimer, I. (2009), *The Time Traveller's Guide to Medieval England: A Handbook for Visitors to the Fourteenth Century.* London: Touchstone Books.

Mortimer, I. (2023), *Medieval Horizons: Why the Middle Ages Matter*. London: Bodley Head.

Mortimer, R. (2009), 'Edward the Confessor: the Man and the Legend', in R. Mortimer (ed.), *Edward the Confessor: The Man and the Legend,* 1–40. Woodbridge: Boydell & Brewer.

Mowl, T. (2024) '"A Sacred Place, A Temenos": Herbert Baker and the Architecture of the War Memorial Cloister', in Richard Foster (ed.), *War Cloister: Winchester College*, 23–36. Ceredigion: Gomer Press.

Murphy P. (2022), 'The Roman Plant Remains', in M. Biddle, J. Renfrew and P. Ottaway (eds), *Environment and Agriculture of Early Winchester. Winchester Studies 10,* 167–84. Oxford: Archaeopress.

Myres, J. N. L. (1936), 'Preface', in R. G. Collingwood and J. N. L. Myres, *Roman Britain and The English Settlements*, vii–x. Oxford: Oxford University Press.

Napier, A. (2013) 'Outgoing Campaign Leader Attacks Winchester City Council for "Capitulation" over Barton Farm', *Hampshire Chronicle*, 12 April. Available online: https://www.hampshirechronicle.co.uk/news/10349745.outgoing-campaign-leader-attacks-winchester-city-council-for-capitulation-over-barton-farm/.

Napier, A. (2021), 'Winchester University Dig at Former Morn Hill Army Camp', *Hampshire Chronicle,* 23 July. Available online: https://www.hampshirechronicle.co.uk/news/19385319.winchester-university-dig-former-morn-hill-army-camp/.

Naismith, R. (2018), *Citadel of the Saxons: The Rise of Early London.* London: I.B. Tauris.

Neal, C. (2014), 'Winchester Mayor's 1919 Pledge Honoured 95 Years on', *Hampshire Chronicle,* 26 June. Available online: https://www.hampshirechronicle.co.uk/news/11302420.winchester-mayors-1919-pledge-honoured-95-years-on/.

Needham, S. P. (2007), '800 BC. The Great Divide', in C. Haselgrove and P. Pope (eds), *The Earlier Iron Age in Britain and the Near Continent,* 39–63. Oxford: Oxbow Books.

Nicolson, R. (2011), 'Fish Remains', in B. M. Ford and S. Teague, *Winchester – A City in the Making: Archaeological Investigations between 2002 and 2007 on the sites of Northgate House, Staple Gardens and the Former Winchester Library, Jewry Street. Oxford Archaeology Monograph 12,* 358–61. Oxford: Oxford Archaeology.

Norton, C. (2018), 'Henry of Blois, St Hugh and Henry II: The Winchester Bible reconsidered', in J. Camps, M. Castiñeiras, J. McNeill and R. Plant (eds), *Romanesque Patrons and Processes: Design and Instrumentality in the Art and Architecture of Romanesque Europe,* 117–41. London: Routledge.

Nubin, O. (2021) 'Why diversity in Tudor England matters', in H. Carr and S. Lipscomb (eds), *What Is History Now? How the Past and the Present Speak to Each Other,* 163–9. London: Weidenfeld & Nicolson.

Oakeshott, W. (1945), *The Artists of the Winchester Bible*. London: Faber and Faber.

Oakeshott, W. (1981), *Two Winchester Bibles*. Oxford: Oxford University Press.

Old, J., J. Backhouse and The Members of WARG (2022), *Fifty Years of Digging the Dirt: Fifty Years of the Winchester Archaeological Rescue Group*. Chandler's Ford: Timeline History and Archaeology Hampshire.

Olalde, I., S. Brace, M. Allentoft et al. (2018), 'The Beaker phenomenon and the genomic transformation of northwest Europe,' *Nature*, 555: 190–6.

Olusoga, D. (2014), *The World's War: Forgotten Soldiers of Empire*. London: Head of Zeus.

Osborne, P. (2022), 'Insect fauna from Lower Brook Street', in M. Biddle, J. Renfrew and P. Ottaway (eds), *Environment and Agriculture of Early Winchester. Winchester Studies 10*, 347–57. Oxford: Archaeopress.

Oosthuizen, S. (2019), *The Emergence of the English (Past Imperfect)*. York: Arc Humanities Press.

Ottaway, P. (1992), *Archaeology in British Towns: From the Emperor Claudius to the Black Death*. London and New York: Routledge.

Ottaway, P. (2017), *Winchester: St Swithun's 'City of Happiness and Good Fortune': An Archaeological Assessment*. Oxford and Philadelphia: Oxbow Books.

Ottaway, P. (2021), 'Conclusions', in K. Qualmann, G. Scobie and J. Zant, *Excavations at Hyde Abbey, Winchester 1972–1999, collated and edited by Patrick Ottaway*, 301–5. Winchester: Winchester Museums Service/Hampshire Cultural Trust Publications Series.

Ottoway, P., and K. Qualmann, eds (2018), *Winchester's Anglo-Saxon, Medieval and Later Suburbs: Excavations 1971–86*. Winchester: Hampshire Cultural Trust.

Partner, P. (1982), 'William of Wykeham', in R. Custance (ed.), *Winchester College: Sixth-centenary Essays*, 1–36. Oxford: Oxford University Press.

Pétrequin, P., S. Cassen, K. Klassen, K., Sheridan and A.-M. Pétrequin, eds (2012), *Jade. Grandes Haches Alpines du Néolithique européen. Ve et IVe millénaires av. J.-C.* Besançon: Presses Universitaires de Franche- Comté.

Porritt, J. (1996), 'Twyford Down: the aftermath', in B. Bryant, *Twyford Down: Roads, Campaigning and Environmental Law*, 297–310. London: E and FN Spon.

Powell, A. (2015), 'Early-Middle Saxon Settlement beside the Winchester to Silchester Roman Road at Abbotts Barton, Winchester', *Hampshire Studies*, 70: 63–101.

Price, J., and S. Cotton (2023), 'Vessel Glass', in F. M. Morris, and M. Biddle, *Venta Belgarum: Prehistoric, Roman and Early Medieval Winchester. Winchester Studies 3.i*, 1048–1109. Oxford: Archaeopress.

Price, N. (2020), *The Children of Ash and Elm: A History of the Vikings*. London: Allen Lane

Pryor, F. (2004), *Britain BC: Life in Britain and Ireland before the Romans*. London: Harper Collins.

Qualmann, K. (1986), 'Winchester-Nunnaminster', *Current Archaeology*, 102: 204–7. Cultural Trust Publications Series.

Qualmann, K. (2025), 'Winchester's Saxon Defences – the Northwest Corner', in M. Maltby and D. Hodges (eds), *Producers, Traders and Consumers in Urban Societies in Southern Britain and Europe*, 71–9. Oxford: Archaeopress.

Qualman, K., H. Rees, G. Scobie and R. Whinney (2004), *The Oram's Arbour Iron Age Enclosure at Winchester*. Winchester: Winchester Museums Service.

Qualmann, K., G. Scobie and J. Zant (2021), *Excavations at Hyde Abbey, Winchester 1972–1999, collated and edited by Patrick Ottaway*. Winchester: Winchester Museums Service/Hampshire

Ramirez, J. (2015), *The Private Life of the Saints: Power, Passion and Politics in Anglo-Saxon England*. London: W.H. Allen.

Ramirez, J. (2023), *Femina: A New History of the Middle Ages, through the Women Written Out of It*. London: W.H. Allen.

Reece, R. (2023), 'Roman coins', in F. M. Morris and M. Biddle, *Venta Belgarum: Prehistoric, Roman and Early Medieval Winchester. Winchester Studies 3.i*, 641–4. Oxford: Archaeopress.

Rawcliffe, C. (2009), *Leprosy in Medieval England*. Woodbridge: Boydell & Brewer.

Reddé, M. (2018), *Gallia Rustica 2. Les Campagnes du Nord-est de la Gaule, de la Fin de L'Âge du Fer à l'Antiquité Tardive*. Bordeaux: Ausonius.

Renfrew, J., and P. Ottaway (2022), 'The natural environment of the Winchester region', in M. Biddle, J. Renfrew and P. Ottaway (eds), *Environment and Agriculture of Early Winchester. Winchester Studies 10*, 26–38. Oxford: Archaeopress.

Richardson, R. C. (1992), 'Winchester and the Civil War', in S. Barker and C. Haydon (eds), *Winchester: History and Literature: The proceedings of a Conference in celebration of the 150th Anniversary of the founding of King Alfred's College held on 16th March 1991*, 55–71. York: Coward Printers.

Ridyard, S. (1989), *The Royal Saints of Anglo-Saxon England: A Study of West Saxon and East Anglian Cults*. Cambridge: Cambridge University Press.

Rippon S. (2010), 'Landscape Change during the "Long Eighth Century" in Southern England', in N. J. Higham and M. J. Ryan (eds), *The Landscape Archaeology of Anglo-Saxon England: Manchester Centre for Anglo-Saxon Studies*, 39–64, Woodbridge: Boydell & Brewer.

Roach, L. (2013), *Kingship and Consent in Anglo-Saxon England, 871–978: Assemblies and the State in the Early Middle Ages*. Cambridge: Cambridge University Press.

Roach, L. (2016), *Æthelred: The Unready*. London: Yale University Press.

Roffey, S. (2012), 'Medieval Leper Hospitals in England: An Archaeological Perspective from St Mary Magdalen, Winchester', *Medieval Archaeology*, 56: 203–34.

Roffey, S. (2020), 'Sanctity and Suffering: The Sacred World of the Medieval Leprosarium. A Perspective from St Mary Magdalen, Winchester', in A. Langlands and R. Lavelle (eds), *The Land of the English Kin: Studies in Wessex and Anglo-Saxon England in Honour of Professor Barbara Yorke*, 538–54. Leiden: Brill.

Roffey, S. (2021), 'SK27, or a Winchester Pilgrim Tale', in R. Lavelle, S. Roffey, and K. Weikert (eds), *Early Medieval Winchester: Communities, Authority in an Urban Space*, 215–24. Oxford and Philadelphia: Oxbow Books.

Roffey, S., and K. Tucker (2012), 'A Contextual Study of the Medieval Hospital and Cemetery of St Mary Magdalen, Winchester, England', *International Journal of Paleopathology*, 2: 170–80.

Rogers, A. (2011), *Late Roman Towns in Britain: Rethinking Change and Decline*. Cambridge: Cambridge University Press.

Rogers, P. (1993), *Essays on Pope*. Cambridge: Cambridge University Press.

Rohnbogner, A. (2018), 'The Rural Population', in A. T. Smith, M. Allen, T. Brindle, M. Fulford, L. Lodwick and A. Rohnbogner (eds), *Life and Death in the*

Countryside of Roman Britain, 281–345. London: Society for the Promotion of Roman Studies.
Rosen, A (1981), 'Winchester in Transition 1580–1700', in P. Clack (ed.), *Country Towns in Pre-Industrial England*, 144–95. London: Leicester University Press.
Rosman, D. (1996), *From Catholic to Protestant: Religion and the People in Tudor England*. London and Bristol: UCL Press.
Rouse, R. A. (2005), *The Idea of Anglo-Saxon England in Middle English Romance*. Woodbridge: Boydell & Brewer.
Royal Archaeological Institute (1924), 'Summer Meeting at Winchester', *Archaeological Journal*, 81: 313–76.
Rumble, A. R. (2002), *The Anglo-Saxon Minsters of Winchester: Property and Piety in Early Medieval Winchester. Winchester Studies 4.iii*. Oxford: Oxford University Press.
Russell, M., and S. Laycock (2011), *Unroman Britain: Exposing the Great Myth of Britannia*. Stroud: The History Press.
Ryrie, A. (2020), *The English Reformation: A Very Brief History*. London: SPCK.
Sabben-Clare, J. (1992), 'Winchester College: History and Literature', in S. Barker and C. Haydon (eds), *Winchester: History and Literature: The proceedings of a Conference in celebration of the 150th Anniversary of the founding of King Alfred's College held on 16th March 1991*, 36–54. York: Coward Printers.
Samson, A. (2005), 'Changing Places: The Marriage and Royal Entry of Philip, Prince of Austria, and Mary Tudor, July–August 1554', *The Sixteenth Century Journal*, 36 (3): 761–84.
Saunders, O. E. (1928), *English Illumination*. Florence and Paris: Pegasus Press.
Schallmayer, E. (1990), *Der Römische Weihebezirk von Osterburken. Teil: 1. Corpus der Griechischen und Lateinischen Beneficiarier-Inschriften des Römischen Reiches*. State Monuments Office Baden Württemberg Publications: Stuttgart.
Scobie, G., J. M. Zant and R. Whinney (1991), *The Brooks, Winchester: A Preliminary Report on the Excavations 1987–88*. Winchester: Winchester Museums Service Archaeological Report Number One.
Scull, C. (2011), 'Social Transactions, Gift-Exchange, and Power in the Archaeology of the Fifth to Seventh Centuries', in H. Hamerow, D. Hinton and S. Crawford (eds), *The Oxford Handbook of Anglo-Saxon Archaeology*, 848–64. Oxford: Oxford University Press.
Seersholm, F. V., K. G. Sjögren, J. Koelman et al. (2024), 'Repeated plague infections across six generations of Neolithic Farmers', *Nature*, 10 July: 1–8.
Seldon, A., and D. Walsh (2018), *Public Schools and the Great War: The Generation Lost*. Barnsley: Pen and Sword Military.
Sharples, N. (2010), *Social Relations in Later Prehistory: Wessex in the First Millennium B.C.* Oxford: Oxford University Press.
Shippey, T. A. (1992), 'Winchester in the Anglo-Saxon Period and After', in S. Barker and C. Haydon (eds), *Winchester: History and Literature: The proceedings of a Conference in celebration of the 150th Anniversary of the founding of King Alfred's College held on 16th March 1991*, 1–21. York: Coward Printers.
Speidel, L., M. Silva, T. Booth, B. Raffield, K. Anastasiadou, C. Barrington, A. Götherström, P. Heather and P. Skoglund (2025), 'High-resolution genomic history of early medieval Europe', *Nature*, 637: 118–26.
Spyrou, M., L. Musralina, G. A. Gnecchi Ruscone, P. Borbone, V. I. Khartanovich, A. Buzhilova, L. Djansugurova, K. I. Bos, D. Kühnert, W. Haak, P. Slavin and

J. Krause (2022), 'The Source of the Black Death in Fourteenth-Century Central Eurasia', *Nature*, 606: 718–24.

Stafford, P. (1999), 'Queens, Nunneries and Reforming Churchmen: Gender, Religious Status and Reform in Tenth and Eleventh Century England', *Past and Present*, 163: 3–35.

Streeter, B. H. (2011), 'The Winchester Chains', in *The Chained Library: A Survey of Four Centuries in the Evolution of the English Library*. Cambridge Library Collection, History of Printing, Publishing and Libraries, 345–6. Cambridge: Cambridge University Press.

Stevens, C. J., and D. Q. Fuller (2012), 'Did Neolithic Farming Fail? The Case for a Bronze Age Agricultural Revolution in the British Isles', *Antiquity*, 86 (333): 707–22.

Stevens, C. J., and D. Q. Fuller (2015), 'Alternative Strategies to Agriculture: The Evidence for Climatic Shocks and Cereal Declines during the British Neolithic and Bronze Age (a Reply to Bishop)', *World Archaeology*, 47: 856–75.

Strickland, M. (2022), 'Warfare and Violence', in B. Pohl (ed.), *The Cambridge Companion to the Age of William the Conqueror. Cambridge Companions to Culture*, 225–43. Cambridge: Cambridge University Press.

Strid, I. (2011), 'Mammal and bird bones', in B. M. Ford and S. Teague, *Winchester – A City in the Making: Archaeological Investigations between 2002 and 2007 on the sites of Northgate House, Staple Gardens and the Former Winchester Library, Jewry Street. Oxford Archaeology Monograph 12*, 339–58. Oxford: Oxford Archaeology.

Stuckert, C., ed. (2017), *The People of Early Winchester. Winchester Studies 9.i.* Oxford: Oxford University Press.

Taylor, B. (1985), 'One Hundred Years of the Hampshire Field Club', *Proceedings of the Hampshire Field Club and Archaeological Society*, 41: 5–20.

Taylor, J. (2013a), 'Roman Urbanism: A View from the Countryside', *Oxford Journal of Archaeology*, 32 (iv): 413–32.

Taylor, J. (2013b), 'Encountering Romanitas: Characterising the Role of Agricultural Communities in Roman Britain', *Britannia*, 44: 171–10.

Teague, S. C., and A. Hardy (2011), 'The Anglo-Norman and Later Medieval Period, c. 1050–1550', in B. M. Ford and S. C. Teague, *Winchester – A City in the Making: Archaeological Investigations between 2002 and 2007 on the sites of Northgate House, Staple Gardens and the former Winchester Library, Jewry Street*, 187–211. Oxford Archaeology Monograph 10. Oxford: Oxford Archaeology.

Thomas, J. (1999), *Understanding the Neolithic*. London: Routledge

Thomas, R. (2022), *History and Identity in Early Medieval Wales. Studies in Celtic History*. Woodbridge: Boydell & Brewer.

Thomas, K., and A. Hessayon (2009), 'The Perception of the Past in Early Modern England', in D. Bates, J. Wallis and J. Winters (eds), *The Creighton Century, 1907–2007*, 181–218. London: University of London Press.

Thomas, E., M. Biddle and F. Morris (2017), 'Royal and Mercantile Centre, 1066 to 1300', in M. Biddle and D. J. Keene (eds), *Winchester: British Historic Towns Atlas – 6. Winchester Studies 11*, 38–47. Oxford and Philadelphia: Oxbow Books.

Thompson, E. A. (1982), 'Zosimus 6. 10. 2 and The Letters Of Honorius', *The Classical Quarterly*, 32 (ii): 445–62.

Thurley, S. (2009), 'A Country Seat Fit for a King: Charles II, Greenwich and Winchester', in E. Cruickshank (ed.), *The Stuart Courts*, 214–39. Stroud: The History Press.

Titow, J. Z. (2022), 'Field Crops and Their Cultivation in Hampshire, 1200–1350 in the light of the Documentary Evidence', in M. Biddle, J. Renfrew and P. Ottaway (eds), *Environment and Agriculture of Early Winchester. Winchester Studies 10*, 86–138. Oxford: Archaeopress.

Tomlin, R. (1974), 'The Date of the "Barbarian Conspiracy"', *Britannia*, 5: 303–9.

Tomlin, R. (2023, 'Altar Dedicated by a *Beneficiarius Consularis*', in F. M. Morris and M. Biddle, *Venta Belgarum: Prehistoric, Roman and Early Medieval Winchester. Winchester Studies 3.i*, 828–32. Oxford: Archaeopress.

Tomlin, R., and M. Biddle (2023), 'Fragment of an Antonine Imperial Building Inscription', in F. M. Morris and M. Biddle, *Venta Belgarum: Prehistoric, Roman and Early Medieval Winchester. Winchester Studies 3.i*, 832–5. Oxford: Archaeopress.

Trigger, B. G. (2006), *A History of Archaeological Thought*. Cambridge: Cambridge University Press.

Trollope, T. A. ([1867] 2010), 'At Winchester', in *What I Remember. Vol 1. Cambridge Library Collection – Literary Studies*, 94–124. Cambridge: Cambridge University Press.

Turley, R. M., J. E. Archer and H. Thomas (2012), 'Keats' "To Autumn", and the New Men of Winchester', *The Review of English Studies, New Series*, 63 (262): 797–81.

Turner, D. (2015), *The Old Boys: Decline and Rise of the Public School*. New Haven and London: Yale University Press.

Tylecote, R. F., and B. J. J. Gilmour (1986), *The Metallography of Early Ferrous Edged Tools and Edged Weapons. BAR British Series 155*. Oxford: British Archaeological Reports.

Urban C., A. A. Blom, C. Avanzi, K. Walker-Meikle. A. K. Warren, K. White-Iribhogbe, R. Turle, P. Marter, H. Dawson-Hobbis, S. Roffey, S. A. Inskip and V. J. Schuenemann (2024), 'Ancient *Mycobacterium leprae* genome reveals medieval English red squirrels as animal leprosy host', *Current Biology*, 34: 1–10.

Virdi, J. (2021), 'How Can We Write the History of Disability?', in H. Carr and S. Lipscomb (eds), *What Is History Now? How the Past and the Present Speak to Each Other*, 113–29. London: Weidenfeld & Nicolson.

Wacher, J. (1997), *The Towns of Roman Britain*. London: Routledge

Wabuda, S. (2018), 'The English Reformation', in D. M. Whitford (ed.), *Martin Luther in Context*, 391–9. Cambridge: Cambridge University Press.

Waddington, K., A. Bayliss, T. Higham, R. Madgwick and N. Sharples (2019), 'Histories of Deposition: Creating Chronologies for the Late Bronze Age–Early Iron Age Transition in Southern Britain', *Archaeological Journal*, 176 (1): 84–133.

Wainwright, C. (2000), 'Travellers to the Round Table', in M. Biddle (ed.), *King Arthur's Round Table: An Archaeological Investigation*, 513–18. Woodbridge: Boydell & Brewer.

Webley, L. (2015), 'Rethinking Iron Age Connections Across the Channel and North Sea', in H. Anderson-Whymark, D. Garrow and F. Sturt (eds), *Continental Connections: Exploring Cross-Channel Relationships from the Mesolithic to the Iron Age*, 122–44. Oxford: Oxbow.

Weir, A. (2008), *Henry VIII: King and Court*. London: Vintage.

West, J. (2008), 'A Taste for the Antique? Henry of Blois and the Arts', in C. P. Lewis (ed.), *Anglo-Norman Studies 30: Proceedings of the Battle Conference 2007*, 213–30. Woodbridge: Boydell & Brewer.

Wheeler, R. E. M. (1954), *Archaeology from the Earth*. Oxford: Clarendon Press.

White, C., and C. Conybeare (2024), 'The Monastic Agreement of the Monks and Nuns of the English Nation (*Regularis concordia*)', in *The Cambridge Anthology of British Medieval Latin*, 369–74. Cambridge: Cambridge University Press.

Whitman, J. (2008), 'National Icon: The Winchester Round Table and the Revelation of Authority', *Arthuriana*, 18 (iv): 33–65.

Williams, H. (2007), 'Forgetting the Britons in Victorian Anglo-Saxon Archaeology', in N. J. Higham (ed.), *Britons in Anglo-Saxon England*, 27–41. Woodbridge: Boydell & Brewer.

Wilson, D. M. (1984), *Anglo-Saxon Art from the Seventh Century to the Norman Conquest*. London: Thames and Hudson.

Wood, M. (2022a), *In Search of the Dark Ages: 40th Anniversary Edition*. London: BBC Books.

Wood, M. (2022b), 'Excavating Winchester: The Dig that Changed (Urban) History', *BBC History Magazine,* September 2002, 66–70.

Woods, D. (2012), 'On the Alleged Letters of Honorius to the Cities of Britain in 410', *Latomus*, 71: 818–26.

Woolley, B (2002), *The Queen's Conjuror: The Life and Magic of Dr Dee*. London: Flamingo.

Woolf, A. (2007), 'Apartheid and Economics in Anglo-Saxon England', in N. J. Higham (ed.), *Britons in Anglo-Saxon England*, 115–29. Woodbridge: Boydell & Brewer.

Worsley, L. (2017), *Jane Austen at Home: A Biography.* London: Hodder and Stoughton.

World Water Day (2022), 'Brook Street Blues: How a Winchester Water Dispute Became a Human Right'. Available online: https://www.winchesterheritageopendays.org/blog/2022/3/22/worldwaterday.

Yorke, B. (1982), 'The Foundation of the Old Minster and the Status of Winchester in the Seventh and Eighth Centuries', *Proceedings of Hampshire Field Club*, 38: 75–83.

Yorke, B, (1993), 'Fact or Fiction? The Written Evidence for the Fifth and Sixth Centuries AD', *Anglo-Saxon Studies in Archaeology and History,* 6: 45–50.

Yorke, B. (1999), *The King Alfred Millenary in Winchester, 1901. Hampshire Papers 17*. Winchester: Hampshire County Council.

Yorke, B. (2021a), 'Royal Burials in Winchester: Context and Significance', in R. Lavelle, S. Roffey and K. Weikert (eds), *Early Medieval Winchester: Communities, Authority in an Urban Space*, 59–80. Oxford and Philadelphia: Oxbow Books.

Yorke, B. (2021b), 'New Minster', in K. Qualmann, G. Scobie and J. Zant, *Excavations at Hyde Abbey, Winchester 1972–1999, collated and edited by Patrick Ottaway*, 21–7. Winchester: Winchester Museums Service/Hampshire Cultural Trust Publications Series.

Yorke, B. (forthcoming), 'Nunnaminster/St Mary's Abbey in the Early Middle Ages', in B. Kjølbye-Biddle and M. Biddle, *The Anglo-Saxon Minsters of Winchester. Winchester Studies 4.i.* Oxford: Archaeopress.

Zant, J. M. (1993), *The Brooks, Winchester, 1987–88: The Roman Structural Remains*. Winchester Museums Service: Winchester.

INDEX

Aethelbert, (860–5) (West Saxon King)
  Cnut upholds his laws, 84
  Viking raid on Winchester during his reign, 64-4
Aethelred, (978–1013, 1014–16), (King of England)
  accession after civil war, 82
  enhancements to New Minster, 74
  increase in moneyers' numbers to produce Danegeld, 80
  land grants in Winchester, 79, 183
  marriage to Emma, 83
  preference for ruling from London, 82
  presence at rededication of Old Minster, 81
  unsuccessful struggles against Scandinavians, 82–3
Aethelwold (904/9–984) Bishop of Winchester
  963 becomes Bishop of Winchester, 71
  Abbot of Abingdon, 71
  changes to Winchester's Minsters, 72–3, 75, 78
  clerk in Aethelstan's court, 71
  commissions rededication of New Minster, 74–5
  establishes Wolvesey as Bishop's Palace, 72
  friendship with Dunston, 71–2
  monk at Glastonbury, 71
  monastic reforms, 69–70, 72–3, 75–6, 78
  patron of Benedictional, 76–7
  patron of *Regularis concordia*, 76
  promotion of St Swithun, 73–5
  reassertion of power at rededication of Old Minster, 71
  regent for King Aethelred, 82
  supported by King Edgar, 72, 76
Alfred the Great (871–99) King of Wessex and England
  association with Winchester, 15, 189, 65, 132
  bones translated to Hyde Abbey, 20, 102
  buried in Old Minster then in New, 68
  established *monasteriolum* for Grimwald, 67
  extends burh network, 65–7
  fictional depictions, 13, 135–6
  millennium commemorations, 128–30
  osteological analysis, 102, 128
  patron of learning, 67
  popularity as an imperial hero, 20, 59, 128
  promotes 'Angelcynn' as united realm, 62, 67
  sponsor of *Anglo-Saxon Chronicle*, 58
Alfred Atheling (1012–36), son of Aethelred and Emma, 84–5
animal husbandry
  early medieval, 79–80
  medieval, 93
  prehistoric, 30–1, 35, 39
  Roman, 49
Anglo-Saxon Chronicle
  begun at King Alfred's Court, 58
  bias towards Wessex's importance, 59, 64
  records major events, 64, 68, 72, 85

Arthur (Legendary King)
    1290 Edward I commissions Round Table replica, 98–9
    association with Winchester in medieval Romances, 18–19, 98
    Emperor Maximilian's interest, 115
    Henry VIII has Round Table refurbished, 115–16
    importance to Henry VII, 115
    Thomas Malory identifies Winchester as Camelot, 12, 15,
Arthur (1486–1502) (Prince of Wales) born at Winchester, 114
Asser (c. 885–909), Welsh Chronicler of King Alfred, 11, 15, 62, 64–5, 67
Athelstan (924–7), (King of the Anglo-Saxons), (927–39) (King of England)
    campaigns to unite Britain as *Angelyn* culminating in his victory at *Brunnaburgh,* 70
    European connections, 70–1
    overcomes Wessex opposition to his becoming king, 69–70
    patron of Guy of Warwick in medieval Romances, 12
    promulgates unified law codes, 69–70

Beaufort, Henry (c. 1375–1447), Cardinal and Bishop of Winchester
    1446 adds 'Almshouse of Noble Poverty' to St Cross, 107–8, 125
    1476 replaces St Swithun's reliquary, 102
Biddle, Martin (Director of Winchester Excavations), 13, 22–7, 62, 98–9, 114–15, 134
Brook Street area
    high-status early medieval occupation and burials, 54, 64, 79
    John de Tyting's house, 88, 91
    Juliana de Floude, 88–9, 137
    late ninth-/early tenth-century occupation, 79
    medieval occupation, 97
    plant remains, 79, 93
    problems of industrial pollution, 110, 124

Roman craft production, 48–9
Roman occupation, 44, 48, 50
Romano-British temple, 45, 51
Victorian cholera outbreaks, 12
Bronze Age
    Beaker pottery, 33
    burials, 35
    Deverell Rimbury pottery, 35
    population change, 33–5, 37
    settlements, 34–5

Cnut (1016–35), Scandinavian, King of England
    buried in New Minster, 84
    depicted in New Minster's *Liber Vitae,* 83
    emphasis on continuity from predecessors, 83–4
    interest in Winchester, 82–3
    marriage to Emma, 83

de Blois, Henri (1096–1171), Bishop of Winchester
    1129 becomes Bishop of Winchester, 100
    1132–5 establishes Hospital of St Cross, 106–7
    commissions Cathedral modifications, 100
    commissions major enhancements to Wolvesey Palace, 105–6
    important role in Angevin Empire, 105–6
    likely patron of the Winchester Bible, 109–10
de la Floude, Juliana, medieval laundress, 11, 15, 88–9, 137
DNA analysis
    Black Death origins, 112
    Bronze Age population change, 35
    Germanic presence, 28, 56
    medieval leprosy, 91, 109
    'Twigstats' developments, 28, 37, 56

early medieval Winchester (*Uintancaestir*)
    660–3 first bishop appointed by Cenwalh, King of Wessex, 58
    animal husbandry, 80

Anglo-Scandinavian sculptures, 84
burials dating to 870–90 with sword cuts, 63–4
craft production, 64
crop husbandry, 64, 79–80
cult of St Swithun established, 65, 73–6
European contacts, 63, 67, 70–1, 73
first property-owning records, 82–3, 88
Godwine (died 1053) (Earl of Wessex), 84–5
high-status burials at Brook Street, 64
imports, 81
meeting to promulgate *Regularis concordia*, 76–8
mint, 65, 80–1
monastic reforms, 72–3, 76, 81
New Minster 17, 20, 68, 71–2, 78, 83–4
new street grid, 65
ninth-century Viking raid, 64–5
Nunnaminster, 64, 66, 69, 72, 75–6
Old Minster, 17, 58, 62–3, 68–9, 71–4, 78, 81
scriptorium produces *Benedictional of Aethelwald* and other manuscripts, 78, 80–3
suburbs, 81
surviving Romano-Britons, 61–2
trading centre, 80
Winchester Reliquary, 81
Winchester School, artistic tradition, 77–8
Edgar (959–75), King of the Anglo-Saxons
963 appoints Aethelwold as Bishop of Winchester, 71
972 oversees refoundation of New Minster, 78
973 reforms coinage, 80
commissions lavish reliquary for St Swithun, 73
depicted in New Minster refoundation charter and *Regularis concordia*, 72–3, 76
legislative reforms, 72
supports Aethelwold's reforms, 75–6
unrest after his death, 81–2
Edward (the Confessor) (1042–66), King of England
crowned king in Winchester, 91
deprives Emma of her property, 91
invasion repelled by Godwine, 90
investment in Westminster Abbey, 91, 93
invited to be joint ruler with Harthacnut, 90
preference for ruling from London, 92
Edward the Elder (870–926), King of the Anglo-Saxons
901 commissions New Minster, 68
arranges transfer of his parents' bones to New Minster, 68
continues Alfred's efforts to create a united England, 68
gains throne after civil war following his father, Alfred's death, 68
Elizabethan Winchester
1582 Francis Walsingham becomes first High Steward, 119
1587 new town charter issued by Queen, 126
economic decline, 120
persistence of Catholic beliefs, 119–20
Emma of Normandy (984/6–1052), Queen Consort of England
banished to Normandy, 84
buried in Old Minster, 85
commissions *Enconium Emma Reginae*, 85
deprived of her property by her son, Edward, 85
marriages, 83–4
probable identification of her bones, 28, 86
restored to power by Harthacnut, 84–5
Georgian Winchester
camp of Hessian troops near Winchester, 29, 122

Daniel Defoe's visit to Winchester, 122
first Hyde Abbey excavations, 20
Jane Austen, 13–14, 122–3
King's House used for prisoners of war, then leased to army, 14, 122
major private and public building programme, 122
Peninsula Barracks becomes a major site for British Army, 14, 124
town council organises social events, 122
Germanic transition
archaeological evidence, 54–7, 60–1
documentary sources, 59–60
incomers, 52
Romano-Britons in the post-Roman period, 61–2
Guy of Warwick, medieval hero of Romances, 12, 19

Harald ('Harefoot') (1035–7), Regent of England and (1037–40), King of England, 84–5
Harthacnut (1040–2), King of England, 84–5
Henry VII (1485–1509), King of England
1486 arranges for heir, Arthur to be born in Winchester, 114
1506 emphasizes Arthurian connections when Philip of Burgundy visits, 115
Henry VIII (1509–47), King of England
1506 accompanies Philip of Burgundy to inspect Round Table, 114–15
1516 commissions repainting of Round Table, 115–16
1519 displays refurbished Round Table to Emperor Charles V, 116
1534 becomes Supreme Head of the Church of England, 116–17
1536 commissions John Leland's antiquarian accounts, 18
Hyde Abbey
1110 building begins, 91–2
1112 bones of Alfred and his family transferred there, 18–19, 102
1141 record of its burning, 103
antiquarian interest, 20, 102
monastic complex, 103–4
osteological analysis, 10, 102
sixteenth-century criticisms, 116
stone robbed after Dissolution, 125
wealth, 104

Iron Age
agricultural settlements, 38–9
arrival of Romans, 39–40, 42–3
coins, 40
DNA analysis, 37
Oram's Arbour, 21, 37–8, 40
Owslebury, 40
St Catherine's Hill, 21, 36–7

Jewish community in medieval Winchester
1264 attacked by Simon de Montfort, 90
Benedict, guildsman and royal servant, 90
Castle's Jews' Tower, 89
first Jews recorded in Winton Domesday, 89
Licoricia, entrepreneur, 11, 15, 89–90
Licoricia statue and charity, 137
Scowrtenestre renamed as Jewry Street, 90

Kjølbye-Biddle, Birthe (led Cathedral Green excavations), 17, 22, 27

Mary I (1553–8), Queen regnant of England
1554 marriage to Philip II in Winchester Cathedral, 118–19
medieval Winchester
animal husbandry, 93
Cathedral Priory, 13–15, 19–20, 87, 94, 97, 99–102, 171
Castle, 14–15, 19, 87, 89, 91–2, 95–8
comparative wealth, 94
craft production, 97

crop husbandry, 93
depopulation and late medieval decline, 111–13
domestic occupation, 111–13
effects of Black Death, 112
friaries and other religious communities, 92, 94
Hyde Abbey, 18, 102–4
imports, 116
leprosy, 10, 28, 91, 108–9
mills, 99
notable citizens, 11, 15, 88–9, 113
Peasants Revolt and other insurrections, 111–13
religious life of the people, 93–4
Round Table, 15, 19, 26, 98–9
royal palace, 87, 92, 95–6, 99
St Cross Almshouse, 106–8
St Giles Fair, 104
St Mary's Abbey, 104
St Mary Magdalen leper hospital, 28, 108–9
St Mary's (Winchester) College, 110–11
St Swithun's importance for pilgrimages, 65, 100
suburbs, 91–2, 94, 103, 112
vineyards, 93
Winchester Bible, 11, 110
Winton Domesday, 11, 87, 89, 108
medieval kings with associations with Winchester
   Edward I (1272–1307), 15, 81, 90, 98, 105
   Henry I (1100–35), 95, 97, 100
   Henry II (1154–89), 89, 91
   Henry III (1216–72), 89, 97, 118
   Henry VI (1422–61, 1470–1), 12, 113
   Richard I (1189–99), 97
   Richard II (1377–9), 111
   William I (1066–87), 86, 95, 97
   William II (1087–1100), 109

New Minster
   901–3 foundation, 68
   966 refoundation, 72
   Aethelwold's reforms, 72–3
   Anglo-Scandinavian sculptures, 84
   demolition, 17, 100, 102
   extended, 71, 78
   Liber Vitae, 83
   transfer of bones of Alfredian royal house there, 69
Nunnaminster/St Mary's Abbey
   970s founded by Ealswith, 66, 69
   community of nuns persists post Dissolution, 69–70
   dedication to St Eadburgh, 69–70
   favourable 'visitation' by Bishop Foxe, 116–17
   first attempt at dissolution defeated, 117
   lack of royal patronage, 76
   Norman rededication adding St Mary to St Eadburgh, 104
   popularity throughout medieval period, 104
   refurbishment under Aethelwald's reforms, 75
   robbing of building materials after Dissolution, 118
   supports 'many poor households', 117
   twelfth- and thirteenth-century additions, 104

Old Minster
   648 first church begun, 58, 62–3
   980 rededication, 72, 81
   depiction in *Benedictional of St Aethelwold*, 76–7
   demolition 17, 100–1
   extensions linked to cult of St Swithun, 65, 73, 78
   Italian influences on design, 63
   modifications sponsored by St Aethelwold, 72, 74–5, 78
   St Martin's Tower added, 63
   tenth-century additions including a spectacular tower, 68–9
   William I's crown-wearing ceremony, 95

Peninsula Barracks
   1796 King's House leased to barracks' department, 122

INDEX

eighteenth century, established as a major site for British Army, 124
nineteenth-century expansion, 124
twentieth-century military museums, 14
prehistoric remains from Winchester and its environs
  agricultural settlements, 32–3, 35, 37–9
  burials, 35, 39
  Iron Age coins, 40
  landscape management, 30–1
  Mesolithic land use and tools, 31
  Oram's Arbour Iron Age enclosure, 37–8, 40
  Owslebury settlement, 40
  Palaeolithic stone tools, 31
  St Catherine's Hill hillfort, 21, 37–8

Reformation and Dissolution of the Monasteries
  1538 destruction of St Swithun's shrine, 117
  1539 all religious houses in Winchester surrender, 17
  Nunnaminster's nuns continue as informal community, 117
  religious dissent in reign of Elizabeth I, 119–20
Roman Winchester (*Venta Belgarum*)
  animal husbandry, 40, 49
  aqueduct, 48
  coins, 49, 51, 64
  craft production, 49
  crop husbandry, 48–9, 54–5
  defences, 48, 50–1, 53
  domestic structures, 48, 50, 58
  evidence base, 44
  enslaved people, 46, 57
  extramural cemeteries, 10, 17, 49, 54–5
  forum, 46–7, 50–1, 53, 62
  foundation, 45–6
  fourth-century decline, 53–7
  Germanic presence, 55–7
  inscriptions, 47, 50
  imports, 52
  Lankhills cemetery, 26, 56–7
  military involvement, 43, 57
  origins of name, 44–5, 47–8
  possible fort, 44
  pottery, 49, 51, 52
  rural links, 54–5
  suburbs, 49
Round Table
  1290 Edward I commissions Round Table replica, 15, 19, 98
  refurbishment for Henry VIII, 115–16
  original decoration, 98
  shown to Philip of Burgundy, 114–15
  twentieth century investigations, 26, 98, 115

St Cross Hospital (Almshouse)
  1132–5 foundation by Bishop Henri de Blois, 106
  1146 Cardinal Beaufort's foundation of 'Almshouse of Noble Poverty', 107–8
  disputes with Knights Hospitallers, 106
  Dr John Dee's interest, 119
  excavations 106
  nineteenth-century reforms, 125
  sixteenth-century revival, 108
  The Warden, 14, 125
St Mary Magdalen leper hospital
  1070–90 first structures and cemetery, 108
  challenge to perceptions of leprosy, 108–9
  curated burials, 28
  DNA results, 91, 109
  osteological research, 10, 28
  religious foundation as well as place of segregation, 109
  survived until sixteenth century, 109
St Swithun (852–63)
  852 Bishop of Winchester, 65
  971 bones translated to Old Minster, and lavish reliquary provided, 73

1093 transferred to Norman, cathedral, 100
1476 new reliquary provided, 102
1538 shrine destroyed by Thomas, Wriothesley, 117
cult promoted by Aethelwold, 73, 77
medieval cathedral modified to accommodate more pilgrims, 100–2
memorial court constructed, 100
Old Minster enhanced to accommodate saint, 74–5
significance throughout Europe and for pilgrims, 65
weather legend, 125
sources for Winchester's past
absences and sampling biases, 14–15, 17, 24
antiquarian investigations, 7–8, 19–21
early medieval documents, 11–12
early to mid-twentieth-century archaeology, 21–2
fictional depictions, 135–6
illuminated manuscripts, 11, 72, 77–8, 81, 115–16
isotopic analysis, 56–7
Leland, John, 18–19
medieval documents, 25
nineteenth-century documents, 12, 123–4
osteological analysis, 28–9, 54–5
recent archaeological investigation, 10, 28–9, 137
scientific research, 26, 28, 30–1
standing buildings, 13–14
Winchester Archaeology and Local History Group, 26–7, 92, 106
Winchester Excavations, 22–5
Winchester Studies, 25–6, 136
Winton Domesday, 25, 87
Stuart Winchester
first archaeological discovery, 20
involvement in Civil War, 120
King's House built, 122
plans by Charles II for 'an English Versailles', 129
town in disrepair, 120

transatlantic slavery, 15, 124
twentieth-century Winchester
First World War, 12–13, 130–3, 137
King Alfred's millennium celebrations, 128–30
M3 protests, 133–5
military museums, 14
purpose-built museum, 21
systematic archaeological investigations, 22–5
twenty-first-century Winchester
archaeological investigations and publications, 28, 136–7
best/happiest place to live in England, 139–40
census data, 139–40
fictional depictions of early medieval Winchester, 135, 137
Hampshire Cultural Trust, 136–7
recognition of importance of Winchester's heritage, 13, 137

Victorian Winchester
antiquarian interest, 19–21
census and trade directory data, 123–4
cholera outbreaks, 124
John Keats' visit and 'To Autumn', 125–6
population growth, 123
public health improvements, 124
major public building programme, 123–4
St Cross reform, 125
tourism growth, 126
Winchester College 'rebellions', 126–7

William 'the Conqueror' (1066–87), King of England
extends Royal Palace, 87, 95
has new Cathedral built, 99
instigates 'crown-wearing' ceremony in Cathedral, 95
orders Castle built, 96–7
receives papal legate in new Castle, 97
Winchester surrenders to him, 86

William of Wykeham (1320/24–1404), Bishop of Winchester
  commissions major modifications to Cathedral, 102, 110
  conducts enquiry at St Cross, 107
  founds College of St Mary (Winchester College), 110–11
  great wealth, 110–11
  oversees changes to Wolvesey Palace, 106
William of Wynford, master mason (flourished 1360–1405)
  oversees building of Winchester College, 111
  transformed Cathedral in Perpendicular style, 102
Winchester Cathedral Priory,
  1093 Norman cathedral building begins, 99
  chantry chapels added in fifteenth and sixteenth century, 102
  dedicated, and St Swithun translated, 99–100
  dissolution, 117
  early research, 19–20
  heritage displays enhanced, 137
  Lady Chapel added, 101
  medieval records destroyed, 14, 101
  modifications to accommodate pilgrims, 101
  mortuary chests, 10, 29, 85–6
  medieval priory buildings, 102
  pilgrimage centre, 100–2
  thirteenth-century remodelling, 101
  towers at west end demolished, 101
  vandalized in Civil War, 14, 120
  wedding of Mary I and Philip II, 118–19
  William of Wynford oversees Perpendicular remodelling in fourteenth century, 106
Winchester Castle
  1066–7 initial construction, 97
  1222–5 Great Hall added, 98
  1290 Round Table installed, 98–9
  after 1302 fire ceased to be a royal residence, 98
  Civil War, 120
  high-status diet, 99
  houses trials in post-medieval period, 14, 120, 123
  Jews' Tower, 89
  proposals for visitor attraction, 138
  refurbishment under Henry III, 89
  refuge and prison for medieval Jewish community, 89
  royal visits, 92, 95, 97–8
  Sir Christopher Wren builds King's House and plans 'an English Versailles', 122
  site of royal treasury, 97
  site becomes major army depot, 129–30
  site sold to Charles II, 122
  slighted after Civil War, site sold to town, 120
  stone keep added in twelfth century, 97
Winchester College (formerly St Mary's College)
  1382 founded by William of Wykeham, 13, 110–11
  1394 first building phase, 111
  1552 visit by King Edward VI, 118
  designed by William of Wynford, 111
  Henry VIII and Emperor Charles V dine there, 116
  'rebellions' in eighteenth and nineteenth centuries, 126–7
  sixteenth- and seventeenth-century persistence of Catholic beliefs, 119–20
  St Catherine's Hill traditions, 21
  War Cloister, 14, 132–3, 137
Winchester Bible, 11, 110
Winchester Reliquary, 86–7
Winchester School, artistic tradition, 81
Wolvesey, Palace of bishops of Winchester
  additions commissioned by Bishop de Blois, 105–6
  demolition of medieval structures to build baroque palace, 122

documentary sources, 11, 92–3
early medieval palace, 72, 104
excavations, 10, 24
fifteenth century, surviving chapel added, 106
first Norman buildings, 104–5
gardens, 92–3
high-status diet, 99
Roman occupation, 48
royal visitors, 106, 114, 116, 118
thirteenth- and fourteenth-century refurbishments, 106